Arish

rama

uez Gulf

LOWER EGYPT

0   25   50 miles

0   25   50 kilometers

Fleeing Herod

Other Titles by James Cowan

Fiction

A Troubadour's Testament
A Mapmaker's Dream
The Painted Shore
Toby's Angel
A Rambling Man
The Deposition
A Voyage around My Pipe

Nonfiction

Desert Father
Francis: A Saint's Way
Two Men Dreaming
Messengers of the Gods
The Aborigine Tradition
Mysteries of the Dreaming
Myths of the Dreaming
Sacred Places
Starlight's Trail
The River People
The Mountain Men

Essays

Letters from a Wild State
Quartet: four essays on power
A Spanner in the Works

Art Monographs

Wirrimanu: Aboriginal Art from the Balgo Hills
Balgo: New Directions

Poetry

African Journal
Petroglyphs

Translation

Rumi's Divan of Shems of Tabriz

For Children

Kunmangur, the Rainbow Serpent

Fleeing Herod

A JOURNEY
THROUGH COPTIC EGYPT
with
THE HOLY FAMILY

JAMES COWAN

PARACLETE PRESS
BREWSTER, MASSACHUSETTS

2013 First Printing

Fleeing Herod: A Journey through Coptic Egypt with the Holy Family

Copyright © 2013 James Cowan

ISBN 978-1-61261-304-8

Library of Congress Cataloging-in-Publication Data

Cowan, James, 1942-
  Fleeing Herod : a journey through Egypt with the Holy Family / James Cowan.
     pages cm
  Includes bibliographical references (pages   ).
  ISBN 978-1-61261-304-8 (hardcover/dustjacket)
  1. Jesus Christ—Flight into Egypt. 2. Cowan, James, 1942—Travel--Egypt. 3. Spiritual biography—Egypt. I. Title.
  BT315.3.C69 2012
  232.92—dc23   2012048046

10 9 8 7 6 5 4 3 2 1

Published by Paraclete Press
Brewster, Massachusetts
www.paracletepress.com
Printed in the United States of America

He now remembered like a dream
The flight to Egypt and his childhood.

Boris Pasternak

CONTENTS

Prologue

EGYPT WILL ALWAYS BE A COUNTRY
of the imagination. No other country in the world provides
us with such a rich source of conjecture and possibility as does
this ancient land of the Pharaohs. It is almost impossible for us
to comprehend how such a narrow strip of arable land, gently
cosseted by the Nile River and stretching more than a thousand miles through a desert reaching from the Sudan to the
Mediterranean Sea, could provide us with such a varied cosmological history, so complete and intact as it is, that even today
we are still trying to come to terms with it as a phenomenon
of human endeavor. More than any other land, Egypt has given
us an extraordinary pantheon of gods, a complete methodology
of death and the afterlife, as well as a resolved architecture to
account for one's passage to Aaru, those heavenly fields of rushes.
Pyramid and tomb, hieroglyph and cartouche announce the very
building blocks of civilization itself, even as we follow the course
of the river to its source.

In the light of recent political events, when Egypt is once more
thrown into turmoil over its future direction as a modern state,
we must be conscious of the millennia of knowledge embodied in its sands. Political theory, civic responsibility, and regnal
authority; these have all been explored in depth by this country's

inhabitants over several thousand years. It is not a young country, but one honed by experience. Recent events such as the so-called Arab Spring, which continues to unfold even as I write, is but one small stepping stone along the long pathway toward freedom. Its inhabitants have laid down many of these throughout the course of history, as we know—so, in effect, nothing is new for them. However, the collective wisdom of ages will, I am sure, allow this remarkable country to navigate a safe passage through what are only temporary shoals.

My own love of Egypt reaches back many years. Even in my youth I had promised myself to one day travel up the Nile in pursuit of its incomparable treasures. Gods, myths, and temples, monasteries, mummies in their tombs, and hermits in their caves—all these formed a backdrop to my desire to plumb the depths of a land whose knowledge of the spirit is unparalleled. Nonetheless, there was one journey more than any other that captured my imagination. It was to explore the journey of the Holy Family upriver between 7 and 4 BC in their bid to escape Herod in Jerusalem, around the time of the Massacre of the Innocents. Was it a folktale or a genuine peregrination? I asked myself. Was it the manifestation of a divine journey, or was it an example of a myth emerging from an ancient land in keeping with so many others of the past? These were the questions that I posed to myself as I prepared to follow in their footsteps.

How strange it is to become absorbed into the events of a story that still reverberates down through the centuries. Even today the various places the family visited during their flight through Egypt are well documented by both scholarship and tradition. It is not hard, therefore, to set out on a journey up the Nile committed to such a task. All a person need do is believe that the journey is possible—that, in fact, when hierohistory and topography are allowed to merge, a new possibility might begin to evolve. In any event, pilgrims such as myself soon find themselves grappling with thoughts and sentiments that go beyond the prosaic. We are drawn into the drama of supernatural events as much as those conditioned by adversity. The Holy Family's journey was, or *is*, no ordinary flight from evil, I soon realized.

Exile, too, is the theme of the family's escape into Egypt. It is part of a long tradition reaching back to Moses when he fled Midian with his family, returning to the land of Egypt.[1] But this is only half of the story. The other half relates to succor and to care, to the offer of protection by strangers. For all the difficulties of the Holy Family's journey that will be found in these pages, one must never forget that they also experienced great kindness from many whom they met. It is not just about travail; it is also about how a land and a people embraced strangers in their midst. To make this journey, then, is to enter into a compact with Egypt itself.

I set out to test my own powers of credulity on this journey as well. How much would I accept as fact? How much would I treat as mere fable? Would I have a right to question the Coptic Church's established traditions? Would I find that modern scholarship was at odds with long-held beliefs? These were questions that only a journey up the Nile could answer. I had put myself not only in the hands of a driver, guide, and interpreter but also in the hands of many people who acknowledged the timeless presence of the Holy Family in their midst, even today. As I was soon to learn, the family made two journeys throughout Egypt during their stay. One, of course, was through the delta and up the Nile; the other, however, was into the indelible consciousness of humankind.

I realized that I was about to become more than a traveler. Egypt, the Egypt of vagabondage and exile, was about to yield up another of its secrets: that of playing host to a divine child and his family in their bid to remain free. The plasma of divinity needed to be shaped by a culture long accustomed to the workings of the spirit, it seemed. My journey was to be one of exploring correspondences and coincidences. In truth, I would have to come to terms with the fact that, for all the exceptionality of Mary and Joseph as the perfect example of Christian parental piety, their story also partakes of an older mythography, one associated with Isis, Osiris, and Horus. Such is the nature of cultural and spiritual accretion, it seems. My challenge, I decided, was to determine where a myth of exile might end and a miracle begin.

The Audience

THE HOTEL WHERE I WAS STAYING
in downtown Cairo was old, outdated, and filled with
Swiss ski posters from another era. The elevator as it ascended
reminded me of a poorly lit Tunisian birdcage. The owner, however, informed me that the Windsor had once been a British
officers' club when Egypt was a protectorate. Leather chairs in the
bar, and the highly polished floorboards that creaked underfoot,
certainly indicated an officious air.

Ramadan had commenced, and the intense drone of voices rose
from the street below. Food was on everyone's mind, even though
people were content to starve themselves throughout the day. The
voice of the muezzin's call to prayer from a nearby minaret sounded
altogether distant.

That morning I was to be driven across town in a taxi to an
audience with Pope Shenouda, the head of the Coptic Church.
The idea of meeting the representative of one of the oldest
churches in Christendom, a church founded by Saint Mark in
AD 60 in the city of Alexandria, left me in a state of trepidation.
He had history on his side; I no more than an inquiring mind.
Could we bridge the gap? What could I possibly say that might
interest a man who had spent his early life in a cave in the desert,
living as a hermit?

Pope Shenouda, it seemed, had heard about my interest in exploring the route of the Holy Family in Egypt after their flight from Judea, and presumably wanted to make sure that I received his blessing. It is a journey dear to the heart of all Copts, who believe that their country has been especially blessed by the Holy Family's stay there. The fact that the Christ child was able to escape Herod by hiding in their land meant that Egypt was essential to the survival of Christianity. If Jesus had been killed along with other children at the time of the Massacre of the Innocents shortly after his birth in Bethlehem, then the world would be a different place. The Coptic Church sees itself as the guardian of the divine child's infancy, the midwife of his message to the world.

My taxi darted freneticly along dusty promenades and through canyons of tall buildings crowded with cars, trucks, and motor-cyclists. The footpaths were busy with people, many wearing *hijabs* over their heads, going to work. Eventually I found myself standing outside the headquarters of the Coptic Church in Cairo, a large neoclassical building. Somewhat shaken by my trip, I was more than grateful to be ushered into an audience room furnished with gold-leafed chairs arranged on each side of a throne. The quiet in the room contrasted the noise from the streets outside. Numerous icons depicting saints hung on the walls. The ceiling was brightly lit and covered with carved arabesques. I had entered an oriental chamber, it seemed, its decorations harking back to a time when potentates wished to impress.

There was a commotion by the doorway. A group of secretaries and bishops appeared, dressed in black. They stood to one side as Pope Shenouda appeared, arrayed in a richly embroidered cape decorated with gold crosses and bearing a staff of office in one hand and a Coptic cross in the other. He wore pointed slippers. His gentle eyes and long beard impressed me. There was something avuncular yet austere about him. Here was a man who had successfully fought demons in the desert in his youth, who had later been imprisoned in his monastery for many years by

President Sadat during the early part of his papacy, and who was now nearing the end of his life, an old man devoid of hubris yet curiously alert.

Two of his secretaries helped him onto the dais and eased him onto his throne. Pope Shenouda sat in silence as one of them formally introduced me to His Holiness. His speech was vaguely oracular. We then exchanged gifts. Meanwhile, I outlined why I had come to Egypt, informing His Holiness of my desire to follow in the footsteps of the Holy Family.

"Your Holiness," I concluded. "It is with your blessing that I wish to journey throughout Egypt. It may be that a visitor to your land will see things with fresh eyes."

Pope Shenouda gazed at me, his twinkling eyes nonetheless concentrated, intense. He placed the porcelain cross on his lap and clasped another made from leather hanging against his chest.

"Like you, the Holy Family were guests in our country," he responded in English. "Our forebears, the ancient Egyptians, welcomed them. Therefore I welcome you to our country in their name. All men who come to Egypt must know that they are entering a land whose experience in matters of the spirit is not wanting. It is an old land. We who oversee it are conscious of the burden we carry. I for one am no more than a lowly monk still struggling to understand its legacy."

I was struck by his modesty. Ascending to the papacy had not for one moment obscured his true calling. The old man before me was, at heart, a simple monk eking out his existence in a cave. At the back of his eyes were the rough walls of his cell, his bed on the floor, a leather water bag hanging from a peg by the entrance. Psalms seemed to emanate from his brow. A sack of bread in one corner promised nourishment beyond all his expectation. Meanwhile, the desert sand lay between us.

"How did the Holy Family survive during the years they spent wandering from place to place?" I asked.

"Why, on miracles of course. Is this not the only way to travel?"

"Alternatively, Joseph may have managed their affairs by selling some of the gifts they received from the Magi," I suggested.

"Ah, yes," the pope sighed. He too had obviously received such gifts during times of intense prayer, or when he emerged from his cave at dawn. "Gold, frankincense, and myrrh were as much spiritual gifts as real."

"Could it be," he further ventured, "that we constantly look for explanations of mystical events, yet are uncertain of their reality? A family journeys into a foreign land; they spend three or four years struggling to survive. How is it possible that they could not have survived other than through the blessedness of spiritual gifts? Joseph was a competent carpenter, we are told. But he was also a man selected by God for a great task. Along with the Virgin Mary, his beloved wife, this was to care for the future God-man, Jesus Christ. Theirs was not a family such as we might know. Of course, miracles were manna to them."

"Egypt is much more a repository of lore and wisdom than we imagine," I said.

"Moses was an Egyptian, we must remember," Pope Shenouda continued. "The Nile formed a part of every Jew who returned to Israel at the time of their exodus from this land. Did they not wish to escape persecution as the Holy Family did? There are clear parallels."

"Is there a similarity between the ancient Pharaonic tradition depicting a realm of multiple gods, and that of our own monotheistic tradition?" I asked.

"We have emerged from such a tradition, yes," the pope replied. "The new dispensation that arrived in our land in the form of the infant Christ was not unfamiliar to our forebears. They, of course, worshiped Osiris and Isis, who gave us the divine child, Horus. These figures made up the Holy Family of ancient Egypt just as we possess Joseph, Mary, and Jesus. Osiris's brother, Seth, cut Osiris into many pieces. In this event we see an echo of the crucifixion of Our Lord. We have been attempting to put Christ back together in our hearts ever since, just as Isis, and the people of Egypt, attempted to reassemble the mutilated body of Osiris. Egypt has a long memory, it seems."

It was a remarkable confession to come from a leader of the Coptic Church. To acknowledge the relationship between an ancient Egyptian avatar and Christ seemed to me to be rather courageous for the leader of the oldest church in Christendom. Pope Shenouda had made a considerable journey from his cave that morning.

"The world forgets sometimes," Pope Shenouda went on, "that many of the questions relating to the nature of God were asked by the ancient Egyptians before they became the subject of inquiry by others. I recall once, when I was attending a conference in Europe years ago, a Greek theologian told me that the philosophers of Alexandria, then a major Greek city of the Roman Empire, had contributed immeasurably to the development of Christianity. Of course, I agreed. But when I added that all these men whom he referred to were born in Egypt—and, more pointedly, that they were Copts and members of the Church of Alexandria—the man became confused. I told him that if men like Tertullian, Origin, Athanasius, and Cyril were Greek, then perhaps I too was Greek!"

"I believe Plotinus, one of the great classical philosophers of late antiquity, was born of Christian parents in the city of Asyut, on the Nile River," I added.

"I ask you: can a man be any more Egyptian than someone born in Asyut?" Pope Shenouda chuckled at the thought, for he too was born in the same province.[2]

A secretary appeared, bearing a tray filled with cups and a pot of tea. I thought the audience may be over, and that Pope Shenouda would politely bid me goodbye and retire. Tea was poured and handed around while I waited for the moment of my dismissal.

"I begin to wonder whether the Holy Family's escape into Egypt was not an act of defiance," Pope Shenouda said at last, sipping his tea.

"Or fear, perhaps, Your Holiness. Herod wanted them dead, particularly the infant Jesus," I replied, as I was handed a cup of tea also.

"To be a king requires the cultivation of wisdom and humility. These are clearly not qualities Herod possessed."

"It seemed that he feared the presence of a lowly peasant family in his kingdom more than he did his enemies," I replied.

"Christ's kingdom was never going to be of this world, Mr. James. We must be thankful to Joseph. He alone listened to the voice of the angel, and so decided to flee. Mary was indeed fortunate; she was betrothed to a man whose capacity for forbearance was matched by his ability to act."

"Can we assume, then, that Joseph holds the key to the survival of the infant Christ?"

"No one acted more courageously than he," replied Pope Shenouda. "Perhaps he had visited Egypt as a younger man, as a wandering carpenter—who knows? What we may assume is that he knew how to get here, and where to go once he had reached the Nile. As you journey through our land, Mr. James, you will hear stories that will confirm the strength of his character, and how the Holy Family overcame their difficulties because of his wise actions. Theirs is no ordinary journey. It is up to you to consider whether their flight was solely to escape Herod, or whether it was to make Egypt central to the birth of Christianity."

"Because of its ancient knowledge, you mean?" I inquired.

Pope Shenouda pressed his weight forward on his staff as one of his staff took the cup from his hand. He was beginning to tire.

"Egypt is handmaiden to the world—your world, as much as ours. Now, I must say 'Good Day' to you, Mr. James," he said.

Two secretaries came forward and helped the pope to his feet. Below his robes, his pointed slippers protruded.

"I trust your journey through our land in the footsteps of the Holy Family will prove fruitful, Mr. James. You will start out at Tel el-Farma, in the Sinai, where it is said that they first entered our country from Palestine."

"I plan to drive there tomorrow," I said.

"We will pray for your safety at all times."

Pope Shenouda extended his hand for me to kiss, made the sign of the cross, and then he proceeded toward the door. Even as he departed, I sensed a hint of the dry air of the desert in his wake.

2

A Vision

IN TEL EL-FARMA THAT MORNING, with the sun playing across the desert as a shadowy light, I climbed out of my vehicle and gazed at the archaeological excavations of what must have been a road into the ancient city of Pelusium. Located on the easternmost branch of the Nile, near the Mediterranean coast, Pelusium had been an important trading city, presiding over the route upriver from Memphis. The coastline has changed, of course, and the Nile no longer passes by, so that the ruins today inspire loneliness rather than the bustle of urban life. Various invaders hoping to conquer Egypt had passed through this city on their way west. It was also an important trading city. Ships from the eastern Mediterranean and caravans from Syria unloaded goods here for transportation by barges up the Nile.

The desert continues to encroach upon the mud-brick walls of a once-thriving metropolis. Transience was in the air: cisterns, shops, ruined basilicas and temples, all of them lay half submerged under sand. This was the first port-of-call in Egypt for the Holy Family after they had crossed over from Gaza. In their day it was surrounded by marshes.[3] A wealthy city, it was considered as late as the ninth century to be a wonder of Egypt. In one report we read, "From Tamnis we came to the city of Faramea, which is a church of Saint Mary, on the spot to which by the admonition of the angel, Joseph fled with the child and his mother. Here there is a multitude of camels, which are hired from the natives by travelers to carry their baggage across the desert [to Jerusalem], which is a journey of six days."[4]

No more a home to a multitude of camels, Tel el-Farma is nonetheless important to the story of the Holy Family's flight from Herod. It was here that they stopped to rest after their escape from Judea, traveling as they did from Bethlehem to the ancient seaport of Ashkelon, where, it was said, Samson had once killed thirty Philistines.[5] It was a center of Hellenistic culture dedicated to the cult of Dercetus, a goddess with the body of a fish and the face of a woman. Herod had already embellished it with fountains and sumptuous buildings, of which only a few Corinthian columns are left.

From Ashkelon, they pursued an easterly course in the direction of Hebron, which, according to the Bible, is older than Zoan in Lower Egypt, then considered one of the oldest cities in the world.[6] Hebron's early reputation rests on the fact that it was here that Sarah, Abraham's wife, was buried in the cave of Machpelah in the field of Ephron. The cave now lies under an enclosure that houses a mosque and a synagogue. One source relates that the Holy Family remained in hiding here for six months.[7]

Proceeding west along an established caravan route, they likely arrived at the Canaanite stronghold of Gaza. Another splendid Greek city, Gaza had only recently been rebuilt by the Roman consul Aulus Gabinus after its destruction by Alexander Jannaeus in 94 BC. The route from this point ran parallel to the Mediterranean Sea until it crossed Wadi Gaza, the presumed site of Gerar mentioned in Genesis as being "near to Gaza."[8]

From Gerar, they would have continued on their way to Jenysos and later Raphia, the frontier town between Gaza and the Roman province of Egypt. Raphia had been the battleground between the contending forces of Ptolemy IV and the Seleucid king Antiochus the Great in 217 BC. Fortunately Ptolemy won that battle, and

Egypt was saved. From Mary and Joseph's point of view, however, Raphia would have been no more than a hurried stop on the way to the natural boundary between Judaea and Egypt, namely, the Wadi el-Arish, known then as the River of Egypt (not to be confused with the Nile). Crossing this inconspicuous brook, they would have pressed on to present-day El-Arish.

The route described so far is purely conjectural, as we have no evidence of exactly where or how the Holy Family reached Egypt. But one assumes the established caravan route would have been their obvious choice, given that any other route necessitated a dangerous journey across the wastes of the Sinai or a more risky, and more expensive, voyage by boat from Ashkelon. In any case, the texts describing their journey insist they traveled by ass. Furthermore, the prophecy of Zechariah states explicitly that the Messiah would come riding upon an ass.[9] Whether this ass was the one upon which he would eventually enter Jerusalem a few days before his crucifixion or the one he would use to reenter Judea after Herod's death is never clearly stated.

Sitting on a wall in the ruins of Farma that morning, gazing at the upended blocks of stone and fallen pillars, I tried to picture Joseph and his family coming over the rise through a heat haze in the distance. Joseph, Mary, and Salome, Mary's servant, each would have been clothed in a *linea*, a long, close-fitting robe reaching from the neck to the feet, and a *tunica*, a type of tunic with short sleeves descending to the knees. They would have also worn a *planeta*, a round piece of material with a hole in the center for the head to pass through. During travel a girdle was added, along with sandals. Such was the wardrobe of most people during the classical era, not the Arab style of dress we see pictured in medieval paintings of the Holy Family.[10] It is easy to picture these three figures, simply attired, trudging toward Pelusium late one afternoon sometime in 7 BC.

This year, 7 BC, is today regarded as the likely year of Jesus's birth for a number of reasons. Herod, we know, was dead by 4 BC. The census and poll tax conducted at the instigation of Caesar Augustus

(Octavian), which influenced Joseph to return to his hometown of Bethlehem in order to register, also occurred in 6 or 7 BC, not seven years later, as our modern calendar suggests.[11] We know too from cuneiform inscriptions deciphered by the German scholar Schnabel in 1925 that a bright "star" was seen to appear over the region as far east as Babylon. These tablets came from the ancient school of astrology at Sippar in Babylon, and detailed the planetary positions in the constellation of Pisces. The "star" was none other than the conjunction of Saturn and Jupiter, which occurred over a period of five months in 7 BC—long enough, it seems, to guide the three astrologers from the East to Israel and later to Bethlehem.

Further confirmation of this event was provided by the noted astrologer and mathematician Johannes Kepler. In 1603 he observed that the two planets Saturn and Jupiter had moved so close to one another in the constellation of Pisces that they produced the illusion of being one large star. Kepler recalled having read the writings of the Jewish philosopher Abarabanel, who in turn acknowledged that the Messiah would appear when such a conjunction should occur. Kepler went on to calculate that the conjunction occurred in 7 BC. It is no accident that the symbol of Christ is the fish, another echo of the constellation Pisces, in which the conjunction of the two planets took place.

Chaldean astrology also determined that Pisces was the sign of the "west country," none other than the land surrounding the Mediterranean Sea. According to Jewish tradition, it was the sign of Israel, and the sign of the Messiah. It does not take too much to realize why the astrologers from Babylon, the so-called Magi, set out on their journey to Israel. They knew that in the west country—that is, in Israel—a mighty king was to be born in the land of their forefathers, as they believed themselves to be one of the Lost Tribes. To experience this auspicious event in person was the main reason for their making the journey. They wanted to see with their own eyes the birth of the king that was, in effect, going to change the world. One should therefore be wary of dismissing the three kings as a picturesque adjunct to the birth of Jesus. It is entirely credible that their appearance in the stable, or perhaps a month or so later in a house in Bethlehem, prompted as it was by Herod's request that they look out for such a child on their journey through Judea, further informs us of the mysterious and momentous nature of Christ's birth.[12]

Nor is it hard to imagine the Holy Family arriving in the city of El-Arish exhausted from their travels. Presumably they had been fearful of being recognized as people from Bethlehem, a town condemned by Herod as the harbinger of a future king of Israel. It is likely they were wary of communicating with their fellow wayfarers. Though they may have been members of a caravan, and not traveling alone, they would have kept to themselves, a modest family with child at breast. Joseph would have led the ass, with Mary and Salome alternately carrying the infant Jesus, all their belongings, no more than a few items of clothing, tied to the animal or strung across Joseph's back. This was the way people traveled in those days—as they often do today on the back roads of Egypt.

The image of the Holy Family trudging toward me across the desert was slowly fading, however, and from here on my sole guide detailing their journey was a text in my possession, purportedly written in the fourth century by the patriarch of Alexandria Theophilus (AD 385–412). The *Vision of Theophilus*, much revered by Copts, is an apocryphal account of the family's journey throughout Egypt. According to legend, Theophilus experienced a vision of the journey at the time of his visit to Mount Qussqam in Upper Egypt while on a visit as part of his pastoral duties. In his vision, the patriarch encounters the Holy Virgin, who implores him not to build a great church over the cave in which the family lived during their stay at Mount Qussqam. It is Mary who relates to him in the vision the difficulties of their journey through the delta and up the Nile to the mountain where, presumably, Theophilus was still deep in prayer.

The *Vision* is a remarkable document. Not only does it describe many of the places along the route, but it also intimates the political situation in Egypt at that time. According to Theophilus, he and his fellow bishops made their tour of duty throughout Egypt at the behest of Emperor Theodosius, who had recently visited Alexandria and ordered the patriarch to close the Serapeum, then the proud symbol of pagan worship standing in the midst of a half-Christianized city. The god Serapis was a Hellenized version of Osiris, whose effigy in wood, covered in ivory and gold, stood in the center of the temple. It was truly an awesome sight, and clearly an affront to many zealous Christians in Alexandria. The destruction of the Serapeum spelled the end not only of Hellenism in Egypt but also of an era that reached back to pre-Pharaonic times, more than three thousand years before.[13]

It is worthwhile exploring Theophilus's vision. For it is here that the moment of realization comes to a man better known for political intrigue and zealotry than for mystical experience.[14] Whether the document is a true account of the facts or a pious fabrication is not known. The Coptic Church certainly believes the *Vision* represents a true description of events of the fourth century. There is a sense of authenticity, however, in the way the *Vision* describes Theophilus's attempt to understand how the Holy Family had come to be at Mount Qussqam in Upper Egypt:

> It happened that after we had finished nocturnes, and my brother bishops had slept in a place by themselves, I went up to the upper chamber in which the Mother of God had slept during the days when she had inhabited the [cave] on this mountain. When I rose [to pray] I stretched out my hands, praying and imploring my God and my savior Jesus Christ, saying: "Hear me, as you heard my father Alexander. . . . Here me, as you heard my Father Athanasius the holy Apostle, whom you helped in all his trials. Hear me in this way—I, who

am unworthy of your service, because I am a sinner. I know that you hear me always, because you are near to all those who love your holy and pure name.

"Oh my Lord and my God, have mercy upon me, and do not let me return empty handed, me who has fixed my mind on your presence from childhood to old age, I beseech you to reveal to me your coming into the world, and to this mountain, which you visited together with your Holy Virgin mother, and to this desolate house in which you established your habitation. I pray to you to help me build a big church here that will glorify and exalt and honor your name. You are the one to whom is due power and glory with your Father and your Holy Spirit, now at all times and forever."

When my prayer was finished, a light shone down on me. It was so dazzling that I believed that the sun itself was shining upon me. A throne of light appeared to me on whom I saw seated the Queen of all women, the Holy Virgin, our Lady Mary, mother of God. Her face was illuminated like the sun from the light with which she was invested, and she was covered in a majestic brightness, and with her were many angels. I was so bewildered that I said: "Is there in all the world one that is able to contemplate this great majesty?" I saw Gabriel and Michael, and a great multitude of other angels with them. When I looked and saw them, I fell on my face to the ground and became a dead man. But Michael raised me, and removed fear and dread from me.[15]

Mary goes on to relate the travails of the family's journey throughout Egypt. Her response to Theophilus is equally declamatory. As the "mother of the one whom neither heaven nor earth are able to comprehend," and as the "mother who gave milk from my breast to the one who feeds the world by His will," Mary explains the events surrounding their escape from Judea. She even gives personal details of how "blessed old Joseph" used to carry her son's clothes and their food. He would, she relates, "carry Him on his shoulders and play with Him when he saw me handing the child to Salome." And Salome used to "take her Son at all times, caress Him and smile at Him." There is intimacy and joy suggested here; it was not all trial and tribulation for the Holy Family, it seems. Moreover, Mary advises Theophilus not to build a great church at Mount Qussqam, but to regard the holy place as a memorial in keeping with the humility of the Savior.

Such is the document that furnished me with information about the Holy Family's journey in Egypt. The *Vision* is more than an itinerary compiled by a patriarch eager to cement his place in the annals of mystical literature, however. The document was destined to underpin all that the Coptic Church stood for in Egypt, as it represented a spiritual contract between a people and the land of Egypt. They needed to justify their right to live there, particularly after the invasion of Islam in the seventh century. The document thus confirmed them as custodians of the so-called hidden years of Christ's early life.

The events that had occurred before the family trudged into Pelusium some time in 7 BC mark the beginning of a series of extraordinary events in the life of Christ. Saint Luke's image of him as a boy "going about his father's business" at age twelve, until his death in his early thirties as a man destined to change the world, confirms what we already know—indeed, what we *want* to know.[16] The portrait we possess is of a man fashioned by Hellenist theologians from Byzantium and Alexandria in the first half dozen centuries of our era. His Semitic nature has all but been obliterated by the Romanized "Good Shepherd" image of late antiquity. It is precisely this image that we see in the tomb of Galla Placidia in Ravenna (ca. AD 440), as well as in the Greco-Roman Museum in Alexandria (fourth–fifth century AD). The Christ of Western Christianity is a man "civilized" by his prolonged encounter with the refinements of Greek philosophy. He is a Platonic "Ideal Man," not a man of flesh and blood who happened to die a painful death outside the walls of Jerusalem.

Even as a child, Christ was about to confront a world very different from his own. So too were his parents. The austere nature of Jewish law, with its emphasis on prohibition at the expense of a more intimate relationship with God, starkly contrasted the timeless spirituality of Pharaonic religion, dominated as it was by a polytheistic worldview and elaborate temple rituals developed over thousands of years. Discounting any Greek influence, which would have been negligible in rural Egypt anyway, it is easy to see that the Holy Family's journey was a journey into another realm of belief. It would have been hard for either Joseph or Mary to reconcile their view of Yahweh as one who harbored jealousy and anger with that of a religion that preached a more intimate relationship between humanity and its gods. Could one imagine Moses saying, as the *Book of the Dead* relates: "My hair is the hair of Nu / My eyes are the eyes of Hathor / My buttocks are the buttocks of the Eye of Horus"?[17] These are clearly the remarks of a people in love with their gods.

Egyptian spirituality was characterized by a gentility born of long years considering how best to express the true nature of the spirit. Even the *Precepts of Kaqemma* of the IV Dynasty reflects a more circumspect and balanced view of morality than do the Ten Commandments. It is well to experience the tone of such a work in order to understand the subtlety of Pharaonic religion, a religion often portrayed as being obsessed with death, crude, and materialistic. Yet in one text we read:

> Not known are the things that make God,
> Even bread is in accordance with his plan.
> Do not inflict terror on men or women,
> This is opposed to God's design.
> If you have land fit for the plough, labor in the field

Since it is God's.
If you would be perfect, make your son
Pleasing in the sight of God.
By your actions satisfy those whom you love;
This is necessary for one favored by God.
God loves your obedience; disobedience he hates.
Truly, a good son is one of God's gifts.[18]

Here the ways of God are clearly inscrutable, yet they also suggest that a genuine give-and-take between people is important. The author acknowledges obedience as positive; so too the necessity to work for one's living. Perfection lies in being pleasing in the eyes of God, surely an indication of high moral intent. Humans are visibly pleasing to God if they live according to his precepts. The Egyptians placed a great deal of value on how a man or woman looked—and whether their physical appearance betrayed the integrity of their inner life. One often forgets this fact when we descend into a Pharaoh's tomb to view their frescoes: that the Egyptians loved not only beauty but also the idea of beauty. Their depiction of the human figure in all their reliefs is one of adoration for the human body.

Joseph and Mary would have been ignorant of such things, however, as they stopped to water their ass at a well in Pelusium, Salome perhaps going off to buy food while Mary cradled the infant Jesus in her arms. One must try to picture them gazing at this throng of wealthy merchants and itinerant hawkers, all of them barely aware of their presence, so busy were they with their affairs. Pelusium was a city at the crossroads of commerce, and Mary and Joseph's personal plight would have been of little or no interest to others. They were just another family on the move; part of that vast migration of peoples seeking work in far-off places. Joseph, an elderly carpenter, and Mary, a young mother exhausted by her travels, stand there in the marketplace, conscious of how different they must seem. Only they know that they bear the future Son of Man in their arms.

I walked back to my driver and guide, who were standing by our car, waiting for me to complete my visit to the ruins of the ancient city of Pelusium. The sun was hot now, and their silhouettes betrayed a casual impatience. They had been watching me, of course—watching this strange man wandering among the ruins of Tel el-Farma, trying to find some clue to indicate that the Holy Family had passed this way long ago. They probably viewed me as a throwback to another era, a traveler under the illusion that people in history do occasionally leave their trace upon the landscape in a form other than a ruined wall or a Corinthian pillar. It was not for me to change their minds, I decided. I had come to this isolated place in the desert to view a mirage, perhaps; a mirage redolent with the image of a family desperate to find succor in Egypt. This was no more than a cicatrice that I had come to observe: Pelusium represented the Holy Family's first encounter with a land that was to change their lives.

Journey into Exile 3

THE JOURNEY OF THE HOLY FAMILY
into Egypt is a story about exile. It is also about their flight
from persecution at the hands of King Herod of Judea. One
member of this family, however, was a divine child, a future avatar,
and so of great consequence to the ensuing transformation of the
world. The others—his stepfather Joseph, his mother Mary, and
midwife Salome—were his chosen protectors. It was their task
to care for this precious child as they attempted to escape from
Herod's soldiers sent to kill him. Only later was the child called
upon to protect them through the exercise of his extraordinary
theurgic powers. Jesus, the future Son of Man, was to be schooled
in the art of exile in one of the world's oldest spiritual cauldrons.
He was to journey through the ancient land of the Pharaohs,
confront its gods, and do battle with what one observer calls the
"chemistry of doubt."

The challenge I had chosen for myself in this ancient drama, if
only as an observer, was to accompany them in their exodus, and
so explore what the Gospel of Saint Matthew says of their flight:

> Behold, the angel of the Lord appeared to Joseph in a dream,
> saying, Arise, and take the young child and his mother, and

flee into Egypt, and be thou there until I bring thee word: for Herod will seek the young child to destroy him.[19]

The Bible, unfortunately, gives us only the barest outline of the flight into Egypt. From the few prophecies in the Old Testament,[20] as well as from Joseph's dream related above, it is clear that the ancient scribes recognized an affiliation between Egypt and the birth of a new religion. Egypt was the country where the idea of religious belief had been forged long before that of Jewish monotheism. It was also a country inhabited by a people wise in the ways of the spirit. Its temple priests had earlier counseled philosophers and poets, as they were to go on doing well into the modern era. It is known, for example, that Pythagoras, Thales, and Plato visited Egypt half a millennium before Joseph brought his family across the Sinai Desert.

It is hard to comprehend the magnitude of the events surrounding their flight. A child is born in a stable near Bethlehem, a star announces his birth, three astrologers from the East visit the stable to pay their respects, and finally the king himself decides that all the children of the town under the age of two must be killed in order to protect his throne.[21] The king of Judea is afraid of a carpenter's son, apparently. More precisely, he is fearful of any child born within the vicinity of Bethlehem that might grow up to supplant him as king. A child born of a virgin whose destiny is to rock the very foundations of Rome, it seems, threatens the very existence of the state.

Indeed, this child will one day change the way the world sees itself. He will set it on a path from which it will never turn back. Is it any wonder that Herod was extremely agitated when told by his chief priests and lawyers that a shepherd would come out of the land of Judea to rule over Israel?[22]

We must reimagine this story in the context of new information derived from modern scholarship. It is no use simply accepting the hagiographies that abound, particularly in Egypt itself. This may satisfy many people, but it does nothing to deepen our contact with the symbolism of the journey or the peregrinations of a family destined to reinvent our notions of suffering and of love. All the elements of this story are steeped in our struggle for freedom and the incomprehensible privilege of encountering the divine. It is we who make this journey each and every day of our lives, even if we pretend otherwise. It is we who travel into exile as soon as we begin to acknowledge the limitations of the material world, and of our capacity to transform it.

I was fearful of making such a journey. Not because of the physical hardships, but because I was uncertain whether in doing so I was merely reiterating events belonging to a folktale. Does one set off on a journey through Egypt to authenticate a few lines in a Gospel, in order to say, yes, it is true? Did Jesus in fact travel into the heartland of an ancient country long noted for its tolerance and understanding so that he might escape death at the hands of a king? This could be counted as a reason, though a flimsy one—almost a whimsy, no more. Even if the event happened, and the Holy Family spent nearly four years in Egypt wandering from one place to another, it is important to realize that the true reason for their journey was perhaps to do with acquiring a deeper understanding of the nature of exile itself.

Before entering the land of Egypt, however, I needed to understand the personalities of the protagonists. It is not enough to toss about names and events, hoping they might stick to the paper. Herod, Bethlehem, a divine birth in a cave, Mary, Joseph, the Massacre of the Innocents, these are all well-known elements in the story, but they have become so timeworn that their portent is diminished. To understand them better one needs to be like a satellite camera scanning the surface of the earth. Instead of observing its contours and marveling at its symmetry, one has to focus on details. The story of the Family's flight into Egypt is clearly delineated by objects and places, by miracles and supernatural circumstance, to the point where these often obscure the ground upon which such events have been played out.

King Herod, for one, fascinates me. Here was a man born of an ambitious father, Antipater, who himself forged successful partnerships with Pompey and later Julius Caesar in order to become the procurator of Judea. Ingratiation was part of Antipater's temperament. He saw the future of his sons and the possession of their budding kingdom as indelibly linked to the imperial order. In turn, his son Herod was appointed by Octavian (later Caesar Augustus) as tetrarch of Galilee and Perea. After the Parthian invasion on the eastern frontier, Herod was later declared king of Judea by Mark Antony. He then made truce with his domestic opponents by marrying one of their daughters, Mariamme, thus paving the way for his eventual occupation of Jerusalem as its king.

Like his father before him, who knew which side to support in times of political uncertainty, Herod threw in his lot with Octavian at Actium in his battle against his former patron. Antony had forced Herod to give up some of the coastal region of Palestine to his paramour Cleopatra, Queen of Egypt. This loss, apparently, had provoked him to switch sides. The reward for doing so came later, in the form of more cities being added to his kingdom, after Octavian's victory at Actium.

An able administrator and skillful financier who did not mind taxing his people to their limit, Herod endeavored to aggrandize his name with spectacular building projects, including a string of fortress-palaces, of which Masada is the most famous. A philhellene, too, he also built amphitheaters and bankrolled the Olympic Games. He lavished donations on Athens, while rebuilding the temple in Jerusalem to appease the ire of his people. To commemorate the latter event, Herod arranged for a golden eagle to be placed on top of the temple gate, much to the disgust of the priests, who began to see him as a dangerous despot. Herod, it seems, had begun to outgrow even his own masterful sense of self-importance.

There was something insatiable yet intemperate about his character. For all his public posturing, Herod was never that sure of himself. Few survived his displeasure. Nor were many members of his large family immune from his anger or suspicion. Some of their intrigues brought about their execution, not least his favorite wife, Mariamme, and her two sons. Even his eldest son and expected heir joined Herod's long list of victims, before the king's sudden death in 4 BC. Herod's madness, it seems, was the result of a family in crisis, as well as a long history of public and private intrigue. His father had set the tone of strategic political alliances and corrupt family values from which he could not escape. Thus he became a victim of his own dichotomous personality.

A half-Jew by birth and a philhellene by choice, Herod sought to shore up his position in Judea by aligning himself with the rulers in Rome. In the end he found himself alone, a man fearful of his future and abandoned by his people. No wonder the threat of a carpenter's son sitting upon his throne was enough to drive him to distraction. The massacre of the infants in Bethlehem was the result of a man living on the edge of despair. Herod was at the end of his tether, it seems; he had made evil his helpmate in his lonely bid to achieve immortality.

It is a scene from which we might wish to extract ourselves. Blood on the streets of a small town in Judea, a mad king in his palace railing at the world and his loss of self, a family in fear stealing by night across the border into Egypt: such is the stuff of tragedy. Yet, if one is to accept the Gospel's interpretation of these events, the star that shone over Bethlehem sometime in the year 7 BC heralded the beginning of a new era, one that was to have far-reaching implications for the world. The astrologers from the East certainly thought this to be so. The fact is that historical events, as much as events of the spirit, intersected in that momentous year. An infant God-man was born into a troubled kingdom belonging to a king who mistook the birth of a Messiah to mean the loss of his throne, when what it actually referred to was the establishment of a new kind of kingdom on earth.

The family's flight was as much a flight from a delusionary king as it was from the decline of an older order of governance. Israel by then was a satrap of Rome, and Egypt now one of its colonies. Herod's extravagant claims to kingship were, moreover, in stark contrast to the birth of a new kind of king into the world. Jesus was the child of poor parents who possessed little education other than knowledge of their religious obligations as good Jews. In a very real sense, they were anonymous members of the vast and ungovernable peasantry that populated the entire Middle East. What few possessions they owned could be loaded onto the back of a donkey. It was this kind of freedom, this *poverty* of freedom, that threatened not only Herod but also the entire cosmopolitan and material nature of late antiquity. Not only did the Holy Family choose to travel away from their homeland to a country whose reputation among Jews was ambivalent given their historical association, going back to the period of the Exodus fifteen centuries earlier, but they had taken it upon themselves to attend to the ills of the world through an act of faith. An angel, after all, had made this possible.

Angels are integral to their story, as are dreams. More particularly, to the role of Joseph as comforter and guide to his wife and son as they confronted the task of survival together. He, more than most men, was a great dreamer. Of the five dreams related in the first two chapters of the Gospel of Matthew, four are Joseph's. Before he marries Mary, an angel appears to him in a dream, imploring him not to be afraid to take her as his wife, even though she is already pregnant. Later, an angel informs him in a dream of the threat Herod poses and advises him to flee to Egypt. "Rise up, take the child and his mother to Egypt, and stay there until I tell you."[23]

We must embellish it a little: a celestial entity appeared to this man as he lay asleep, possibly in the stable, urging him to care for his newborn stepson. Joseph thus becomes an interlocutor between the angels and ourselves; he interprets. Moreover, he takes upon himself the role of father to the child in defiance of convention. The uncertain events surrounding Mary's pregnancy (was she ravished, did an angel appear to her as she maintained?) failed to impede the steadfastness of his purpose. Joseph sought strength in dreams, in the interpenetration of images that informed his every action as a man. In this sense, Joseph became a man possessed. His every gesture from here on transformed him to the point where all his movements, all the decisions that he made on behalf of his family, were divinely ordered.

Joseph is a figure of incomparable stability and discretion. While he might at first have doubted Mary's account of her conception at the hands of an angel, what in the *Protevangelium* is called the "seed of an angel," he again acquiesces to the voice of an angel, who tells him of Jesus's destiny as the future savior of the world: "'Fear not this child, for that which is in her is of the Holy Ghost, and she shall bear a son whose name is Jesus, for he shall save his people. . . .' And Joseph arose from sleep and glorified God, which had shown this favor to her: and he watched over her."[24]

Clearly, Joseph was a man prepared to listen and act upon information that he received from his dreams. He is a watcher too—what in the *Gospel of Thomas* is known as a "passerby," someone who observes.[25] Such qualities were much prized by the ancients. These were often expressed as "anticipatory awareness" (*pronoia*), "internal reflection" (*ennoia*), and "foreknowledge or intuition" (*prognosis*). They constitute what is known as "luminous *epinoia*," or insight. It is this quality of spiritual intuition that sets Joseph apart from most men. He lived a secret life that remained concealed behind his persona as a carpenter. Wood was the chamber into which he pressed his true nature. A widower who wandered from place to place seeking work, he was less a man wielding a mallet than someone committed to the preservation of that special aspect of divinity that now resided in his newborn stepson. He traveled about in order to remain anonymous, given his powers. Joseph never wrestles with an angel, but heeds. If not a begetter, at least with Mary, he is certainly a man of great inner strength and resolve. It is as if he personally chose his role as the comforter.

The family's flight into Egypt brings into focus two men least likely even to have been aware of one another's existence. Herod, the lonely king pacing the corridors of his palace in Jerusalem, trying to eliminate those threats to his fading patrimony, and Joseph, an old man able to dream himself and his family into a new existence, far from the clutches of royal obsession—these men affect one another in the most unlikely circumstances. It is almost as if a script had been written emphasizing their opposing characters.

Nonetheless, Herod deserved everything he had brought upon himself, torn apart as he was by ambition, doubt, and megalomania. There was little to redeem him, not even the pathetic nature of his crimes. In contrast, his chief antagonist was little more than a wandering carpenter, a homeless tradesman. Between them, they would struggle over the life of a child born in a stable to a mother who insisted that she had been visited by an angel. It is hard to imagine a more unlikely scenario: that of a king succumbing to the might of a disenfranchised family, while transcendent events are already being formulated in the mind of an unlikely infant.

I was about to journey through a country that had long ago been prepared for the imminent arrival of such a family. The events surrounding Joseph and Mary's departure made it imperative for the them to seek refuge in a land now under the direct control of Caesar Augustus, who, in spite of negative remarks by Tacitus, had made it a relatively safe place to live.[26] The population of Egypt, which at this time was around eight million, included, on top of the Egyptian majority, a privileged Greek minority, a few citizens of Rome, and numerous Jewish communities living along the Nile, notably in Alexandria. Corn was the staple product, a good deal of which was paid as tribute to Rome. In the first three centuries of the Roman era, Egypt sent 150,000 tons of grain to Rome each year as the *annona*, or tribute. Furthermore, the last of the Ptolemies, Cleopatra, was long dead by her own hand (30 BC), and the colony was under the rule of a prefect appointed by the emperor himself.

Jewish settlement stretched along the Nile as far south as the First Cataract. They had built a temple to Yahweh on the island of Elephantine at Aswan, a sign of how entrenched they were as a community in their adopted land. Free by official decree to live according to the precepts of their religion, they were not immune to the attractions and influences of Greek culture, especially in urban centers like Alexandria. We know from Diodorus of Sicily that the city had a population of 300,000 free inhabitants, which meant that its true census must have made it much larger.[27] It is noteworthy that the Greek translation of the Old Testament, known as the Septuagint, was rendered here in the third century BC. Philo, a wealthy Jew of Alexandria steeped in Greek philosophy, produced voluminous works in Greek, some of which are still read today. The Jews of Alexandria enjoyed many privileges conferred by the Ptolemies, later to be reaffirmed by Augustus, including that of their own council of elders, a privilege denied to Greek citizens. Is it any wonder that Joseph decided, on the advice of the angel, to escape from Israel to Egypt, where his people already enjoyed a life of relative stability and calm?

Moreover, he could be assured of work in his adopted country. Timber, though scarce and therefore costly, was in great demand in boatbuilding, windows and doors, as well as furniture for the wealthy. Chaparrals, acacia, sycamore, fig and tamarisk, and the woods of dying fruit trees were all readily available. Even the trunks of palm trees were put to good use: sawn into boards, they were employed especially in roofing, where their light weight proved an advantage. Although the *Arabic Gospel of the Infancy of the Savior*, an early apocryphal text, suggests that "Joseph was not very skilful in carpentry,"[28] the text goes on to say that Joseph was called to Jerusalem by Herod's successor, Archaelus, on his return to Israel from Egypt and was asked to make a throne for the new king. Apparently he spent nearly two years making it.[29] According to the same text, the various woods used in the construction of the throne were much celebrated, all of which indicates that Joseph possessed great skill in carpentry.[30]

It is no accident that the Holy Family journeyed into the land of the gods. For here an established archaeology of belief had long ago laid bare the mysteries of the otherworld for people to experience. To suggest that Jesus was not about to assume the mantle of other authorial figures in the Egyptian pantheon because of the nature of his unique persona would be to dismiss the evidence. Even in his infancy, Jesus was about to confront an older order of gods, absorb their timeless wisdom, and return to Palestine immeasurably nourished. It was the destiny of the infant Jesus, in the company of his beloved family, to journey up the Nile River in order to discover the legendary "Alter of the Lord" said to reside at the very center of Egypt, equidistant from the rest of the world.

Such is the nature of mystical journeys. They take us to places where memory, intellect, and belief intersect. Egypt was to become the place where significant events in the early development of Christianity would be played out against a backdrop of extreme antiquity, none other than the realm of the Pharaohs. This country on the Nile, long celebrated for its knowledge of the afterlife, was to be transformed into the cocoon from which the infant Jesus would one day emerge as a fully fledged avatar, a God-man, thus reaffirming the Old Testament prophecy of Hosea when he announced, "Out of Egypt I called My son."[31]

My task looked simple enough: to journey in the footsteps of the Holy Family in a bid to separate fact from fantasy, reality from myth. It would not be easy, however. There were so many layers to the story, so many interpretations and opinions to sift through if I were ever going to find out what really happened to them during their travels in Egypt. I was about to explore one of the least-known aspects of Christ's early life—those years before he entered the temple in Jerusalem to debate with the priests at the age of twelve. Was he not equipped then with rare insight and wisdom, as the Gospels suggest?[32] His years spent in Egypt until the age of approximately five are therefore important to understanding the nature of the man he was to become in later life. How much of the lore of Egypt did he absorb as a child, one wonders? It is not unreasonable to assume that, as Egypt determined the character of Moses, so did it determine the character of Jesus. It seems that both men are children of one of antiquity's greatest rivers, the Nile. The river, as much as the country and its people, was to be integral to understanding the early development of Christ before he became the Savior we know and love.

4 *Confronting the Old Gods*

THE INFANT JESUS WOULD HAVE been around eight or nine months old when the Holy Family set out from Pelusium on their way to the delta region. If one is to accept that Jesus was circumcised within eight days of his birth, and a month later presented at the temple in Jerusalem as prescribed by Mosaic law, this would make it unlikely that the family had left Bethlehem any earlier.

We should assume also that his birth did not reach Herod's ears immediately—and probably not until Anna, Zachariah's wife and mother of John the Baptist, had spoken of it publicly. She lived only a half a mile away from Herod's palace, and is the most likely one to have spread the rumor, given her friendship with Mary. Nor do we know when the astrologers from the East received their audience with Herod, nor how long it subsequently took them to find the Holy Family in Bethlehem. If one adds this unaccounted-for period of time to the six months the family reputedly spent in Hebron, and a further lapse of time for travel to Pelusium via Ashkelon, then we arrive at Jesus's conjectured age of nine months.

It was important for me to ascertain this sequence of events as I drove westward through the desert along a straight road, toward the narrow isthmus of land known as El Qantara ("the bridge"), which once linked the two lakes of Menzaleh and Balah south of the Nile estuary. The country was flat and bare of herbage. Nothing grows there save memories. After my visit to Tel el-Farma, I was about to enter a region steeped in biblical history. This was the gateway to the province of Goshen mentioned in Genesis, the land Joseph gave over to his brethren in the hope that they might remain with him in Egypt, and the place from which Moses and his people fled to the Red Sea.[33] Moreover, I was traveling along the same route taken by Abraham and his party when they first entered Egypt nearly two thousand years before the birth of Christ.[34] Much later, it became a Roman road linking Pelusium and Daphnae on the western side of the isthmus.

Herodotus mentions that the Pharaoh Sesostris (XII Dynasty) used this same route in order to reach Daphnae after subduing the whole of Asia and Europe as far as Thrace. The ancient historian tells an interesting story of how Sesostris's brother, who had been acting as regent in his absence, attempted to burn him and his six sons alive at a banquet given in his honor. "He piled wood around the house and set it on fire," Herodotus relates, invoking the image of an elaborate funeral pyre. Sesostris, naturally fearing for his life, asks his wife what they should do. "She counseled him to lay two of his six sons on the fire to make a bridge through the flames, whereby they might step over the bodies of the two and escape."[35]

Daphnae was also the home of the so-called Deserters at the time of Psammetichus (XXVI Dynasty). They had been ordered to guard the eastern approaches to Egypt against invasion, and did so without any relief for three years. Finally they became bored, and decided to desert their post by journeying overland to Ethiopia. Psammetichus pursued them with his army in an attempt to persuade them "not to desert the gods of their fathers," nor their children and wives. The Deserters scorned his entreaty, pointing instead to his "manly part," thereby suggesting to him that wherever they might end up there would be no shortage of "wives and children" in Ethiopia. It may well be that this large migration of soldiers (more than 100,000 according to Herodotus) taught

Egyptian customs to the local inhabitants when they settled in Ethiopia as guests of its king, who in turn instilled in them "milder manners." It may also be that this early migration paved the way for the Coptic Church to spread into Ethiopia at a later date, as the country was already sympathetic to Egyptian beliefs and customs.[36] It is interesting to note also that Sesostris was reputedly the only Egyptian king to rule over Ethiopia.

Sesostris's son succeeded to the kingship and so to the control of the delta region. However, according to Herodotus he was mysteriously blinded after a narcissistic encounter with the Nile. Following a very high flood one year, the water rose to a height of eighteen cubits, causing it to spread across the fields as never before, and a strong wind blew up and roughened the surface of this vast, temporary lake. The king was so infatuated by the phenomenon that he hurled a spear into the midst of the river. Immediately he was afflicted with a disease of the eyes and became blind. After ten years, an oracle from the city of Buto notified the king that his punishment was drawing to an end. But in order to regain his sight he would have to wash his eyes with the menstrual blood of a virgin.

First, he attempted to use the blood of his own wife, but to no avail. Then he approached a succession of women in an attempt to overcome his affliction. None of these were able to help him until one last young virgin. When he had finally regained his sight, the king herded all the women who had failed him into one town and burned it to the ground. He later took the young virgin as his wife. The moral of the story is evident: the Nile, it seems, has a way of exercising its authority.[37]

The province of Goshen was thus the adopted land of the Jews. Crossing under the Suez Canal by way of a modern tunnel, I made my way toward the tel of Pithon, after visiting Daphnae. This city was associated with the Pharaoh's so-called treasure cities built by the Jews.[38] The same Pharaoh, Ramses II, known as the "oppression Pharaoh," insisted that their sons should be killed, including the as yet unborn child known as Moses.[39] It was no accident that the Holy Family should journey to a province associated with an earlier attempt to destroy a prophet. Nor was it an accident that in his adult years Moses longed to return to Israel after a long period in exile of his people. The mythographers, obviously, had been hard at work. Christ needed to be linked to an earlier prophetic dispensation so that the old law might be joined to the new. Such narrative elegance appealed to those early Christians interested in validating their religion. Moses was a great prophet and leader; ergo, Christ was to adopt his mantle in the new kingdom.

The symbolism associated with Pithon extends to the city being the home of the god Tem or Nefer-Temu. As "young Tem," he was the god of the rising sun born of the cat goddess Bast, from the nearby town of Bubastis.[40] Bast was known as the Lady of the East, and she bestowed upon her son Tem the gentle, fructifying heat of the early morning sun. Tem is associated with the beauty of dawn, with his headdress made from the lotus blossom, itself a symbol of life.[41] In the Pyramid texts Tem is described thus: "Unas has risen like Nefer-Temu from the lotus to the nostrils of Ra [the sun-god], and he goes forth from the horizon each day, and the gods are sanctified by the sight of him."[42]

Pithon was his home on the eastern edge of the delta, a god sacred to the freshness of morning and capable of transforming himself like a lotus. These connotations merge with the idea of Jesus as the "Sun of the sun," as later indicated by Philo, since Tem was also the first *living* man-god, and as such always represented with a human head.[43] Was it not Jesus who said later, "I am the light of the world," thus alluding to his dawn-like nature? It would seem that one of Ramses's "treasure cities" housed more than wealth; rather, it became the repository of the nascent avataric nature of the future God-man, Jesus Christ.

These associations brought to life the archaeological mound known as Tel el-Maskuta, near El-Mahsama, which was once the city of Pithon. The road nearby followed a branch of the Nile, so it was easy to imagine the Holy Family proceeding by stages along this ancient route, enjoying for a change a green and verdant land-scape. Even I was struck by the sudden change in the countryside now that I had quit the Sinai. To think that they had visited cities steeped in an age-old spiritual tradition was not lost on me, either. I kept thinking of my conversation with Pope Shenouda a few days before, when he had alluded to a similarity between Christianity and Pharaonic life. A new world was opening up to them, as to me—of fertile fields, palm groves, water buffalo yoked to wooden ploughs, hippopotamuses yawning in the shallows, herons standing on dykes watching for insects or frogs, and of a warm sun forever linked to the lotus blossom. Surely it had some effect upon their behavior. Surely they found themselves laughing aloud at times, and sharing their joy with those they passed along the road, just as I did.

It does not take much to imagine them traveling the high road, even today. Of course the traffic and the pollution, as well as the sight of bizarre, surrealist trees standing by the roadside bearing exhaust manifolds that look like metallic fruit, may detract from any illusion one might have of encountering an idyllic scene from the Bible. Egypt is no longer some rustic arcadia, a land populated by date palms and timeless village scenes. It is an intensely populated land confined to a river already controlled and managed by the Aswan Dam project in Upper Egypt. The annual inundation is a thing of the past, the Nilometer in Cairo that once measured the height of floods little more than a tourist curiosity. Yet one senses the country's antiquity and its reliance on the perpetuation of certain memories.

Mary and Joseph would have encountered these too. They would have observed the great temples of the gods, and possibly experienced their annual festivities, as they passed through town and village and through cities such as Sais, where the goddess Neith, "the mistress of heaven," was venerated by the Egyptians. Even in the ubiquitous scarab beetle they would have noticed in the fields, its hard carapace reminiscent of the upper hemisphere of a human skull—in it they would have found themselves rubbing shoulders with an animated spirit and solar symbol.

It is not hard to understand why earlier chroniclers of the Holy Family's journey sought to invest it with their own interpretations. The Spanish king Sancho IV (1257–1295) related what is perhaps the first recorded miracle of their flight. The king followed in their footsteps as a personal act of piety after his conquest of Tarifa in Palestine. He came across a cave in the desert where the Holy Family had reputedly camped after an encounter with a dragon. "The dragon fell down and worshipped the child," relates Sancho, inferring also that a number of wild animals from the desert approached Jesus for his blessing. Isaiah's prophecy was thus fulfilled: "The wolf also shall dwell with the lamb, and the leopard shall lie down with the kid . . . and a little child shall lead them."[44]

It is this kind of magical tale that leaves us feeling incredulous today. But we must remember that in the thirteenth century everyone who came to the Holy Land, or indeed Egypt, wanted to reinforce their own imaginative encounter with the life of Christ. That a dragon and a number of wild animals were subdued by way of a theurgic act of a divine child further substantiated their belief. The message is simple enough: the miracle that the infant Jesus performed was not to pacify wild animals but to learn how to suppress the innate opposition we might have toward one another. In a desert cave far from civilization, it seems that Love had sought rest in its bid to overcome violence and hate.

A few kilometers further along the road, which skirted canals and palm groves, I came upon the village of El-Qassasin, considered to be where the ancient city of Succoth once stood. It was here that the Israelites camped at the time of their Exodus from Egypt. I tried to imagine "six hundred thousand" people camped here with their flocks. In their possession they carried the bones of Joseph, their first leader—much as Coptic Christians store the relics of saints in their churches today. Ramses and his army were some distance behind, intent on catching up with them before they escaped. It was here, or near here, that an angel descended upon the Israelite camp and cast a wall of cloud between them and Pharaoh's army. The trick worked: the Egyptians found themselves surrounded by darkness, while the Jews were able to press on to the Red Sea.

It seemed strange to think that such a sleepy town as Succoth, with its poorly built apartment blocks and narrow, dust-laden streets crowded with bicycles, old cars, and hawkers' carts, could have been chosen for a visionary event to occur. How does such a dust bowl of a town become selected to host an angel? Indeed, like Bethlehem, how do any of these insignificant habitations, noted more for their poverty than their beauty, find themselves thrust into the limelight of history, to grace us with their portent?

At Ramses, or Tel el-Kebir, as it is known today, which happens to be another of the treasure cities, a few miles further along the road, I suddenly realized that I was about to enter the fertile lands of the delta. For Joseph, Mary, and Salome, the sight of these broad fields stretching to the horizon, rich with crops and date palms growing between a fretwork of canals, must have afforded them an immense feeling of relief, not to mention surprise at the sheer variety of natural growth that greeted their gaze. After their long trek across the desert, the lands of the Nile must have surely seemed to them like paradise. Not even in Judea would they have encountered such abundance. Their landscape, after all, at least in memory, was one filled with little more than flocks of sheep and goats, as well as the ubiquitous olive groves. Could it be that they were destined to make the idea of verdancy central to their lives? In one sense, surely, as this is among the many gifts that Christ later bestowed upon the world.

But all is not always right in paradise. The Holy Family, under Joseph's guidance, would have slowly made their way toward the city of Bubastis, dedicated as it was to the cat goddess. It would have been their first encounter with any Egyptian city of note, so one must assume that they were looking forward to their arrival with a mixture of anxiety and hope. Would there be Jewish families living there who might help them? Would Joseph find work? Salome, of course, may have hoped to find employment as a midwife among Egyptian women, as this was her calling. Between all three of them there must have been a sense that, after the difficulties of the journey so far, better times lay ahead. The life of the infant Jesus was dependent upon a little good luck coming their way at last.

But before they had reached the city, tradition tells us, they were in for a rude awakening. Life on the road is anything but a smooth transition from one place to the next. There are always people ready to prey upon the gullibility of strangers. Theophilus, in his *Vision*, is the first to alert us to the dangers that lie hidden around every corner. "It was a warm day," Mary relates. "We had been walking for some hours. When we reached the outskirts of the city, Joseph, because of his age, pleaded with us to lie down and rest. Salome also decided to sleep."

At this point, it seems, Mary sat down under a nearby tree to feed the infant Jesus. Mary's recollection of this moment is vivid: "My son was wearing clothing the greenish color of grape, a color similar to that of the clothes I wore when I was presented in the temple." Linking Jesus's clothing to her own at her time of presentation in the temple is significant, for green is the color of vegetation and spring, of life over death. It is also the color of the Epiphany season, which marks the visit by the Magi to the cave in Bethlehem. Mary seems to be inferring that, while she is the origin of all renewal by carrying the Christ child in her womb, he is its source. It was a garment "I never put off again," she relates. "Nor did I put off the veil I am wearing." Mary is bound by a moment celebrating purity, her own as well as her son's. The color green is a testament to their difference from all others.

Mary goes on to describe another aspect of her son's apparel, that of his tiny sandals. Reading in the *Vision* that these sandals were also colored, this time in gold and silver hue, I asked myself what kind of world did Theophilus—or Mary—wish to invoke? Silver was a precious metal tested by fire, and so a symbol of purity and chastity. Did it prefigure Christ's later life as a celibate? And what of gold: the symbol of pure light, and thus of the heavenly element, which God inhabits? Clearly the author wanted us to understand that the infant Jesus was already marked by destiny to become a God-man whose feet were contained by the felicity of precious metals. These sandals would henceforth determine his stance in the world as much as any utterance he might subsequently make.

Little did Mary know that at this point two brigands, one Egyptian and the other Syrian—a "Hebrew from our land"—were observing her movements. These men were intent on stealing her clothes, since they resembled the "garments of Kings." The Egyptian thief, however, became wary, suspecting that this child was like no other. He attempted to persuade his friend to leave the family alone, but to no avail. It was not until Jesus demanded a drink of water that Mary chose to walk into town and find a well. While she was gone, the robbers decided to act. They crept into Joseph's camp and stole the sandals while the child and Salome slept. The deed was done: two sanctified objects, possibly gifts from the Magi, were now in the possession of thieves. It was as if Theophilus wanted us to know that chastity and purity are always going to be the object of scorn by others.

We will meet these brigands again, later in the Holy Family's sojourn.

Driving through the outskirts of Zagazig that afternoon, into a crowded city of crumbling apartments and dirt-laden alleys, which in turn has now enveloped the ruins of the once-grand temple of Bast, I realized that ancient Bubastis represented an important transition for the travelers. They had escaped Herod perhaps, but now they were entering a city alien to their better instincts. Not only had Jesus lost his magic sandals to a pair of thieves, but the Holy Family was also about to come face-to-face with the ultimate provocation: a goddess whose links with other deities would all but swallow up their integrity as representatives of a new dispensation.

The family was to confront a mirror image of themselves. They were about to find out whether their fears, their doubts, and their courage were capable of combating the power of the old gods.

Meanwhile, my taxi slowly negotiated the streets, picking its way through jostling crowds, beasts of burden, and stalls offering cigarette lighters, penknives, and shoelaces. The city seemed like one huge bazaar, selling everything imaginable. Women behind veils, men in ill-fitting suits or jellabas sidled past, gazing into my vehicle as they did so. I was new to them, a figure from an alien place. This was a city where contrary currents had once flowed, transforming the home of Bast into that of the Greek goddess Artemis. The events that unfolded here, however, would send shock waves throughout the world.

5
City of Women

HERODOTUS IS THE MOST ENTER-
taining of observers. One must try to picture him
traveling throughout Egypt, quill in hand, an oil lamp in his
bag, and sheets of papyrus carefully laid out before him, trying
to come to terms with the mystery that lay at the heart of this
ancient land. He was preeminently a biographer with a keen eye
for all that he saw, and always ready to talk to everyone he met.
One gains the impression that he reveled in the task of absorbing
as much as he could. Nothing escaped his curiosity. He rendered
the panorama that was Egypt in insights that are human, balanced, and reflective.

Visiting the temple of Bast in Bubastis, he was at pains to describe
its layout. "It stands on an island," he relates, "surrounded by two
channels of water running in contrary directions. The outer court
of the temple is adorned with notable figures six cubits high. The
temple is in the midst of the city that overlooks it, since the land
was raised by Sesostris. Trees overshadow its walls, which are carved
with figures. A great shrine is enclosed by these walls, wherein the
image of the goddess stands." One senses that Herodotus must
have entered this precinct in a state of awe.

Mary's impression of the city was less favorable. When she entered
it with Jesus in her arms, no one welcomed her. "I asked for water,"

she states, "but no one cared to quench my son's thirst." The people of Bubastis were indifferent to her plight. Living at the gateway to Egypt, its inhabitants were inured to the influence of foreigners, probably because they were suspicious of their motives. Though a small Jewish community may have been present in the city due to earlier colonization by the Israelites, Theophilus does not allude to this possibility. Rather, he is at pains to present a city that spurns visitors, that has little sympathy for travelers or their needs.

"I cried," Mary admits, as much out of frustration at their treatment by the people of Bubastis as by the recent robbery. "I never saw a people with less faith and compassion than its inhabitants. The only gain that accrued to me in this town is that my son's sandals have been stolen!" It was at this point that her beloved son heard her weeping. In an act of childish compassion he wiped away her tears "with his holy hands," as Theophilus writes. Then, in a significant gesture that prefigures all his future dealings with the world, Jesus "stretched out his small finger and made a sign of the cross on the earth." Instantly a spring of water bubbled forth from the ground as "sweet as honey and as white as snow." The hagiographer in Theophilus reaches new heights: Jesus is able not only to speak but also to pronounce upon matters pertaining to the future evolution of the human spirit. "Let this water help," the Christ child utters, "make whole and heal the souls and bodies of all those who shall drink of it. With the exception, however," he adds, "of the people of Bubastis who will remain forever subject to disease."

It seems that the Waters of Life have been released from the earth for the first time. Jesus is no longer swaddled in silence, a child without voice. He has come into his own, a divine child with the power of transforming reality through an act of will. It is easy to skate over such an event as little more than a pious act in keeping with his miraculous nature. He is not subject to contingency other than as a man of flesh and blood. But as God and therefore supra-normal, the world is there for him to manipulate in whichever way he pleases. Yet his actions are not arbitrary. They are steeped in a new mystical and moral dimension. Body and soul can now be healed by the Waters of Life that are none other than the Logos, the divine Word of God. In the past, as stated in the Gospel of John, the Word *was*—that is, it was a divine act associated with creation.[45] One needs to understand the event that occurred in Bubastis for what it implies: from henceforth every action on the part of Jesus would be open to interpretation as something altogether current. His gestures and his remarks had entered the domain of words for all to consider.

The loss of his sandals has caused him to open his lips. Mary, his mother, has been comforted. She is now under his aegis, rather than the other way around. Jesus is capable of guiding his parents through the shoals of adversity. That the healing of the body *and* the soul has become essential to the realization of wholeness says much about the new dispensation for which Jesus is responsible. He is now one who longs to take up the matter of the world's woe and make it his own. Is it any wonder that Bubastis should become the place where he reveals his true nature? For this is the home of the goddess of the East, of sunrise, of the dawn of the new sun.

At the entrance to the temple grounds early that morning, I paid the necessary fee to a guard in order that I might view the ruins. My first instinct was to wander among them at random. The area seemed to go on forever. Scattered blocks of stone, many of which were elaborately carved with hieroglyphs, littered the open space. Broken statuary and lotus columns lay about, all but lost among weeds. I came upon two seated Pharaonic statues, a husband and wife, their faces worn away by the weather. Inscriptions on stones, as well as carved murals, told of an age when the word was as important as it was later to become for John the Evangelist. Rather than being the Living Word, however, what lay before me was the utterance of a people in love with self-aggrandizement. Pharaonic culture regarded the word as magical, the cartouche as the frozen yet declamatory statement of self.

Entering a broad avenue by a crossroad halfway along, I looked left toward the statue of a sphinx gazing down the avenue. At the opposite end of the expanse I could see another statue that immediately lured me along the path. My heart raced. Suddenly I was standing before the goddess Bast, her feline features in marked contrast to the delicacy of her body. I gazed at her narrow waist and pubescent breasts, aware that she was both beautiful yet mysterious. Her hair was arranged in a plait on her back, suggesting that she had been sculpted during the Ptolemaic era. On her head she wore the vulture-headed uraeus, symbol of the union of the two lands of Egypt. Here was the goddess who gave to dawn its brightness, its freshness, and its sense of the birth of a new day. Everything about her denoted the regenerative influence of the early-morning sun.

The inscription below in stone celebrated her magnificence.

> Homage to you, O Bast-Ra, mistress of the gods, bearer of wings, lady of the red apparel, you who wear the crowns of the South and the North. In the Boat of a Million Years, you are pre-eminent, and rise in the seat of silence, queen, mistress, and lady. Mother to the horizon of heaven, beloved of all and destroyer of rebellion, you stand in the bow of the boat of your divine father. You are a mighty flame, mistress of enchantments, and object of adoration. You, Lady, arise above the Eight Gods of Hermopolis. The living souls who are in their hidden places praise the mystery that is in you.

It is a paean to the principle of femininity, which prompted me to ask: could the Virgin Mary overcome Bast as a symbol of divine mercy?

One could not stand before the cat goddess and not ask such a question. In the Holy Family's party there were two women, Mary and Salome. Up to this point Salome has been silent, a figure of loyalty but without a clearly defined character. We know she was reputedly Mary's cousin and the midwife who attended Christ's birth. One must assume that she loved Jesus as if he were her own. That she chose to accompany Mary and Joseph to Egypt further engenders our admiration. Our image of Salome is that she is no ordinary young woman. She is someone practical yet loving, a confidant to Mary in her moments of self-doubt, a counselor to Joseph when he needs to discuss issues that affect them all. In contrast to Mary, who lived only for her son, Salome engages with the world.

Mary is a far more complicated figure. We know a good deal about her early life from various apocryphal texts. Her father, Joachim, was a wealthy Jew denied the right to make offerings in the temple because his wife, Anna, had not produced a child. Deeply shamed, Joachim pitched a tent in the wilderness and fasted there for forty days. Meanwhile, Anna wept to see her husband isolate himself like this. She too felt that she was flawed in some way. In despair, Anna took herself into a nearby garden and sat under a laurel tree to weep. Looking upward she spied a nest of sparrows, which only made her weep more bitterly. "Oh, how I long to have a child!" she cried out. "To what am I likened? I am not like the earth that brings forth fruit in due season." At this point an angel appeared and announced to Anna that she was to give birth. When Joachim heard of this, and as an expression of his profound gratitude, he vowed to send his daughter to the temple to be educated once she had reached the age of three.

Mary did not set foot on the earth until she was three years old. Anna had made a vow to this effect, and so made a sanctuary in the child's room, where nothing unclean was permitted to enter. "She is a miraculous child," Anna said. Then at the age of three Mary was handed over to the temple priests as an "undefiled torch." A priest received her and placed Mary on the third step of the altar where she danced for the first time. "Her bright spirit could not be contained," says the *Protevangelium of James*, as her parents turned to depart. For the next few years the child excelled, revealing qualities that were both "fearless and gentle." Truly, she was a wise young woman, so the *Arabic Gospel of the Infancy of the Savior* explains. But she was also a dancer, one capable of flight.

Subsequent to completing her temple duties, the young Mary cared for the aged. One day, while bathing the brow of a sick young woman who was not expected to survive the night, Mary heard angels singing. She presumed the utterance might have come from her patient. When she touched the girl's forehead, Mary discovered that the fever had passed. At once she was aware that a miracle had occurred. "Mary," a voice whispered. "You have been brought into the world without stain of sin. You have used your talents to care for others. In so doing, the Lord honors you." This was a moment of realization for Mary. She knew that henceforth her life must be dedicated to the realization of some supreme event. As a dancer, she was there to represent all the hiddenness of divine mercy with her entire body.

At fourteen she was betrothed to Joseph, an elderly carpenter from the south who lived in Nazareth with his son Clopas, in a modest house that presumably he had helped to build. Joseph had always been a wanderer, moving from place to place seeking work. Why was this man chosen to become the husband of Mary? It is never made clear, except that his age appears to be a factor. It is unlikely that he might wish to have intimacy with so young a woman as Mary. Another reason lay in him successfully passing a test for suitors performed in the temple. As the priests kneeled in prayer, Joseph struck the ground with his staff, and at once a lily blossomed.[46] Joseph was astonished, as was everyone else. "Why have I been chosen?" he asked. "I have children of my own nearly as old as this girl." But the augury was plain to all who observed it: the white lily of purity, the lily that was to be offered by the archangel Gabriel to Mary at the time of the Annunciation, had blossomed between them, thus pronouncing his suitability to be her husband. For Mary, this was enough. She extended her hand to Joseph and said, "I accept."

The marriage contract was duly signed, and the wedding was planned to occur in a year's time. Mary returned to her parent's home, while Joseph resumed his wandering in search of work. It was said that he had accepted a commission to build a temple in a distant town, but this may be conjecture. What we do know is that while he was searching for a midwife on the eve of Christ's birth near Bethlehem, he beheld a vision that mitigated his earlier concern about Mary's probity during his absence. One account suggests that initially, at least, until Joseph was advised by an angel that Mary's conception was the result of a visitation by the Holy Spirit, he believed an "evil thing" had defiled her house. His subsequent vision alerts us to the fact that he was aware of the miraculous nature of her pregnancy.

Let Joseph tell us in his own words:

> I looked upward and saw the air in amazement. And I looked up at the pole of heaven and saw it standing still, with the fowls of heaven without motion. And I looked upon the earth and saw a dish set, and workman lying by it, and their hands were into the dish. Though they were lifting food to their lips, they were not chewing even as if they appeared to put it in their mouths. They too were looking upwards. And behold there were sheep being driven, and they appeared to move forward but in fact remained still; and the shepherd raised his hand to smite them with his staff, but his hand remained suspended in the air. And I looked upon the stream of the river and saw the mouths of the kids upon the water and they drank not. Then suddenly, as if someone had struck a bell, all things began to move again as before.

Once again we are alerted to Joseph's power to envision. While many accounts, including the Gospels, complain of his doubts as to Mary's constancy, given that she became pregnant during his absence, it appears he is more forthcoming. The world "stopped in its tracks" for a short moment. At this point we begin to understand the divine nature of their calling: Mary, whose feet barely touch the ground, and Joseph, the man of visions; together they were selected to care for a child conceived in virginity and by an act of the Holy Spirit. This couple was made a chosen vessel from the very outset.

How Mary dealt with the loss of the sandals outside Bubastis says something about her character. Of course she blamed their situation and the general indifference expressed by the people living there. She would not have known that the goddess Bast was held in particular veneration by the people of the city, so to find herself and her son ignored in this way would naturally have left her feeling disenchanted. Had she known of the city's association with the Greek goddess Artemis, herself a dancer in the service of untrammeled nature, she might have realized the strength of her competition. Artemis was known as the "most beautiful" and the "light-bringer" (*phospheros*) whose connection with the moon allowed her to glance at all with a "starry eye." She was also known as the "sovereign lady of women," an epithet not alien to Mary as the mother of God. Artemis represents transfigured woman just as Mary later became for Christians. Her nature is to be starry-bright, sparkling, the embodiment of sweet strangeness. Would the people of Bubastis be tempted to abandon these characteristics that Bast had subsequently claimed as part of herself? It is doubtful.

One has only to return to Herodotus for an explanation. He speaks of a magnificent festival to Bast-Artemis held in this city each year, attended by tens of thousands of people. Let him tell us what he saw:

> The people go by river to Bubastis, men and women together, a great number of them in every boat. Some of the women make noises with rattles, others play flutes all the way, while the rest of the women, and the men, sing and clap

> their hands. Whenever they come near to any other town,
> they bring their boat near to the bank; then some of
> the women do as I have said, while some shout in mockery
> at the women of the town; others dance and still others
> bear their breasts. When they have reached Bubastis, they
> make a festival with great sacrifices, and more wine is drunk
> at the feast than in the whole year beside. Men and women
> assemble there in their hundreds of thousands, so the people
> of the place say.[47]

Bubastis was a city dedicated to the power of women, where their sensuality was on display for all to see at least once every year. Bast's fructifying energy was made over to another side of her character, that of the huntress, in keeping with her feline personality. She is a lioness able to flaunt her powers even as she nurses little children when they are ill. It was this combination of disparate and complementary aspects in her character that made Bast-Artemis such a formidable opponent to the new dispensation that had entered the city unannounced. Mary had not yet come into the fullness of her being as the mother of God, whereas Bast still reigned as a goddess of the morning, of sensuality and warmth.

If one considers how Bast appears in the statue among the ruins of the temple grounds, and through her Artemian persona, it is not hard to see why the people of Bubastis treated Mary with indifference. Mary was a strange kind of woman to them. Her very demeanor seemed so alien, her sensuous nature all but lost in the folds of her dignity. Is it any wonder they turned their back on her? The fourth-century monk Epiphanius, of course, saw the Virgin Mother in a way that we are more familiar with:

> She was grave and dignified in all her actions. She spoke little
> and only when it was necessary to do so. She listened read-
> ily and could be addressed easily. She greeted everyone. She

was of medium height, but some say she was slightly taller than that. She would speak to everyone fearlessly and clearly, without laughter or agitation, and she was especially slow to anger. Her complexion was of the color of ripe wheat, and her hair was auburn. Her eyes were bright and keen, and light brown in color, and the pupils were of olive-green tint. Her eyebrows were arched and deep black. Her nose was long; her lips were red and full, and overflowing with the sweetness of her words. Her face was not round, but somewhat oval. Her hands were long, and her fingers also.[48]

It is the image we see in most European paintings of the Holy Virgin. The licentious women of Bubastis have been transformed into a new image of woman. This goes to the very heart of Mary's confusion as she walked the streets of the city, child in arms, asking for food and water. Her mendicant status had yet to be recognized.

When I came upon the dry well among the temple ruins that morning, the well that Jesus reputedly caused to bubble forth, I realized this was the location of a cataclysm known only to those who understand the power of symbols. The circular brick well plunged into a pile of debris lying on the bottom, its waters long since dried up. According to Theophilus in his *Vision*, a momentous event occurred here "within the hour" of the Holy Family's departure from the city. "The temples of the idols which were in the town fell and were smashed to pieces," he relates. "Likewise, the idols fell onto one another and were smashed." About me, the ruins of Bast's temple clearly indicated the effects of an earth tremor. Great fluted columns lay on the ground in disarray, entablatures and blocks of stone stood abandoned in the grass. Slabs of hieroglyphs uttered their entreaties to a mute and limpid sun. Bast, it seemed, had been forced to give up her divine status as the result of some extraordinary natural disaster.

I paid a final visit to the statue of the goddess, standing at the end of the avenue, her slim figure in marked contrast to the surrounding rubble. I tried to picture her acolytes dancing in the streets, bearing their breasts and drinking themselves into a stupor. The joys of sensuality had been smashed to the ground in one mysterious, tectonic act. While Theophilus's opinion about the future of Bubastis may have been one of understandable condemnation for the treatment meted out to the Holy Family, this only partly accounts for what had really happened. Two powerful opponents had confronted one another in Bubastis some time in the year 6 BC, causing the world to be shaken to its foundations. The sphinx at the other end of the avenue was doing more than gazing at the statue of Bast. It was surrendering its unique personality to a greater power than hers.

In Bubastis that day, it seemed that Jesus had performed his second miracle on behalf of his mother. In so doing, he had served notice on an older, less deserving ideal of womanhood. From here on Mary, his mother, stood for something. She was a dancer who had flouted the laws of gravity. As a result, she had determined the future course of femininity for the modern world. She was to be, for all, a new kind of woman whose integrity surpassed an outmoded archetype.

The Tree That Cried

6

FIFTEEN KILOMETERS SOUTH OF Bubastis lies the city of Bilbeis, on the eastern edge of the delta. My taxi driver, a Copt by the name of Samir, broad shouldered and full of easy grace, wanted me to visit the church of Mari Girgis, or Saint George the Martyr, on our way back to Cairo that evening. He felt it was important that I visit a genuine Coptic holy site after spending the last few days exploring ancient Egyptian antiquities. From his point of view these were all "in the past," and as such did not reflect what he called "Christian Egypt." The old gods were dead as far as he was concerned.

Bilbeis was typical of the cities of the delta. It appeared to emerge from the surrounding fields like a bonsai—disfigured, a twisted mass of streets bedeviled by too many people and livestock. Its apartment blocks were pressed together in a way that suggested space was at a premium. Probably it was: with Egypt's burgeoning population exceeding seventy million, large spaces for building are limited. I always felt slightly claustrophobic when I entered one of these delta towns: they bore down on me like images in a horror movie. It was always with a sense of relief that I approached a church or monastery gate located downtown. Behind their high walls lay a haven of relative tranquility.

I was hungry. Ramadan had made it all but impossible to grab a bite to eat during the day. The thought of entering the sanctuary of Mari Girgis, and watching the iron gate close behind me, made my mouth water. Surely the good priest would satisfy my hunger with a glass of tea, and possibly a plate of olives.

Theophilus does not mention Mar Girgis. Quite a number of sites linked to the Holy Family's journey, in fact, do not make it into his account. I sympathize with his predicament: a dream is a dream, and it often fails us in its detail. Nonetheless, the church of Mari Girgis is significant to their story, for it was here that they stopped to kneel before a tree known as the Tree of the Virgin. It was here too that the infant Jesus performed another miracle, this time bringing the son of a bereaved widow back to life.

It appears the Holy Family encountered a funeral procession on the streets of the village one day, and the infant Jesus was moved to commit his act of compassion. In a scene reminiscent of his revival of the dead Lazarus, Jesus practiced his theurgic powers and was successful. In response, the man fortunate enough to experience this second taste of life pronounced: "This man, born of the Virgin Mary, has accomplished a mystery which the human intellect cannot comprehend." A holy tree and a man raised from the dead had become inexplicably entangled.

Unfortunately the tree no longer exists. Once a popular place for medieval pilgrims to seek shade, it had also existed at the center of a necropolis built to bury Muslim saints in the years after Islam over-ran Egypt. Muslims cared deeply for this tree, and even today relate with sorrow how soldiers from Napoleon's army attempted to cut it down with an ax. According to Samir, my driver, the tree began to exude blood, frightening the soldiers so much that they ran away.

"They were tears of blood," Samir explained. "The soldiers, because of their wish to profane her memory, attempted to cut down her limbs," he added, alluding to the precious body of the Holy Virgin. In the end, the tree was cut down by local workers for firewood around 1850.

Mari Girgis is the only church in town, so one can be forgiven for thinking the tiny Coptic population of Bilbeis feels isolated. Islam surrounds them, a vast ocean of popular piety threatening their very survival. The bell tower on the church, domed and illuminated like a mosque, stands at the end of the street ready to toll soundlessly in honor of our arrival.

Inside the monastery compound, I gained the impression we had entered a fortress. Outside, the street was filled with traffic and noise; inside, children played and birds twittered as they swooped on breadcrumbs. Samir went to find the priest, while I sat in the courtyard and considered the reasons why Coptic Christianity had become so embattled a religion in a country so important to the creation of the Christian church as a world religion. Many of the early theologians, as well as the monastic movement itself, were born in Egypt. The country has long been the crucible of Christianity. Yet now it was an outpost, struggling to survive official disdain and the world's indifference, which in the past saw Coptic Christianity as little more than a heretical offshoot of the universal church.

To sit in the courtyard of Mari Girgis, surrounded on all sides by a predominantly Islamic populace, was to understand why Copts feel so oppressed. Not only did their brethren of the universal church show them the door, but now they are subject to the stern injunctions of a religion that sees itself as the chosen vehicle of God. Where there is a church or monastery, one always sees the ubiquitous minaret standing outside the walls. The muezzin's voice invades even the quietest and remotest places. Monk and nun are subjected to endless calls to prayer from the mosque, even as they prostrate themselves before their beloved iconostasis in their chapels and churches.

Meanwhile, Samir returned accompanied by an elderly priest, Father Hosias. I was struck by the man's dignified demeanor. He wore glasses, a skullcap decorated with crosses, and a long gray beard, and seemed to float toward me under his vestments, as if his legs were an unnecessary adjunct.

"Wel-come," he said, hyphenating his salutation for my benefit. "I trust your journey so far has been rewarding."

"I suspect it will never end, Father," I replied, wondering which journey he was referring to—mine or the Holy Family's.

Again Father Hosias smiled. For him, isolation was a cross he might have to bear, but he was not about to forget that repartee or a friendly gesture make normal human contact much easier. He was like an anchorite in the desert—though a desert surrounded by a city, not dunes.

"I see that your wit has not failed you, Mr. James. Perhaps you might like to share tea with me before we look at the church."

Food. It was something I had all but forgotten. I thanked him as we were shown into a reception room furnished with ornate Louis XV–style chairs. About the walls were numerous icons, as well as portraits of Pope Shenouda and the local bishop of the region. A servant appeared a few minutes later with a tray of tea and refreshments. I sipped my tea slowly, savoring its bitter taste.

"I notice by the bonnet you are wearing, Father Hosias, that you are a monk as well as a priest."

He nodded. "My bishop requested I become a priest, as he needed someone to perform Mass here at Mari Girgis."

"Your heart is still back there in the desert, I take it."

Again Father Hosias nodded, his smile dimming for a moment.

"I must go where I am needed. This church is my monastery. I am a monk alone."

I continued to sip my tea.

"The age of the hermit is behind us, Mr. James," the good father began, his voice this time more ruminative. "All those men who once lit up the desert like myriad flames, who fasted and stayed awake in the name of our beloved Jesus Christ, who subjected their bodies to excruciating trials, their legacy is now a thing of the past. Of course we mourn its loss, but we must remember times have changed. How can we expect a man to live in a cave in the desert without electricity, or without a phone? It is ludicrous to expect the average monk to submit to such a basic existence anymore. I admit it myself: I would be unable to live the life of the Desert Fathers. It is too hard."

"If I recall, one of the jewels of Egyptian asceticism gave up his life of ease in the Byzantine capital, and the love of a woman, in order to live as an anchorite in Egypt. Surely he must have felt as you do now: that such a life was just too hard," I remarked.

I was referring to one of the major theologians of the early Christian Church. Evagrius Ponticus (AD 346–399). It was he who formulated a theory of *apatheia*, or stillness, as constituting the "health of the soul." According to Evagrius, contemplative knowledge was considered to be the perfect "food of the soul." It could only be successfully ingested, however, when the soul was separated from the body. This was the task of the anchorite: to subject his or her body to prolonged and intense physical austerities in order that it might finally become amenable to the soul entering into a state of *katastasis*, which meant achieving perfection and a quality of peace that extends even to the unconscious. A revolutionary new doctrine, *katastasis* implied doing away with the psychological debris that had bedeviled an earlier generation of hermits such as Anthony and Paul of Thebes, whose temptations were more from engaging in elaborate fantasies drawn from the outer world than that of interior clarification, which were more subjective.[49] Evagrius, however, introduced a more subtle interpretation: a person intent on spiritual realization needed to renovate his or her soul by way of self-analysis guided by prayer. It was the method of the psychologist, not the warrior, that became the essential weapon in an ascetic's armory.

Meanwhile, Father Hosias considered my remark about early anchoritism in silence, his eyes closing a little. Then he spoke: "Evagrius was much advanced in spiritual understanding before he came to Egypt, Mr. James. One must discount his difficulties with the flesh as being of minor importance. We all suffer these— even I, a simple priest. Not one day goes by that the demon of lust does not knock at my door! Evagrius Ponticus had become as a harp whose strings were, temporarily at least, out of tune. He needed to find someone, or a place perhaps, where the process of attunement could begin anew. Only in the desert of Egypt could such a transformation happen. Did he not say that in the end a perfect man does not work at remaining continent?"

"I believe he linked the idea of *apatheia* to stillness of the heart, Father," I countered.

"It is imperative for a man to go beyond continence, if he is to attain to a state of *apatheia*, Mr. James. This can only come about by having these impulses in the first place. Not to feel passion prevents one from going beyond the troubling emotions they inspire. Steadiness of heart comes about by exercising patience at first, then going beyond patience itself."

"Evagrius wrote somewhere that the soul that attains to *apatheia* is not simply one that remains undisturbed by changing events, but the one which remains unmoved by the memory of them," I said.[50]

"When I was younger and living in the desert, I often found myself plagued by the need to go beyond patience, beyond continence too," replied Father Hosias. "I realized that we must summon the courage to step beyond all valuations in our pursuit of God. We must not allow ourselves to become victims of the need to determine *what* is wrong with us, rather than concentrating more on the divine ray itself. This light remains concealed behind the holy veils of upliftment, which we in turn must learn to push aside."

"Such a thought, Father Hosias, concurs with Evagrius's belief that *apatheia* is achieved only when the soul is capable of seeing its own light," I said.[51]

"We are now entering into the very heart of mystical theology, Mr. James. And all this over a glass of tea!"

Our discussion that afternoon at Mari Girgis had taken Father Hosias back to his earlier years as an ascetic in the desert. He was remembering the battles he had fought with his nature, with the demons of boredom, with the spiritual isolation that springs from knowing one has started on a path without end, and from which one cannot turn back. The life of a Coptic monk, conditioned as it is by nearly two thousand years of ascetic practice, enjoined him to consider severance as the true condition of life. Such a man must leave this world if ever he is to experience *katastasis*.

"Would you like to visit our church, Mr. James?" Father Hosias asked, signaling that our conversation was now over.

We crossed the courtyard and entered the church. I was immediately struck by its iconostasis of wood arabesque mingled with ivory inlay. It was patterned yet looked plain, like a panorama in the desert. Above the main entrance to the holy sanctuary, covered by a velvet curtain with an image of the Coptic cross sewn onto it, was a picture of the Last Supper, a popular image in Coptic iconography. To the right and left of the sanctuary doorways were portraits of Christ, Mary, the Annunciation, Baptism, the archangel Michael, and Saint George killing the dragon. Above these were portraits of the twelve apostles. Two lecterns, both richly inlaid, also stood on either side. This was Father Hosias's domain, and he held onto one of the lectern posts with evident pride.

"The holy tree of our Virgin Mother may well have been cut down long ago," Father Hosias commented, "but at least we preserve its memory."

"As you preserve the memory of the man who was miraculously reborn here in Bilbeis," I replied, recalling Theophilus's story in his *Vision*.

"Did the man not say that his resurrection was a mystery that could never be understood by the human intellect?" Father Hosias remarked. "Bless him. He must have known, then, that from henceforth his life would never be quite the same."

"If you say so, Father."

"I am an old man, Mr. James. All I know is we must bare our souls to the wonder of events, however strange they might appear. In Bilbeis, it seems that a tree grew up in the wake of a resurrection. The miracle, surely, is that it benefited a pagan!"

"Does this bother you, Father?" I asked.

"It might have, in my youth. But now I see it as another kind of inclusiveness. You see, Jesus understood the need to reach out to everyone, believers and nonbelievers alike."

"As you try to do, Father Hosias," I said, indicating with a nod of my head the city beyond the courtyard walls.

"God obliges us to include everyone in our love," he replied. He bowed before the curtain, genuflected, and backed away from the sanctuary.

As he spoke, I realized that Father Hosias was already clasping hands with that pagan of the past in his new life. Together they were dealing with the miracle of their mutual resurrection in a town blessed by the visit of the Holy Family. The sea that I feared might wash over this town, namely, the power of Islam, was now calm. Father Hosias had managed to quiet the waters.

On the Road

7

DRIVING NORTH INTO THE DELTA
after a few days' break at the Windsor Hotel in Cairo, I planned to visit the Church of Mary in the town of Daqados. From there, my itinerary took me in a wide arc through the region to other places associated with the Holy Family's journey. It seemed simple enough. The only problem was, my thoughts were filled with stories I had read in the *Arabic Gospel of the Infancy of the Savior* the previous evening. Lying half awake in my bed, I soon found these stories merging with others I had encountered. The story of Osiris's dismemberment by his brother Seth, and the subsequent journey through Egypt by his wife Isis in search of his various limbs, seemed to pale by comparison. I realized then that Egyptians, even today, enjoy embroidering whatever their minds happened to touch upon.

Every city or village we passed through on our way north reminded me how the demonic has its own role to play in the story of the infant Jesus. In one we are told of a madwoman who was unable to live in her house or wear clothes. Chained to a post, she would often break free and run naked into the fields or stand at crossroads, throwing stones at passersby. When the Holy Family visited the town, Mary took pity on the woman. As she did, the evil spirit departed in the form of a young man pleading for mercy.

Returning to her senses at last, the woman blushed with shame because of her nakedness, then hurried inside to find clothes. Later, when relating her story to the head men of the village, she paid tribute to the divine mercy of the Holy Family. They were then treated honorably by the villagers and given food for their onward journey.

In the next town, so the *Arabic Infancy Gospel* relates, they came upon a marriage ceremony in which the bride had lost her power to speak or hear. It almost seemed like a parody: a dumb bride in the midst of festivities celebrating the consummation of her betrothal. Again Mary approached, this time with Jesus in her arms, and the bride was immediately drawn to her. She reached out and took the infant Jesus in her arms, kissing and cradling him. In that moment her voice returned and "her ears were opened." She praised God for restoring her faculties, and was exultant. The bride truly believed that an angel in the guise of the infant Jesus had visited her.

The Holy Family remained in the village three days before moving on to a larger city. There, they came upon a deeply pious woman who had gone down to the river to bathe. "Lo, an evil spirit in the form of a serpent leapt upon her and twisted itself around her belly," so the text relates. In despair, the woman recognized Mary with the child in the street and pleaded that she might take him in her arms. "Give me the child," she cried, "so that I might kiss him." Immediately she was released from the evil spirit.

These stories multiplied in my thoughts as I gazed out the window of the taxi. I saw a young woman, as the text suggests, who had been "white with leprosy" and was cured through Mary's intercessions; on another occasion the palace of a prince where the ruler's son was also afflicted by leprosy. His mother, it seems, no longer knew what to do. "Either I kill him, or abandon him in a field so that I will never see him again," she confessed to the woman recently cured of leprosy. "Take the bathwater in which Jesus has been washed, and bathe your son in it," the young woman suggested. The princess agreed to do so. First, she invited Joseph to a banquet at the palace. Then she prepared scented water to wash the infant Jesus. When Mary had completed her son's ablutions she gave the water to the princess, who at once bathed her leprous son. In an instant he was cured. "Blessed is the mother who bore you, Jesus," the princess cried. "Your nature is so pure that even your bathwater is capable of cleansing the afflicted."

Impotence, a man turned into a mule, numerous cases of leprosy, illness, madness, and many other human afflictions—the Holy Family encountered all these on their journey through the cities and villages of the delta. It was as if they had plunged into the pit of hell. Yet the power of the infant Jesus, with the help of his mother, was ever able to cure their various ailments. While there were times when people refused to welcome them, or provide them with food, one gains the impression that the local inhabitants of the delta were glad to have them in their midst. The Holy Family, it seems, was able to administer a new kind of medicine: that of the deep lustrations of humanity married to a purity of spirit.

The *Arabic Infancy Gospel* was written to reinforce the idea that the Holy Family was representative of a rich tradition of the wandering holy men that pervaded Middle Eastern society. Though this figure became more prominent with the rise of early Christianity, nonetheless his pagan prototype did wander the back roads of Egypt, dispensing wisdom and medicines. His powers were entirely self-created, and so he was often confused with the *theos anir*, or divine man of late classical times. He too was able to perform miracles as the infant Jesus did, being in possession of *palaios logos*, or the "ancient wisdom" he had acquired in the Egyptian temple. A stranger in society, the holy man was able to act as a mediator in village disputes, as well as to arbitrate over questions of law. As a so-called god-bearer, he lived through the final stage in the long history of oracles and divination in the ancient world.

Theodoret of Cyrrhus wrote that anyone wanting a holy man's help must "pray to derive benefit from the power he now wields, and from his intercession."[52] To visit a holy man was to go where the power was.[53] Men often trusted themselves to him because he was thought to have won his way to intimacy with the gods—to a so-called state of *parrhesia*. This delicate art of intimacy, derived originally from the manner of rulers in Hellenistic times, enabled a holy man to enact miracles among a people hungry for wonders. Was it a case of smoke and mirrors? Judging by the Arab chronicler, who detailed so many miracles conducted by the Holy Family, it was real rather than illusion.

I tried to imagine the world of Egypt at the time Joseph and Mary traveled through it. If one subjects these ancient texts such as the *Arabic Infancy Gospel* and Theophilus's *Vision* to critical analysis, then they probably do not stand up. Many of them were written in the centuries after the events described and are therefore influenced by the political and social conditions of their time. All of them are steeped in a credulity disconcerting to the modern mind. How can one believe in miracles? Why should we believe that temples collapse and wells are created with a flick of the fingers? Why should so many people be possessed by demons, and others so readily lose control over their faculties? Yet if we asked similar questions about our own time, several centuries hence, we would probably regard this age as credulous also. The family's journey through Egypt needed to be miraculous, just as our own age is in thrall to science. Each age, it seems, finds a way to justify the miracles it experiences.

When we arrived midmorning in the city of Mit Ghami, on the Damietta branch of the Nile, I became aware that although the land did not look fertile for the growth of miracles, the fields I had traveled through had, at one time at least, been fertile nonetheless. I came to the church of Daqados, located on a back street. It's name is a corruption of "Maria Theotokos," meaning Mary the Mother of God or "birth-giver." It was originally built by Helena, the mother of Emperor Constantine, when she passed through Egypt at the end of her trip to the Holy Land early in the fourth century.

The Holy Family rested here for three days—in what is now the crypt of the main church. The brickwork below was very old, made from sun-dried soil from the Nile no later than the fifth century. Carved into the central niche, above which a scallop shell still rests, are the words *Hoden Alaab*, meaning "Father's Embrace." Symbol of the rising sun, the scallop shell also represents Isis holding her son Horus on her knee, in contrast to its symbolism in the West, where it is associated with Saint James the Elder of Compostela and pilgrimage. For the Copts, the shell means *Noor Yasoo*, the "Light of Jesus." However one looks at this ancient and holy spot, one thing becomes evident: the Holy Family's visitation, the image of Isis embracing her son, and the light of an emerging Christian vision have all mysteriously converged. No wonder the priest showed me around his church with a mixture of awe and pride. Like the scarab protecting its egg, it had rolled up everything of spiritual value into one luminous ball.

After tea with the local priest, we pushed on to Samannoud further north along the Nile. Market day was in progress as we approached the street where the church of Abba Noub stood. It was all but impossible to drive the car through the milling crowd and the donkeys laden with produce, the open-air butcher's shops shaded by flour bags and the barrows filled with vegetables, or indeed the hawkers selling everything from key chains to fake watches. In the end, we decided to park the car on a back street and walk.

Dedicated to Abba Noub, a third-century Christian anchorite of the desert, the church is a monument to martyrdom. It is said some eighty thousand people were executed for their beliefs in this region during the reign of Diocletian. For the Copts, the idea of martyrdom as a justification of their faith runs deep. Abba Noub typified the clash between two opposing cultures of the time, that of the emperor as deity and the Christians' refusal to acknowledge him as such. Abba Noub died after deliberately provoking the local governor into ordering his execution. By openly professing his

Christianity instead of remaining silent, he invited his own death. Rather than an ordinary death, however, Abba Noub found himself crucified on the mast of a ship.

Even today, Copts speak with bitterness of Emperor Diocletian and the age of martyrdom. What they do not know is that it was not Diocletian who ordered the persecution but his prefect Galerius. Born of peasant stock on the Danube, Galerius was later made Caesar by his friend in AD 293. He became concerned at the rising popularity of Christianity throughout the empire and urged Diocletian to be alert to the danger of this radical group fomenting rebellion. Christians were known to deny allegiance to the emperor instead giving their loyalty to an extremist known as Jesus the Messiah. This infuriated Galerius. His native cunning told him what might happen next if ordinary folk chose to deny the emperor his due. Though Diocletian urged leniency toward the Christians, Galerius wanted blood. As far as he was concerned, Christians were fanatics.

The Christians, especially those in Egypt, obliged Galerius in every way. When the general edict of persecution was published, thousands of men, women, and children offered themselves up for martyrdom. By renouncing the gods and the institutions of Rome, Christians throughout the empire set a dangerous precedent. Galerius feared they might one day acquire a military force and so rise up in rebellion. With its own laws and leaders the church encouraged community wealth to flow into its coffers rather than into the treasury in Rome. The stage was set for what Edward Gibbon called a "new species of martyrdom" to be enacted. If it was not death in the coliseum, then people who refused to disavow their beliefs could expect a lingering one in a public place. Roasting on a slow fire, crucifixion, disembowelment, or having limbs severed one by one, these were just some of the ingenious ways used to torment Christians in their final hour. Galerius may have exacted his revenge on a people he despised, but it was Diocletian who reaped its most dubious reward. Within weeks of the edict his palace in Nicomedia was twice put to the torch. And so the massacres began. It was not to end until AD 311 when Galerius, now emperor, wearied by his failure to contain the rise of Christianity, finally admitted defeat. He signed an edict ending the persecution on his deathbed.

Abba Noub and his kind had triumphed. But their deaths have left an indelible mark upon the collective psyche of all Copts. Even today, they seem to enjoy speaking of the time when their ancestors surrendered their lives in the name of Jesus Christ. I tried to imagine what must have gone through the minds of those early Christians eager to profess their faith in such a way. Was it a need to identify personally with Christ's death on the cross? Did they wish to experience the pain of Christ's agony? Did they want to make their martyrdom an echo of his? In the past the Copts, perhaps more than any other Christians, saw the need to identify with the crucifixion as a way of reinforcing the courage required to survive periods of Islamic oppression they later experienced.

The church of Abba Noub has various artifacts celebrating the Holy Family's visit to Samannoud. The priest took me on a tour of the nave after I had paid my respects to the saint in front of a beautifully decorated twelfth-century iconostasis, or haikal. The wooden inlay radiated countless ivory crosses and mandalas. Above the ornately carved door to the sanctuary a number of ostrich eggs hung like lamps, symbols of Christ, who is always caring for us, just as the ostrich is always looking after its eggs. Above the cavalcade of apostles on the iconostasis, the statue of Christ crucified was flanked by two crocodile-like figures carved in wood, each flaunting wings. Perhaps they were dragons.

The priest then took me aside to view the casket containing the relics of the saint. They were contained in a box not much more than eighteen inches long, and wrapped in red cloth. Pilgrims had inserted bank notes through a small aperture in the protective glass cabinet as an accompaniment to their prayers. Old icons graced the walls of the nave, as did a large circular granite bowl reputedly used by Mary to knead dough. It was possible to put one's head through a Perspex covering in order to kiss or touch this sacred object. Outside in the courtyard, through the doorway, was the well where the Holy Family had quenched their thirst.

At the rear of the nave the priest stopped before a windowsill on which were various pieces of equipment used by people with physical disabilities, including a number of rusty calipers, some orthopedic shoes covered in dust, several walking sticks, and an old wheelchair. The priest then explained to me how they came to be there. "Abba Noub has worked his miracles over the years, Mr. James. Anyone can be cured by his power, provided people have faith. His crucifixion at the mast made him particularly susceptible to those with a disability."

The Holy Family's visit to Samannoud was rich with significance. The bread that was kneaded to feed them was probably less important than the intersection of the two lives that had occurred here. The infant Jesus had passed through the town going in one direction, while a young martyr called Abba Noub was limping toward his death in another. Surely there was a message in all this. Perhaps we need "fanatics" to invest us with a reason for living, as well as dying, if the cause seems worthy enough.

Wastelands

8

WE KNOW THAT HERODOTUS VISITED
the Burullus region of the Nile Delta in his travels
because he spoke of meeting with a priest in the Egyptian city
of Sais. Although he believed the man was jesting with him,
he did admit the priest possessed "exact knowledge" about the
source of the Nile. "The springs of the Nile rise between two
hills known as Crophi and Mophi," Herodotus wrote. "Half the
water flows northwards towards Egypt, the other half southwards
towards Ethiopia. Thus its source cannot be fathomed."[54] If this
were true, and Herodotus doubted it, then we can be sure these
mountains exist somewhere in the hinterland of Africa, remote
peaks bathed by summer rains, their summits forever carpeted in
wildflowers. It is the image we all wish to have of the mythical
source of a river that flows as much through our imagination as
it does through Egypt.

My destination that day was Saint Damiana, a monastery for
women located in an area known as the wastelands. Local lore
suggests Mary and Joseph passed through the region on their way
westward to Sakha. In a village known as Shagaret el-Teen they
were refused bread, an act of ingratitude that in time was said to
promote a decline in the fertility of the land. Herodotus makes
no mention of such wastelands existing in his time, so one must

assume something drastic occurred here to bring on its state of aridity. After my trip to Samannoud the previous day, a land fertile with miracles, I was prepared to believe anything could happen in the wake of the Holy Family's passage, given its penchant for transformation.

The entire region held significance for the ancient Egyptians. It may have been no accident that the Holy Family seemed to be traveling from one important Pharaonic site to another as they traversed the delta. Were they in fact trying to link up these places, or at least absorb them into their own particular pilgrimage? I had already visited Daphnae, Pithon, and Bubastis in my travels, all cities associated with various Egyptian gods. It is likely that the Holy Family also visited such important cities as Tanis, Mendes, Buto, and Sais as they made their way westward, for these too were associated with important Egyptian deities. Could it be they wanted to see for themselves something of this ancient society and their gods? Theophilus may well have had this in mind when he dreamed his dream.

So it was with some trepidation that I drove into the Burullus wastelands that morning under an intense blue sky. What had dried up here in the course of history was the magical effect of mythology upon a people. No, that is not quite right. More probably, what had brought about growing spiritual aridity was the belief that the old gods of Egypt had departed. Those great festivals of the past, such as the Feast of the Lamps in Sais, where people once placed saucers full of salt and oil outside their houses to burn all night in honor of the goddess Neith, may have been a thing of the past; but I suspected people today secretly believe in her continued existence. She had probably adopted a new disguise.

When we reached Saint Damiana monastery later that day, I was feeling unsettled in the stomach. I hardly noticed the high wall and solid wrought-iron gates at the entrance. The monastery stood alone in the landscape, as if it had been placed there as an afterthought. The rest of Egypt appeared to have mysteriously slipped away, over the horizon. Moreover, my initial reaction after being shown around the grounds by the guest mistress, Mother Nadeen, was less than enthusiastic as I tried to come to terms with an illness I was experiencing. Probably I had eaten something the previous day that did not agree with me. Or perhaps Ramadan had its first casualty—fasting during the heat of the day is not easy. Whatever the cause, clearly the *djinns* had caught up with me!

Mother Nadeen was a young woman in her late thirties, clear-faced and articulate. She told me she had been born in Cape Town, not Egypt, and had converted to Coptic Christianity while living in her adopted homeland of Australia. Mother Nadeen radiated a particular dignity that was reflected as much in her smile as in her voice. She represented a new kind of recluse, one whose education and upbringing had prepared her for a vocation in the church that was vastly different from nuns in the past. She was, in her own words, a "bride of Christ," but one able to act with independence and a clear sense of destiny. Nadeen's long journey to Saint Damiana must have begun with a spiritual crisis unlike that experienced by an earlier generation of nuns. In an age of acute individuality and selfhood, she had opted for obedience and trust rather than material fulfillment. In turn, Saint Damiana had welcomed her into her house.

We entered the ancient chapel of the old Damiana church in the center of the convent. Its altar was shrouded in tasseled cloth, with the virgin martyr Damiana, the "Princess of Martyrs," surrounded by her Forty Virgin Martyrs, embroidered on one side. The brick-work in the apse, bare now of frescoes or decorations, reminded me of the harsh earth beyond the monastery. It was as if the old church had been constructed out of the very earth of the wastelands.

"I can see that you are not feeling very well, Mr. James," she said, noticing my pale condition.

There are moments in life when it seems right to simply give in. This was one of them. I gazed at Nadeen, knowing it was better to surrender to her care than to pretend I was not ill.

"Some hot broth, I think, might help," I suggested.

Nadeen's eyes lit up, and her veil fluttered like bird's wings. To minister to a man in the heart of God's house seemed to her to be entirely appropriate. I was immediately led away to a reception room, there to await the arrival of some freshly prepared food.

While Nadeen departed the room, I took the trouble of acquainting myself with Saint Damiana's story from a leaflet on the tea table. She was born to wealthy parents. Her father, Mark, was the provincial governor of Burullus and a baptized Christian. At the age of fifteen Damiana received a marriage proposal, which she declined, believing herself destined to serve Christ as his bride. Elated by her decision, Mark decided to build a retreat for her in a remote area of the province in order to house his daughter and forty of her friends. It was hoped that in time their retreat might be recognized as a convent. During the persecutions under Diocletian, however, Mark chose the safer road of apostasy, an act that disappointed his daughter. She journeyed back to his palace and convinced him of the error of his ways. Later, Mark was beheaded as a martyr, because of his daughter's influence. When Diocletian heard of this tragedy, and that his friend's daughter had been responsible for what had happened, he ordered her to be tortured for a period of three years. Though strengthened in her resistance by appearances of Jesus, Mary, and the archangel Michael in her cell, she finally succumbed to her last torment—that of being torn limb from limb. In a very real sense she had undergone the trials of Osiris, and with a similar result: her own apotheosis as a saint, along with her forty friends. Mythic history, it seems, had prepared her for a parallel destiny to that of the lord of the dead.

Since then, sixteen hundred years have gone by, yet still her light shines in this remote province of Egypt. The mysterious power of martyrdom touches us deeply, and we are forever beholden to what it means. Martyrs desire to give of themselves for others—not to save them, but to demonstrate their link with Christ. It is a dismemberment of being which allows others to put back together the pieces, and so create a measure of wholeness. No wonder Nadeen had been drawn to this monastery. In doing so, she had made her own small contribution to the reconstitution of the world.

"Here is your soup, Mr. James," Nadeen announced, as a trolley with an assortment of food on it was wheeled into the room. "One of the mothers prepared it especially for you. She is also from Australia."

"Quite a connection, Sister," I remarked, slowly spooning the fresh vegetable soup from the plate. It tasted delicious, and I could feel my stomach responding to it immediately. "It may be that Australia and Egypt have something in common."

"They are both old lands," replied Mother Nadeen. "Here, I feel as if I am home. The mystery that is a part of the landscape of Australia is similar to the one I feel in this country."

"So many layers of myth have accumulated over time here, as it has done in Australia," I mused. "Do you think it possible the earth actually contributes in some way to the unfolding of such events?"

"I am sure it determines how we embrace its mystery, Mr. James," Mother Nadeen said, ladling more soup into my plate.

"You are inferring, of course, that the Nile in some way sanctifies our presence here, even as it goes on to nourish the earth."

Mother Nadeen smiled, half in agreement. My observations, however, tested her belief in Jesus Christ as the world's sole redeemer.

She remarked: "As you know, the Holy Family came here on their journey west. We believe this implicitly, as did our beloved Saint Damiana. Her death as martyr became an affirmation of the enduring nature of a new dispensation entering the world. The old gods were in disarray, it seems. They had been with us for too long, and had lost their power to transform our lives. The infant Jesus, in all his simplicity and as a persecuted being, passed by here with his mother and his father, hoping to find succor. It was their vulnerability that allowed them to triumph over their adversities. It is this vulnerability that makes us want to adore him, because it gives us strength. The truth is, we are often weak, impoverished human beings who are unable to release ourselves into his care."

"Does it always have to be a case of revealing our weakness in order to find a motive for the spiritual life, Sister Nadeen?" I asked, hoping to draw her out from the security of her faith.

"Here we live in a constant state of vulnerability," she replied, choosing her words carefully. "It is not for nothing we pray each day. Prayer allows us to leave the security of ourselves, to venture forth into the divine naught that is God. We try to embrace this state of nothingness, as if it were our own personal martyrdom. Saint Damiana may be our guide in these matters, given that she suffered inordinate torture, but our torture is that we feel so distant from his presence. We long to suffer so he might notice us."

"Is this not a trifle masochistic?" I ventured.

"Masochism is an aberration designed to instill pleasure, Mr. James. It is not pleasure we seek, but knowledge of the divine itself. We are trying to break through the barrier of our limitations in matters of the spirit. For us, this is the greatest adventure."

"Like Isis journeying throughout Egypt in search of her husband's limbs," I replied, thinking of Osiris and his dismemberment. "It may be that to adore Jesus now is to adore the mystery of creation in every age."

"At one level this may be so," responded Nadeen, pushing toward me a plate of mixed vegetables. Her clear face became intense and passionate as she contended with my arguments. I sensed a deep resolve in her slight shoulders, hidden as they were behind vestments.

"But at another level?" I asked.

"We are brought into a state of stillness by the mercy of Christ, Mr. James. Mercy is a unique quality and gift. The world suffers from a lack of it at this time, as we are all well aware. His love is an outpouring provoked by his expression of mercy toward us. I feel it at Morning Prayer, sometimes—not often enough, I must admit. His mercy spreads through me and I am filled with light. Is it possible to glow, I ask myself? I think so. On rare occasions, I feel my body has become as a pinpoint of light in the darkness. I am alight to myself! This is the gift of his mercy."

Nadeen's outburst stunned me. It seemed to come from deep within, as if it too had lain secluded behind the walls of her monastery. It was not that she felt suppressed or lonely, but that she was bursting with some inner knowledge she wished to impart. With a few generous ladles of soup, she'd managed to restore my health. Now, with her words, she had helped to invigorate my thoughts. It seemed the wastelands of Burullus concealed more under its parched earth than memories of past injustice.

"Can any of us," Nadeen continued, "know the answer? Each of us is committed to a journey, just as the Holy Family was. Are we not called upon to do the same? Christ is my Osiris, perhaps. His mutilated body is my anguish. I am called to the task of putting it back together in my soul because it is the body of our beloved Jesus Christ."

The soup ladle lay before me in the bowl. I had entered the wastelands of Burullus feeling ill and a little dispirited, only to discover a new form of sustenance. While my body was calling out for help due to illness, it seemed I had found another cure in Mother Nadeen's wise words. In her, numerous traditions had become integrated. Perhaps this is the way Egypt works on any of us who is prepared to listen to its message.

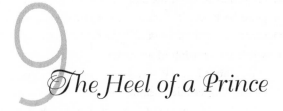

9
The Heel of a Prince

I DROVE WEST TOWARD SAKHA,
through palm groves and irrigation canals, river tributaries
and fields, all of which made the Nile Delta appear as one vast
lung breathing in disparate airs. Men on donkeys trotted past,
or led beasts carrying a load of newly cut hay for storing back in
some village compound. I had now entered the rural heartland
of Egypt, where families tended fields as they had for thousands
of years.

The wastelands were behind me, but not the lands of Lower Egypt
as a rich source of symbolism. The nuns of Saint Damiana were
like the temple priests of old, preserving and caring for the so-called
exact knowledge relating to the way people kept the faith. The neck-
lace of cities across the northern fringe of the delta, from Tanis to
Sais, was thus an "abode of hymns" that celebrated a more transcendent image of the world.

In turn, Herodotus could speak of nearby Sais as the "burial
place of him whose name I dare not utter," alluding to the temple
of the goddess Neith, whom he linked to Athena.[55] Immediately
one feels in the presence of stone obelisks, temple walls, a shrine
and a lake "adorned with a stone margin in the fashion of a circle"
where, at night, the story of the god's sufferings was enacted. Being
there, it was not hard to imagine the glow of oil lamps across the

water, the splash of oars, temple priests in elaborate costumes performing rituals on the decks of river craft, and the crowds onshore gazing in wonder at the performance. This was how the land of ancient Egypt was transformed into an abode of hymns for earlier generations. Neith, the mighty mother who gave birth to Ra, could then utter what all wished to hear: "I am what has been, what is, and what shall be."

These were words Mary would have understood perfectly had her son uttered them. Neith was considered to be the mother of Osiris, just as she, Mary, was the mother of the infant Jesus. Mary was not a goddess, however, so one must be careful not to attribute to her more than her share of deific virtue. Along with Joseph and Salome, she would have been intent upon reaching Sakha on her journey westward. Was this to ensure that their travels became an intrinsic part of the ancient land of Egypt? What we know is that when the Holy Family reached the city, the infant Jesus planted his foot on a stone there, leaving his imprint upon it. He also created a spring. To protect the stone from treasure hunters visiting the place from medieval Europe, as well as local Muslims intent on desecration, it was later buried and eventually lost. This may have occurred in 1194, when the monastery of Pikha Eesous (the "Heel of Jesus") was finally abandoned. In 1984, when archaeologists dug near the entrance to the Church of the Holy Virgin in Sakha, an eighty-centimeter length of stone was unearthed. On its surface appeared to be a brown-colored footprint. Since then, the stone has been responsible for a number of miracles.

Entering the compound of the Church of Saint Mary, I was met by Mother Adrosis, who agreed to show me the relic. She invited me into the church, where I was immediately confronted by a finely crafted iconostasis all but bare of icons. This was unusual, given that most of the haikals I had seen so far featured all the apostles, as well as numerous saints and angels. On the left of the altar screen was a beautiful icon of the Virgin Mary holding her son. He in turn was clasping an orb depicting the sky, sea, and earth, the three elements traditionally associated with the cosmos. The icon was extremely pleasing to the eye; one sensed that Mary was in full command of her world here in Sakha, knowing her son had stamped his imprint in its earth.

Mother Adrosis seemed older than I had thought. It may have been because of the way she peered at me through an antique pair of glasses. Or it may have been how she walked along the carpet in the nave. She moved deliberately, as if she were approaching a relic of great power. It was only when I looked to the left to see a cabinet by the wall that I recognized a large block of stone encased in glass. Obviously we were walking toward an artifact of great significance. Mother Adrosis's comportment reflected her undiminished awe at the sight of this object.

"Here, Mr. James," she began as we stood before the cabinet. "You may see the footprint of our precious Lord Jesus."

The stone's surface was uneven, as if a chisel had gouged it out. It reminded me of a piece of petrified wood. After studying it for a short while, I noticed a brownish indentation in the surface that could easily have been interpreted as the sole of a child among the chisel marks. For Mother Adrosis, however, there was no question of its being the footprint of the infant Jesus.

A badly chiseled block of stone inscribed in Arabic on one side seemed hardly sufficient an object to justify the construction of a monastery and later a church. It seemed more like the product of a pious imagination. Experience among tribal peoples in many parts of the world has made me wary of such assertions. Certain objects, blessed by tradition and by what the ancient Egyptians called *paut*, or "divine substance," were obviously capable of imparting their effect on pilgrims. In my experience, the *churinga* stones of the Australian Aborigines are capable of imparting the same power. Known as *kurunba*, only men of high culture are permitted to touch them.

The block of stone containing the footprint of the infant Jesus was thus a form of *churinga*. Mother Adrosis certainly acknowledged its power, and urged me to touch it for myself. Something constrained me from doing so, however. Not that I felt reluctant to show the object due reverence, but rather—I had nothing to request of it. At this point I realized how different I was from my Coptic friends. Belief may be a part of my makeup, but not a belief in miracles. Somewhere along the way I, like many of my contemporaries, have lost the art of seeing objects as anything other than an accumulation of matter. I have lost the ability to see them from the perspective of their *paut*, their divine substance.

"You must understand, Mr. James," I heard Mother Adrosis's remark. "The Holy Family felt under siege at this point in their journey. Wherever they went they were only ever able to stay a few days, a week at the most. There was never a time when they could truly lie down and rest. What jobs Joseph was able to secure gave them a little money to buy food, no more. At the back of their minds, I feel sure, there was always the specter of Herod's soldiers. How far behind them were they? What should they do if they were discovered? How long could they stave off capture by men in the pay of a king? Can you imagine the mental state of Joseph and Mary during these months? They must have thought God had abandoned them."

"Hence the need for the occasional miracle, Sister Adrosis," I reflected.

"It is important that the world undergo some sort of fracture at times; is this not so? Otherwise, we would remain seduced by its favorable appearance. The infant Jesus, wise child that he was, understood the need to transform reality wherever he went, whether it was by some miraculous intervention or by showing us how mysterious reality really is."

"A natural disaster on the one hand, or a footprint in stone on the other, perhaps?" I suggested.

"Natural disasters are acts of discord, Mr. James. They are the cry of the earth as it heaves in pain. We forget sometimes that the earth suffers as we do. It longs to be relieved of its anguish too. This is why we have eruptions, tidal waves, cyclones, and earthquakes. They tell us that the world also bleeds."

"And the footprint?" I asked, peering down at the stone.

"Miracles are God's way of healing the wound," replied Mother Adrosis. Her glasses seemed to mist over as she spoke.

"Miracles are therefore an expression of the world struggling to come to terms with forces bent on trying to undermine it," I reasoned.

"That is so, Mr. James. They are the wings of a butterfly the instant it breaks free from its chrysalis. We see these as real, but are they not in fact a wonder? How one creature is born anew from another is one of the great mysteries, surely. Such is the nature of the miracle: it is also one reality born anew from another."

"So this footprint is none other than the cicatrice of deity," I remarked.

"Is it not a miracle?"

"Not far from here, Mother Adrosis, I am told a goddess called Neith once reigned. In doing so, she made the delta region into her chrysalis. Out of it she rose and spread her wings."

"Just as Christ has done in our age. Gods are the butterflies of being, Mr. James."

I bent over and kissed the glass. It was as near as I wished to be to this mysterious piece of rock that bore Christ's footprint.

"Now you understand why I believe how the world is sustained by miracles. They are our true nourishment, Mr. James."

It was a statement that I no longer felt able to disagree with. Christ's footprint had given the city of Sakha a new set of wings.

Into the Desert

10

TRAVELING SOUTHEAST ALONG THE
desert road from Alexandria toward Cairo, I was conscious
of entering a new phase of my journey. The Holy Family, having all but quit the fertile river lands of the delta, would have
begun to make their way inland along the Nile. Probably they
had crossed the Rosetta branch at the ancient city of Terranah, a
popular staging point between Memphis and Sais for river traffic
in days past.

I could feel the pressure of the chase at this stage: Herod's soldiers were back there on the road somewhere inquiring as to their
whereabouts in village and city. Joseph would have known they
must be constantly on the move if they were to avoid capture and
possible death. For all its timelessness and gentle rhythm of agricultural life, the delta was still a place of whispers and of gossip.
Three itinerant people, a child and a donkey, all without fixed
abode, inevitably provoked questions from the local peasants. It
was time to move on.

In Terranah it was possible to see from afar the desert of Scetis
and the depression known as Wadi Natrun. In ancient Egyptian
times the region was referred to as *Sekhet Hemat*, the "Field of
Salt," because of the string of salt lakes that dotted the region. The
Greek name *Scetis* was derived from the Coptic *Sheit*, meaning "to

weigh the heart," presumably in recognition of its unique historical importance. It was in this region that some of the earliest attempts at living the hermit life were conducted by men fleeing persecution. Remote and exceedingly arid, it was not a place that could be approached without due care. As Rufinus describes the Wadi Natrun in his *Historia Monachorum*, "The place is a desert, and offers great dangers to those who go there. If a man makes a slight mistake in direction, he wanders about the desert at his peril."[56]

No wonder it became popular with anchorites of the fourth century and after. It was the perfect place to contemplate a vision of last things, in keeping with the millennial pessimism of the age. "Who cannot see," wrote Saint Cyprian of Carthage in a letter to a friend, "that the world is already in its decline, and no longer has the strength and vigor of former times?"[57] Wadi Natrun was the perfect eschatological retreat for those who doubted whether the world had any future.

Although the Holy Family probably did not actually visit the region, tradition tells us, through the *Arabic Gospel of the Infancy of the Savior*, that the infant Jesus remarked to his mother as they passed through the region, "Know O Mother, that in this desert there shall live many monks, ascetics, and spiritual fighters, and they shall serve God like angels." One senses that the Wadi Natrun needed to be preordained by deity as the world's first natural monastery; it was, no less, the new chosen land designed to replace Palestine as the primary place of spiritual gifts.

From the fourth century onward, at a time when the Christian message needed to develop a language of its own, it was important as a bastion of asceticism. The desert, sand, aridity, heat, waterless space—these became the basis of a revolutionary new metaphor to encompass human existence. Only by living under the rule of these extreme conditions was it possible to become a *theophoroumenos*— that is, an initiate into *teleios*, or state of perfection. The infant Christ had, it seems, ordained this region to be the boiler room of Christianity for the world. Men would enter it at their risk, suffer extreme privation, and emerge, if they were lucky, as transformed human beings, undivided and in a state of unshadowed clarity (*katherotes*, "to be pure").

It was not until around AD 340 that some order was brought to bear on the thousands of desert hermits living in the region. Although Macarius was not the only hermit to take up residence in the desert of Scetis, it was he who founded the first monastery there, known today as Baramus.[58] Said to have been a camel driver who traded in salt throughout the region, Macarius was eventually attracted to the ascetic life and so decided to take up residence in a cave in a rocky outcrop. Deeply influenced by the life of Saint Anthony, who was then living in a cave at Mount Colzim in the eastern desert, Macarius practiced an austere existence from the age of thirty, and his fame soon spread.[59] Other monasteries were quickly built, to the point where there were probably more than a hundred of them dotted throughout the region. This was the golden age of asceticism, when men (and some women) from all over the empire flocked to Wadi Natrun to join in this great human experiment. Evagrius Ponticus, John Cassian, as well as Ephrem the Syrian were just a few of the prominent intellectuals who chose to give up their lives of relative comfort elsewhere in favor of a life of extreme asceticism in Egypt. They were enamored of the prospect of becoming *theos anir*, a perfect man.

Today, there are only four monasteries left in the region. Baramus, Deir es Suriani, Saint Macarius, and Saint Bishoy are located a few miles west of the desert road, some 120 kilometers from Cairo. They glow like flickering lamps in the window of a past age, casting their gentle light upon the world. One can see their high walls at the end of avenues of eucalypts, enclosing a rich history of asceticism. As my taxi drove through a village toward the Monastery of the Syrians (Deir es Suriani), I became conscious that they were as much historical monuments as living monasteries. Civilization had already encroached upon them, however: piles of worn tires, rubbish, abandoned cars, and machinery in the street signaled that the tranquility of desert life was a thing of the past. The monastery brought to mind the image of a ship floating in a sea of sand, its rusted hull encrusted with all the detritus of modern life. Somehow I could not escape the feeling that I was about to enter an archaeological site, in spite of the numerous visitors' cars parked outside the walls.

Deir es Suriani was an imposing edifice. Its massive, fortress-like walls were like those built by the Hospitallers around the city of Rhodes in the late Middle Ages. They were bulky and impregnable. The narrow, gated entrance invited visitors to make their final exit from the world: after all, within those walls lay a prototype of the celestial city. My allusion to a ship of the desert did not seem inappropriate as I ducked my head upon entering the gate. I was later to discover during a discussion with one of the monks that the monastery had been modeled on Noah's Ark.

Dedicated to the Mother of God (Theotokos), the monastery was founded during the sixth century at the height of the Julianist heresy.[60] Its name, Deir es Suriani, is derived from the fact that the monastery was later purchased by a group of wealthy Syrian merchants living in Old Cairo after the heresy had died out, thus leaving the place all but abandoned. As a result, the monastery became home to a group of Syrian monks interested in learning. Under the guidance of Moses of Nisibis, a deeply cultured man, a library was soon established and manuscripts from Syria brought in to form the basis of the collection. This is perhaps the primary reason why Saint Ephrem of Syria, the greatest poet of the patristic age and the only theologian-poet to rank beside Dante, came to stay in Deir es Suriani. It is likely he came here from Edessa, after fleeing Nisibis at the time of the Persian invasion. Legend has it that he planted his staff in the ground within its walls and a sycamore tree sprouted. This tree can be viewed standing by the orchard to this day.

The majestic tower, or keep, just inside the doorway, further accentuated the image of the monastery as a fortress. Built in the ninth century, it comprises a ground floor and three stories above. One gains access to it via a drawbridge to the second floor, which made it impossible for raiders to breech the fortification. The ground floor housed a granary and storage for oil and wine. The second floor was where the precious library was housed, until it was largely pillaged by European bibliophiles eager to augment institutions such as the British Museum and Vatican Library during the nineteenth century. The top floor housed living quarters and a chapel dedicated to the archangel Michael. Secure in the keep, the monks were able to continue their monastic lives without interruption from marauding nomads. The keep was the final act of introversion on the part of Egyptian monasticism: here a man remained inward for long periods of time, both physically and mentally.

I wandered about the central courtyard area for a short while, absorbing the elegant cupolas and archways that were a feature of the Church of the Holy Virgin standing against the southern wall. In the late afternoon, the tawny colors of each building reflected the color of the sand outside. Somehow it felt as if the desert had encroached by way of these colors, softening corners and perpendicular lines. At the western end of the monastery, next to the orchard, stood the Tree of Ephrem behind a grill, a gnarled gathering of branches and boughs. A few lines of one of his hymns sprung to mind as I reached in and touched its trunk, their beauty a contrast to the ageless impression given off by his miraculous tree. "The tree that holds back its buds withers, and the birth of green buds miscarry. But if fruit buds appear from deep within the womb of this sappy tree, then let my faith rejoice!"

But it was the Church of the Holy Virgin that I had come to visit, and now that most of the day visitors had departed, I was able to enter one of the oldest churches in Christendom (ca. AD 645) to study its interior. My guide that afternoon was Father Lucas, a monk in his midfifties with a staccato turn of phrase that belied his gentle expression. Behind his beard lay an intense gaze wizened by years of austerity.

Stepping inside the dimly lit nave, I found myself standing on an expanse of floral-patterned carpets. The church seemed like an interior garden, its smoke-stained walls as if daubed in darkness. Growing accustomed to the light that shone down from ventilation apertures high up in the cupolas, I began to recognize how beautiful the church really was. A number of very ancient frescoes graced the far end of the nave and the choir area as well. One particular fresco of Mary, together with Archangel Gabriel and various prophets at the end of the nave, had only been discovered recently by French restorers when they peeled away a later painting of the Annunciation.

"Very old," Father Lucas reminded me in his pinched, staccato voice. "Very old indeed."

"From the ninth century, perhaps?"

"Very old, yes, very old."

Four prophets, Isaiah, Moses, Ezekiel, and Daniel, stood on both sides of Mary enthroned, each holding a scroll dangling before them so that the text was clearly legible. The scrolls were pointing toward the Virgin, as if imploring some response. Each prophet spoke from his own book, thereby ensuring that his version of sacred events might be heard. "You watched while a stone was cut out without hands," Daniel insisted.[61] To which Ezekiel added, "And the LORD said to me, 'This gate shall be shut; it shall not be opened, and no man shall enter by it.'"[62] Whereupon the archangel chimed in, "Rejoice, highly favored one, the Lord is with you."[63] And Isaiah rejoined, "Behold, the virgin shall conceive and bear a Son."[64] Finally, Moses, his face ablaze, uttered his own entreaty, "The bush was burning with fire, but the bush was not consumed."[65] Here, perhaps, was an example of the very first comic strip. The Holy Virgin was surrounded by a babel of words.

I proceeded down the nave into the second choir area. Before me, as part of the iconostasis, stood a set of six tall and narrow doors, each leaf made of seven panels of ebony inlaid with ivory patterns. Above them was an inscription on the screen frame that dated this so-called Door of Symbols to around AD 913. Each of the seven rows of six panels revealed a set of different ivory patterns, beginning at the top with icons of Jesus Christ, the Holy Virgin, Saint Mark, Pope Dioscorus of Alexandria, and Saints Ignatius and Severus, both of whom represented the church of Antioch, which at that time enjoyed good relations with the church of Alexandria. The door represented the perfect entrance into paradise.

"These doors tell us the story of the Christian church," Father Lucas remarked.

"Their symbolism seems rather obscure," I replied.

"The row below the icons is made up of identical crosses intertwined, and surrounded each by a circle. They represent the early Christian era, with its strong faith, unity of purpose, and courage in the face of persecution. The third row has larger circles, as you see. These represent the era when Emperor Constantine converted to Christianity, and established large centers throughout the empire. In the fourth row you will note the appearance of crescents around every cross. This represents the advent of Islam in our midst."

"And the fifth row?" I asked, noticing a pattern made up of tiny swastikas.

"The swastika, which is an ancient symbol found in the Hindu culture also, I believe, speaks of discord in our own house, even as it is a sign of protection. It was the time of heresies. A bad time, a bad time indeed."

"And the small crosses in the sixth row?"

"They represent the growth of a multitude of beliefs and doctrines in the church. It was a time of lukewarm love and weakness among our people. In the seventh row you will see crosses radiating outward. They represent the second coming of Christ, when he will appear in the sky to us all. We believe this to be the time of the Coming One."

The entire history of Christianity had opened before me. Meanwhile, in his quietly officious manner, Father Lucas directed my gaze toward the southern half-cupola in the choir, where a fresco depicted the Annunciation combined with that of the Nativity. Mary was reclining by the manger in which the infant Jesus lay tightly swaddled, like an Egyptian mummy. Joseph, ever the watcher and guardian, stood to their right. While angels proclaimed the good news, the Magi approached with their gifts of gold, frankincense, and myrrh, representing the three ages of life—youth, maturity, and old age.

"You are, of course, familiar with the fact that the Holy Family passed through this region," Father Lucas announced.

"It is said that the infant Jesus created fresh water in the middle of one of the salt lakes not far from here," I replied, recalling a photograph I had seen of a pathway constructed of stones reaching out into shallow water, where a metal pipe containing the spring reached down into the lake.

"Is it not true that the world wishes to be revived, however inhospitable the terrain might appear?"

Since it was late on Saturday afternoon, Father Lucas kindly invited me to stay the night in the guest quarters, a building located outside the walls of the monastery on the edge of the desert. I readily consented. Together we left the Church of the Holy Virgin and made our way through the monastery gate. Father Lucas, ever the organizer, put in a call on his mobile phone, which mysteriously appeared from a fold in his vestment, presumably to arrange for my room to be prepared. Then we crossed the parking lot and proceeded to the guest house.

Once I had stowed my overnight bag in my room, I rejoined Father Lucas, now on the balcony overlooking the desert, for a glass of tea. It was a mild evening, and the sun slanted across the low dunes, casting a soft light upon the scene. In the foreground was an orchard that signaled the frontier of cultivation and order. Beyond lay a wide expanse of sand with a few simple structures barely visible in the distance. Even as we sat there, sipping tea and talking, there was movement on the desert road in the distance as a number of figures slowly made their way toward the monastery.

They were not walking as a group, but separately, the color of their clothing dark against the sand.

"Who are these men?" I asked.

"They are hermits. Each Saturday evening they come in to attend liturgy in the early hours of tomorrow morning."

"These men are genuine anchorites?"

"We have perhaps a dozen attached to our monastery. They are former coenobitic monks who have chosen to live the solitary life."

I watched the monks slowly drift toward the monastery. It was like observing a movie in slow motion, such was their steady but unhurried pace.

"How and when is this decision made to become a hermit?" I asked.

"Not every monk wishes to be an anchorite. It is a personal choice, and is only made after many years of ascetical training in the monastery. But some men, at a certain time in their lives, believe the desert offers them a greater opportunity to explore a more meaningful relationship with God. In consultation with the abbot they obtain his permission to build a small house in the desert. Once they have made the decision to live the full anchoritic life, there is no turning back. A monk might only come into the monastery to die—and even then, he might choose not to do so."

"Do any of them live in caves such as their forebears once did?"

"One or two, yes. But in these times, it is harder to give up small comforts. We monks are not as severe on ourselves as Saint Macarius or Saint Anthony were in their time. Those men were true athletes of the spirit. By comparison, we are no more than amateurs."

It was a confession I had not expected to hear. But Father Lucas was only being honest. Seventeen centuries after the era of the first hermits, when thousands of men had quit the world to live in caves throughout Egypt, it was clearly harder now to maintain either the intensity or dedication to the full anchoritic life. Something had departed from ascetic life—innocence perhaps, or at least a strong belief that a life of solitude was the best and only way to experience full revelation. Who but these men drifting toward the monastery as shadows at dusk really knew what it was like to live such a life? I wanted very much to ask them such a question, so I inquired of Father Lucas whether it might be possible.

"Do you think I might be able to talk to one of them? Ask him a few questions, perhaps?" I asked.

Father Lucas looked at me severely. His eyes, always intense, made me feel as if I may have overstepped the bounds of decorum.

"These men do not speak as you or I do," he replied. "Your interest in inquiring of their motives will fall upon deaf ears. They hardly utter words, except in prayer. And then, for the most part, they speak through silence. As Isaac of Nineveh once said, conversation in prayer comes about through stillness. And stillness is only acquired by the stripping away of the self."[66]

"What is prayer, exactly?" I asked.

"Prayer is the emptying of the mind of all that belongs here, in this world, and a heart which has completely turned its gaze to a longing for that future hope of oneness with God. From Evagrius, we know that prayer is a state of mind which is only cut off from the light of the Holy Trinity by a sense of wonder. Wonder is the key to the door of prayerful insight; this much we must accept. In prayer we journey toward the unknown, to a state that is unsurpassable. I myself have only been there once or twice. But it is enough. I know now it is attainable."

"It must give you some comfort, Father Lucas. At least you have experienced that feeling of bliss the ancient writers speak of."

"Bliss, yes. But it is more. When one reaches such a state, one finds oneself swallowed up by the Spirit. From this point onward the mind goes beyond prayer. No longer does the mind actually pray. Instead, one finds oneself gazing with wonder at the inaccessible things which do not belong to this world. The mind becomes stilled because it no longer has any knowledge of anything in the here and now. Only then does one experience a state of unknowingness. Such a state, I am told, resembles the color of sapphire. It is a most perfect condition."[67]

"These men I see coming toward us: have they experienced the color sapphire?"

"I have no doubt of it. They are far more accomplished in the spiritual life than I am. They have sacrificed everything to attain to perfect solitude. Prayerful contact with friends in the monastery, meeting with their families occasionally: such things are denied to them. I have yet to make such a commitment," replied Father Lucas, his voice sounding rueful. He slowly sipped his tea.

"The time will come, surely, Father. One day soon you will set out for the desert and not return."

"If that should happen, then I will be the most fortunate of men."

Later, when Father Lucas had taken his leave, and I was left with time enough to recall our conversation, I tried to picture the hermits arriving for liturgy that afternoon. It seemed like a dream, seeing them all dressed in black with embroidered bonnets on their heads, trudging along the road more like shades than men. It was as if I were encountering an image from the distant past: of men who had discovered how to live an angelic existence through a lifelong commitment to prayer, fasting, and abstinence. Everything about their lives seemed to be so confronting, yet in their very act of denial they had discovered a new way of living. Were they in fact masochists? I recalled Mother Nadeen's definition of masochism: its intention was a form of perverted pleasure, whereas the ascetic never has such an aim in mind. The ascetic's desire is oneness with God.

The light soon faded. I could make out a few lights by the monastery gate and a glow above the walls from the lights within. The monks would likely be gathering for evening prayer in preparation for liturgy early next morning. Sitting alone on the balcony, I kept thinking of Father Lucas's remarks about the idea of wonder being contingent to prayer. Dipping into the small collection of books that always accompanied me on my travels, I took out one by Isaac of Nineveh and flipped through its pages. Certain words of his became an echo of Father Lucas's:

> When there is awestruck wonder, prayer ceases. Only a certain divine vision remains, and the mind is unable to pray. Prayer is one thing, and contemplation during prayer is another. Prayer is the seed, and contemplation is the harvesting of its sheaves. When the reaper stand in ecstasy before the unutterable sight of such rich ears of wheat suddenly bursting forth before his eyes, he knows that he has sowed the seed of prayer wisely. Only then does he remain entirely motionless in contemplation.[68]

These words seemed to be telling me something. Clearly, I had yet to plant the seed. If I could not experience for myself the first rule of the ascetical life, namely that of prayer, deeply and with heartfelt intent, then how was I ever going to understand the nature of bliss? Father Lucas and his fellow monks were the true masters of the ascetical life, it seemed. They had learned by patient application of the principles of prayer the proper workings of their inner life.

11

A Chance Conversation

LITURGY AT DAWN IN THE CHURCH of the Holy Virgin was a moving experience. I joined Father Lucas and the rest of the monks in the early hours of the morning in the chapel, at once feeling at home among its floral motifs on the floor, its flickering candles, and the aroma of incense wafting through the barrel vault above. The Door of Symbols in the iconostasis was wide open now, revealing the sanctuary and an altar made of black stone. There was something timeless about this moment: the sound of voices raised as they chanted ancient hymns, as well as the slow unfolding of the liturgical experience itself, seemed to spread out like a carpet as colorful as any weaver could achieve with his shuttle. The icons above the Door of Symbols looked down on us all, bestowing their gaze of continuity and grace. Looking up at the ceiling of the nave, I found myself gazing into the dark hull of Noah's Ark.

The desert hermits were gathered in a group, standing slightly apart from their monastic brethren. Even as the priest performed the ritual of the Mass, these men seemed to embrace every word he uttered with quiet fervor. Each one of them had deliberately enclosed himself in a sphere of silence. The words of the liturgy became a diaphanous substance that screened them from the world. Older than the other monks, the hermits conveyed an infinite capacity for forbearance in their posture. They were like dolmens standing in some prehistoric site. I looked at their embroidered bonnets, each with the twelve crosses representing the disciples, six on one side of the head and six on the other, wondering what might be going on in their minds. I decided then that these men were emptied of thought. They had embarked upon their weekly journey into a state of endless existence.

When the service was over the hermits gathered outside the church to take leave of their brothers, and then slowly drifted off toward the monastery gate. They crossed the parking lot and made their way onto the desert road as they headed toward their respective caves and hermitages. In the dawn light, with barely a shadow on the ground, they trudged into the distance, their vestments moving easily with their bodies. Suddenly they were gone, this apparition from another age, this choir of angelic beings for which silence was the ultimate hymn. They had graced our lives for a few short hours, barely speaking, hardly smiling, and yet for all that always giving of their presence.

After breakfast with Father Lucas, I made the short walk to Saint Bishoy Monastery rather than go by car. It was only five hundred yards away, and easily visible down the road. I felt in need of a walk, anyway, in order that I might give further thought to Father Lucas's remarks of the previous evening. The fact was, there were issues that needed to be explored if I were ever going to come to terms with desert monasticism in Egypt.

What did I understand by the word *asceticism*, or by its Greek eponym, *ascesis*? The word finds its root in *ascaein*, which means "to exercise," thus aligning asceticism with athletic activity among ancient Greeks. The Olympians of old regularly practiced *ascaein* in order to raise their physical performance to another level. It was only natural, therefore, to regard a champion athlete as someone who had made *ascesis* a part of his training. The anchorites of Egypt, whose achievements were first written about by Greek-speaking authors living in Alexandria, naturally found themselves described as "ascetics." It was probably not a term they used to describe themselves. Nonetheless, it was important to know that anchorites were first and foremost "athletes of the spirit."

I also had to come to terms with their other eponym, that of the "anchorite." This term is derived from the Greek word *anachoresis*, meaning "withdrawal." An anchorite is one who withdraws from society in order to practice an ascetical lifestyle. The entire basis of ascetic life was removal from the world, and that meant quitting the settled region along the Nile and retiring into the desert. The desert became a gymnasium in which ascetics trained to become capable of expressing a superabundance of spiritual gifts. It was the one place where a man—or woman—might engage in a spiritual transformation of his or her entire being, providing the perfect opportunity for transformation to occur. In time, as the exploits of the early anchorites spread throughout the Roman world, the desert was able to spread its gossamer threads of supernatural power across the fertile fields of the Nile. Many pious folk actually believed this power contributed to the inundation by the great river each year. What the monks had renounced for themselves—that is, an abundant supply of food and plenty of water to grow vegetables—became for the many living along the Nile a symbol of holy beneficence. The ascetic life of the desert was made, paradoxically, into a conduit of grace for ordinary folk who were unable, or unwilling, to make the break from society themselves.

The walk had been invigorating that morning. A clear blue sky, almost dome-like in appearance, dominated the flat landscape of sand and low dunes. Ahead of me stood the monastery of Saint Bishoy, a walled compound that looked like it had emerged from the sand rather than having been constructed. Finally I reached the gate.

Saint Bishoy was founded by the holy monk Bishoy, one of seven children born to a family in the delta region. His father died early, making it difficult for his mother to raise her brood. According to legend, an angel appeared to Bishoy when he was not yet twenty, urging him to withdraw into the desert and devote his life to God. Journeying to the desert of Scetis, he attached himself to one of the great figures of early asceticism, a man named Pambo. According to Palladius, Pambo possessed heroic virtue and was capable of knowing the moment when he was about to die. Weaving a basket one day, he announced to the Lady Melania from Jerusalem, "Receive the basket at my hands to remember me by, for I have nothing else to leave you." With that he died in her arms.[69]

On the death of his teacher, Bishoy was again commanded by an angel to retreat further into the desert in order to lead a life of total solitude. His cell lay where the monasteries of Deir es Suriani and Saint Bishoy stand today. So great was his piety, it is said of him, that Jesus Christ visited him one day, whereupon he bathed the Savior's feet. Bishoy did not recognize his guest, however, until he saw the marks of his crucifixion. Today, his relics lie in the northern transept of the choir, and are much venerated by monks and visitors alike.[70]

I followed the western wall inside the monastery, past the keep, until I had reached the courtyard and gardens. Before me stood the ancient ninth-century church of Saint Bishoy, with its imposing array of sixteen domes rising above the roof on either side of the nave. It reminded me of a beehive. Its many domes and icons on the wall, most of them extremely old, spoke of Bishoy's unrivaled sanctity. The key to his life was that he had always been prepared to listen to angels. That, and the austerity of his ascetical practice, made him a hero to many. Bishoy used to pray all night, never leaving his feet for a moment. So as not to fall over because of fatigue while doing so, he tied his hair with a piece of rope to the ceiling of his cell.[71]

While standing before the haikal inside the church, and gazing at the richly patterned wood and icons on either side of the sanctuary, I was approached by a monk who asked me whether he might explain the history of the place to me. His voice sounded almost musical, lilting, as if he might have studied singing earlier in his life. He was perhaps in his early forties, with dark, almond-shaped eyes. His beard had not yet turned gray, which made me think he might be younger than he appeared.

"My name is Father Abadir," he said. "I have heard that you were among us."

"From whom, Father?"

"Father Lucas called from Suriani. He told me to treat you as our honored guest, Mr. James."

"It seems my well-being is his command!" I replied, half in jest.

"I pray that your walk this morning was as fruitful as sharing holy Mass with the monks." Father Abadir's face was inscrutable as he spoke.

Then he conducted me around the church, explaining various points of detail that were as much legendary as they were historical. I had grown used to such commentary, and would have been worried if I had not been subjected to at least one or two miraculous stories. Coptic Christianity thrives on the supernatural, so one hardly expects to hear of anything so prosaic as a date being attributed to such tales—unless, of course, it happens to be while recounting a story about martyrdom.

Later, Father Abadir invited me to take tea with him in a large reception room available to visitors. On weekends in particular, families drive out from Cairo or Alexandria to spend the day at the monastery. There they are able to make confession or talk over their problems with a friendly monk. It is this easy familiarity between layperson and monk that contributes to the richness of Coptic life. Everyone belongs to a monastery, even if he or she is not a religious.

I decided to ask Father Abadir about his own life. Surprisingly, he did not seem reluctant to tell me how he had become a monk.

"I owned a successful pharmacy in Cairo when I was younger," he confessed. "In those days I had all I wanted. I owned a car, and was saving up to purchase an apartment in a better part of town. This is what we Copts are expected to do in preparation for marriage."

"Did you succeed in your task, Father?"

"Of course. But it did not bring me the satisfaction I had anticipated. All the money, success, and feeling of security these things
brought to my life, not to mention the respect of my family, none
of them made me feel that I was worthy."

"Worthy of what, Father?"

"Of believing that in some way I had been chosen, Mr. James.
This is a strange way of speaking, I know. But the truth is that all
I had done up to this point was of my own volition. I was always
in control of my destiny. A time came when I realized how shallow
this perception was. Since I was always in a position of choosing, I
had alienated myself from the prospect of being chosen. Does this
sound so strange? Perhaps my English is wanting."

"You are expressing yourself perfectly, Father," I said, trying to
encourage him. "Being 'chosen' suggests to me that you felt your
real worth lay outside yourself."

"Indeed, it lay with God, but I could not see it at the time.
I was too busy arranging my life in accordance with prescribed
rules of behavior. Success meant a great deal to me. So too did
my possessions. I had seen how difficult it was for my parents
to live after our country's defeat during the first war with Israel,
and I did not want their life to be one for myself. So I decided to
pursue a professional career as a pharmacist. At least, I thought,
I am helping people."

"Weren't you?"

"Of course. But I began to feel this was merely an excuse on
my part, a justification of my own power to choose, when what
I really needed was to let go of my life altogether. In a very real
sense, I wanted to give it away. If that doesn't sound like too great
an act of largesse, Mr. James!"

Abadir's face lit up with a smile as he spoke. His eyes, normally
so radiant, opened and closed with the slow precision of a cat's.

"I realized then," he went on, "that life is like a symphony. Each
of us is called upon to take up an instrument and play. The trouble

was: I seemed to have no talent for music! All I could do was make a noise."

"Perhaps you were destined to be the conductor, Father," I remarked.

Again Father Abadir gave that special smile of his, one that took you into his confidence as if you were his brother.

"In the end, I sought advice from a friend of the family," he continued. "It was he who recognized the strain my predicament was causing me. He could see that I was suffering from possessing too great a capacity to choose. 'Let us go out to Wadi Natrun,' he said to me one day. It was on that day, when I met the monks here in Saint Bishoy, that I first began to realize my vocation. From here on, I told myself, the instrument I must learn to play is myself. I had to learn how to submit my body and my mind to the discipline of the desert. Then, perhaps, I might begin to play music of an altogether different tone."

"Yet today you live without possessions and without a future other than to reside here in the presence of God, Father. It was a radical decision, to say the least," I said.

"It is enough. Since the Lord Jesus has chosen me, I feel I am in his hands. Such is his gift that I do not feel I belong to myself any more. The experience of being no longer present in the world, yet at the same time feeling intensely open to its wonder, makes me realize that before I came here I lived in a kind of—how do you say—miasma? Yes, a miasma! I was walking about in a fog most of the time."

"This new perspective of yours, Father: do you believe it has come about because of your commitment to the ascetic life?"

"Inevitably. Asceticism leads to a refinement of being. I cannot put it in any other way, Mr. James. Ascetical life has offered me the opportunity to cleanse myself of all my impurities. I sometimes think of this process of refinement as one might the task of extracting steel from iron ore in a foundry. The longer one subjects raw material to heat in a furnace, the more slag runs off as waste.

Personal faults and failings are no more than slag; they need to be subjected to the fiery heat of ascetical practice."

"Do you ever feel you might be missing out on something because of the limited life you now lead here in the monastery?"

"What could I be lacking? The freneticism of modern life, perhaps? The agitation and insecurity brought about by economic pressure? The need to hurry everything that one does because of time constraints, or a feeling that not to do so is to imply a lack of busyness? One always has to be doing something, as you know.

"Here, in contrast," Father Abadir continued, "we are also busy—but busy dealing with the virus of overcoming the need to be busy! Ah, the English language: it allows one to play with concepts so easily. I think you know what I mean, Mr. James. Our principal objective, living as we do, is to realize a state of stillness, impassivity. This is about as busy as we get! By subjecting our bodies to prolonged periods of discomfort, by limiting our desire for sleep, by ensuring that we hear only the inspired words of the Gospels and other sacred texts when we are attending liturgy or at mealtime in the refectory, by eating little and fasting often, we are able to slowly refine our sensibilities to the point where they are no more a mixture of iron ore and slag. They have become like steel. They are sharp—how do you say it in English? Keen. Yes, that is the word. It says so much."

"It has many meanings, Father," I replied.

"To be incisive, yes?"

"Bold too, and brave. Enthusiastic."

"Learned, clever, and wise, perhaps?"

"Yes, and sharp. Biting. Even acrid to taste," I added with a smile. I could see that Father Abadir was enjoying our banter.

"Oh, how beautiful a word it is, Mr. James. Your language is so rich in meaning. Yet all of these meanings apply to the ascetical life. It is a 'keen' process. It helps us to be wise sometimes, certainly more incisive in our perception of the world. Denial can also be regarded as acrid, biting, do you not agree? You see now why we monks are so committed to the ascetical life. It is not a life of denial for its own sake. Not at all. Denial is the heat of the furnace. It subjects us to a transformation of what we were into a person that is annealed. Is there such a word?"

"There is," I said. "It would seem by what you are saying that the ascetical process is more than simply one of discipline. It embodies something subtler. Nor is it about controlling—no, bridling—one's passions, so much as bringing them to order. They are like colts in a field, ready to run in all directions without thought of the consequences. Asceticism becomes a halter; it subjects us all to some form of control so that our appetites might be led safely through the gate."

"We often see ourselves as asses, do we not? This is why we rely so much on a trainer in our early years as a monk. Saint Pambo, as we know, taught Saint Bishoy. He also taught Ammonius, Plotinus's teacher, as well as Origen's. A teacher is there to give us the benefit of his experience, and that of his teacher as well. Everyone who enters monastic life begins as a student. In doing so, we draw comfort from knowing we are partaking of a long tradition of ascetical insight. Without this, where would we be?"

"Why are monasteries always located in the desert, and not in more salubrious surroundings?" I asked.

"Because it is only here that thoughts are permitted to become concentrated," replied Father Abadir, pouring me another glass of tea. "Distillation is the essence of our journey throughout the spiritual life. As with refinement, we are attempting to reduce all our thoughts down to one simple belief—our invisibility in relation to God. We do not wish to be seen. Strange, is it not? To want to become selfless, to be absolutely effaced in the eyes of God. This is the principal objective of any monk. He is not here to astound himself. No, he wants to diminish himself—his self, rather—to the point where its existence is no longer acknowledged. It is the very reason why Father Lucas advised you against talking with the hermits last night."

"How do you know of this, Father?" I inquired, somewhat surprised that my confidence had been betrayed.

"It is the request all visitors make of us. They want to talk with men whom they believe can answer questions of selfhood that they find troubling. You did ask this of Father Lucas, no?" Father Abadir inquired, his eyes dancing, almost playfully.

"I confess I did. It seemed important at the time."

"It was important—to you. But to the hermit, such a question is difficult to understand. Because the state of mind you wish him to discuss has gone from his recollection. He can no longer remember what it was like to be immersed in self. In a very real sense, a hermit much advanced in the spiritual life is no longer a 'psychological' being at all. He has gone beyond it. His self has been purged from him after years of ascetical practice. Nothing of his past is left other than his name, perhaps, or where he was born. And these he will not reveal to you because they savor of his old persona. The hermit does not live for the past, but for the eternal present. Can you understand now why any converse with a hermit would prove to be fruitless, Mr. James?"

"Why should these men exist at all, then, if they cannot communicate how they feel to us who need to know and understand?" I asked, frustrated by where the conversation was leading me.

"Because such men can only communicate with those who have already made a commitment to following in their footsteps. Until this has occurred, and you have made that commitment yourself, all talk is pointless."

"It becomes very much an intellectual exercise on my part, is that what you mean?'

"Only you can decide," replied Father Abadir. "But I do know that until I had resolved to end my old life as a pharmacist and begun my new one here at Saint Bishoy, there was no point even airing my doubts. I had to acknowledge that what I expected of myself bore no relation to the life of the spirit. Before we enter the spiritual life we are little more than infants: our diet is very simple—we can only stomach milk, not solids."

"Milk you equate with basic human nourishment, I take it—the kind we receive while living a normal life in the world."

"Already you are beginning to understand the language of the angels, Mr. James. True nourishment is a spiritual food. You must prepare your mind to receive such food, as a child prepares its stomach for the absorption of solids."

"I can only say that indigestion has been a lifelong affliction of mine, Father!"

Father Abadir seemed pleased by my allusion. He blinked his almond-shaped eyes with the slow grace of a curtain falling at the end of a performance.

"At least now you have been provided with a remedy, Mr. James," he remarked.

It seemed that Father Abadir had landed in my life like a bird. His remarks possessed all their tonalities of abundant and varied plumage. Had he been sent to speak with me—not by Father Lucas, but by some hidden adjudicator? Through him, Saint Bishoy was obviously working one of his miracles. Nor did I feel this would be the last time that Father Abadir and I should meet.

12
Under the Tree

CROSSING THE ROSETTA BRANCH of the Nile at a place called El-Kanater el-Khairiyah some miles southeast of Wadi Natrun, I tried to imagine what it might be like to gaze down upon the delta region from high up in space—the expanding vortex of green fields emanating from Cairo toward the Mediterranean coastline like a flower pressed between the pages of a book; the long veins of the river, with their myriad capillaries made of canals reaching across the land, the delicate markings on a petal. Crossing back into the fertile lands of the delta once again was like entering a faded blossom whose ancient cities formed an interlocking pattern of protective leaves. From Daphnae, through Tanis, Mendes, Buto, and Sais, they guarded the frontiers of Egypt from invasion. More importantly, they protected the most sacred of all cities, that of On, or Heliopolis, now an outer suburb of Cairo.

The Holy Family probably would have crossed the river at the same point as I on their way to El-Matariyah, in Heliopolis. Although Theophilus does not say so in his *Vision*, Joseph and Mary must have known they were traveling toward one of the most important cities in Egypt, famed not only because of the marriage between Joseph of the Old Testament and Asenah, the daughter of Potipherah who was high priest at the temple of the sun-god

Ra-Tem in that city, but because it was here Moses spent his early years as the adopted son of Pharaoh's daughter. At the time of the family's visit to the area, Heliopolis would have been deserted, as Strabo attests on his visit sixteen years before. It had been destroyed during the Persian invasion by Nebuchadnezzar (525 BC), and had still not recovered. This had already been prophesied fifty years earlier by Jeremiah, who spoke of the gods of Egypt being destroyed by the king of Babylon.[72]

They visited Heliopolis probably because there was a large Jewish community living in the nearby village of El-Matariyah, with a synagogue of their own dedicated to Unias. The existence of such a community would have lured them there, as Joseph might have hoped to find work. A fine sycamore tree stood outside the village under which the Holy Family rested. Today, the tree is known as Shagaret Mariam, or the "Tree of Saint Mary." I was on my way there, not only to see this tree, but also to drink at a nearby spring reputedly created by the infant Jesus with a wave of his hand.

During the Middle Ages, El-Matariyah was a popular place for pilgrims visiting the Holy Land and Egypt. Entrance to the garden surrounding the tree cost six ducats, a sum that allowed the pilgrim to bathe in the pool and take advantage of its medicinal properties. In 1480, the Dominican friar Felix Fabri noticed a small chapel in the bowl of an immense fig tree by the entrance. In it, he says, two lamps hung in memory of the Holy Virgin's visit. What he does not mention is that a tradition associated this tree with an act of concealment: the family was miraculously enclosed by the tree after yet another attempt to rob them by the two brigands that they had met at Bubastis. The place was also known as the Garden of Balm because of the presence of sweet-smelling balsam plants growing nearby—which, according to Josephus, were a gift to King Solomon by the Queen of Sheba. These were later transplanted from Israel to El-Matariyah by Caesar Augustus. There was widespread belief that the trees could not produce balsam without water from the spring.

Such was the high number of visitors to the garden that only five people at a time were allowed entry. This was to protect the balsam trees, whose fruit and branches were eagerly sought after by pilgrims. By boiling the branches, for example, a concoction known as myron oil was obtained for use as a chrism at baptism. Sultan Abdul Malik (1217–1238), a friend of Saint Francis of Assisi, attempted to relocate these trees to a neighboring plot of land, but they did not blossom.[73] Only after the trees were irrigated by water from the holy spring did they bring forth an abundant crop. Though the balsams have long since disappeared, the ancient sycamore under which the Holy Family rested still remains, even if only as an offshoot of the original, which, weighed down by age, finally fell in 1672.

The family's visit to Heliopolis, however, did not all go according to plan. The tree offered them some relief from the heat; but when Salome asked some of the local inhabitants for yeast to make bread, they refused her request. To this day it is reported that in a few streets of the city, namely Sharie Eid (the "Street of Feasts") and Sharie Shaq el-Teeban (the "Street of the Snake's Crack"), bread does not rise. Whether this is because yeast is not used in the dough-making process by bakers in these streets, no one knows. The fact is, after two thousand years a belief still lingers here that, because of this act of inhospitality, the bread of the region remains as hard as a snake's anus!

As my taxi driver negotiated the crowded streets of the city on our way to the sanctuary at El-Matariyah, my thoughts that morning were of the seeming coincidence that Jesus Christ, none other than the "New Sun," paid a visit to the home of Ra-Tem, the legendary sun-god of the ancient Pharaonic cult. Tem was considered to have been the first *living* man-god known to the Egyptians, just as Osiris was the first *dead* man-god. Tem usually held the *ankh*, or emblem, of life in one hand and the *uas*, scepter, representing supreme kingship and stability, in the other. Whenever he was portrayed in a boat on the Nile, Tem was also portrayed in human form, with his abstract nature, that of the Ra sun disk, encircling him in the form of a mandala. To the Egyptians, he was a manifestation of God (Ra) in human form, almighty, inscrutable, unknowable, the maker and creator of the universe. Like Christ, who was seen as a manifestation of God on earth, Tem was held to be the equal of Ra and so the protector of the human race. And like Christ he bore immortal life in his hands. It is no accident that Tem's *uas* was the symbol of a tree branch, cut off along with a piece of a larger branch. Together they signified the act of creation, its vitalizing sap present to cause division in oneness while at the same time generating the mystery of opposites. At El-Matariyah, it seemed the branches of a tree reiterated Christ's beneficence to a people longing to receive some sort of balm.

The Heliopolitan mysteries acted as a magnet to many thinkers of the past, not least Pythagoras and Plato.[74] Both men, at different times, visited the city to study under the guidance of temple priests. Both men became aware of the law of harmonics and their association with ethics. Plato spoke of the belief that melody, properly expressed, was the doing of a god, or a godlike man.[75] He called such melody one of "intrinsic rightness," sometimes attributing its creation to Isis, whose lore he had studied at Heliopolis. According to Plutarch, Plato regarded Isis as the principle of Nature in her nurturing and generative essence.[76] Moreover, Plato explored his own trinity of essences that became, in the hands of his Christian readers, the basis of the Trinity. He spoke of the "high honor" of the most "beautiful of triangles" in which the divine nature manifested itself in the forms of the conceptual, material, and what the Greeks called the cosmos.

Plato was taught all such ideas by temple priests during his time in Heliopolis, much as Pythagoras and Thales had learned them here before him.[77] Heliopolis became the seat of wisdom for the entire ancient world. From here many early conceptions of religion and philosophy developed and were disseminated throughout the entire corpus of Western thought. On may be termed the mother-city of thought, the place where Ra-Tem manifested himself as a divine being and as a precursor to Christ.

Heliopolis, too, was once the home of a very ancient obelisk known as *bnbn*, or "the radiant one." According to tradition, the land where the city was built represented the primordial hillock, the first manifestation of matter in the world. On this hillock a phoenix from Arabia landed each year, bearing his father wrapped in myrrh. "First the phoenix moulds an egg of myrrh as heavy as he can carry," writes Herodotus. "Later, he hollows out this egg and places his father in it. The phoenix then carries him off to the temple of the Sun in Egypt."[78]

It would seem from all accounts that Heliopolis was a city not only associated with the sun cult of Ra-Tem, the ever-renewing God of light, but remained the most important center of learning well into the last centuries before the birth of Christ. It appears to be no accident that the Holy Family, bearing the new "radiant one" in their arms, might wish to associate themselves with the city and its precinct, even if it were largely a ruin. One senses many similarities between the sun-god Ra-Tem and his Christian counterpart, both of whom died and were born again in the figures of Phoenix/Osiris and Christ.[79] The city became an *omphalos* for Egyptians as well as others, thus linking the realm of the spirit with ordinary people on earth. It is ironic, I suppose, to think that while important god-men were "resurrected" in Heliopolis throughout the millennia, to this day bread does not rise!

Heliopolis today is an urban nightmare. Driving through the outskirts of the city, I found myself surrounded by high-rise apartment blocks, streets jammed with traffic, and a sense of frenzied locomotion as everyone pressed forward to meet appointments or reach their destinations. It was hard to imagine that somewhere under all this masonry and macadam there was once a bridle path along which the Holy Family made their way across country to El-Matariyah. In an attempt to blot out the sheer ugliness and agitation of present-day Heliopolis, I tried to transport myself back into their time in order to understand how a tree and a spring might have transformed their lives.

We arrived outside the garden, which was located below a hill crammed with poorly constructed apartment blocks. I could hear schoolchildren playing behind a high wall on the other side of the garden. Birds flitted through the air as I entered the gate and paid my respects to a group of policemen there to protect the place from unwanted visitors. The young men, shabbily dressed in military-style uniforms, were slouched on chairs by the entrance, trying to overcome sleep and the pangs of hunger. Guiltily, they stood to attention as I wandered by and made my way down a path to the fountain.

From nowhere, it seemed, a man approached me. He appeared to be in his late thirties, and had an open gaze and rather muscular appearance. Introducing himself as Mohe el-Dein, he told me he was the resident guide to the sanctuary. Initially I was surprised, since this was the first time in my travels so far I had encountered a Muslim in a Christian sanctuary. It did not faze him in any way, and he happily informed me about the significance of the pool and Saint Mary's tree. I realized then these were as important to him as they were to Christians.

"The Lady Mary washed the baby Jesus's clothes in this pool," Mohe el-Dein told me.

"So I am told."

"Baby Jesus's sweat was sprinkled on the balsam plants too. It was this act which made them so fragrant," he added.

"Where are these plants now?" I asked.

He shrugged.

"They have died through want of faith," he said simply.

Together we gazed into the grotto, where a stream trickled down over an artificial formation of rocks into a pool. Each of us pondered the significance of his remark. I felt that Mohe el-Dein wanted me to confirm his observation, so I said: "It is believed that these plants didn't flourish until after the Holy Family's visit. What is you opinion?"

"Miracles only occur when sanctity is acknowledged. We Muslims believe in the Lord Jesus. He may not be Allah, but he was surely a very pure person. We honor him in our thoughts and our prayers."

"Certainly Sultan Malik recognized the mystery of his presence," I replied. "I know for a fact that he and Saint Francis of Assisi deeply respected one another, both acknowledging the power of their mutual faith."

"Is it not true that men of good faith put aside what divides them in order to emphasize what brings them together?"

"I suspect you are right," I said.

A few yards further along the path we came to the Tree of Saint Mary. I was completely taken aback by what I saw. The ancient tree, located in a circular garden, spread its boughs in all directions in an intaglio of dead or dying branches. Many of these were propped up with posts to prevent them from breaking off. The tree reminded me of an image from a Salvador Dali painting: how often had I witnessed the fantastic, surrealistic shapes in his work, particularly his trees, thinking perhaps they were the product of an overheated imagination. In front of me now stood a venerable sycamore tree, struggling to survive against all odds, its branches reaching out, expressing all the perturbations one experiences in a horror movie. Yet, in the same moment, I did not feel afraid. The tree was too old, too craggy, too bedeviled by a sense of deadness to arouse any fear. Mohe el-Dein was right: the decline in faith had starved it of nutriment.

"Such a tree speaks to us of its anguish," he remarked. "Though I have worked here for many years, I always reach out to it in my heart. We are an old people, we Egyptians, as you know. Our history goes back into the dim reaches of time. Up and down the Nile you will find ruined temples and churches, their stones chipped and broken by neglect and the weather. How can it be, I ask myself? What is so special about this fertile yet arid land that made its people want to take upon themselves the task of trying to measure the worth of the human soul? It seems so strange, when abundance was always at hand. Why begin to question what is given gladly by nature, I thought to myself? On school excursions when I was young, I saw tiny figures on tomb walls of gods with animal heads. At first I was aghast, telling myself how barbaric my ancestors must have been. How can you see Allah with the head of a hawk or an ibis, or even a cat?"

"Surely the Qur'an has something to say about the beauty of nature as a repository of sanctity," I remarked.

"It does indeed. Let me quote you a few lines. They come from the Book of Abraham:

> A good word
> is a good tree—
> its roots are firm,
> And its branches are in heaven.[80]

"For your people, Mohe, language is the prism which colors all that you think and believe. You must be thankful that words still have the power to heal."

"Let us not forget that you as a Christian and I as a Muslim, we draw our sustenance from the same root."

"As people of the book, perhaps?"

Mohe el-Dein glanced at the Tree of Saint Mary, its tangled branches bending over, a battered sentinel, a lighthouse perhaps, its beacon flashing intermittently.

"Everything we think and believe finds its origin here, in Egypt. This country precedes the Book," he said.

After saying goodbye to my new friend, and paying him a small fee for his services, I walked back along the path toward the entrance to the garden. At the gate I turned to look for the last time at the Tree of Saint Mary. It stood there, its fragility suddenly apparent, a bedraggled mass of dried-out branches and boughs. It was hard to believe I had traveled through such a pall of ugliness to reach it that morning, only to find myself in the presence of its strange and ancient beauty. The tree, as old as it was, embodied much more than I had expected. It spoke of all the trees I had gazed upon in the past, and of all the trees whose shade I had enjoyed. It had become a metaphor for the tenuous nature of belief when it is allowed to suffer the imposition of conflicting demands and attitudes, which cause it to wither.

The Dream 13

RETURNING TO CAIRO AFTER A COUPLE of weeks in the provinces brought me down to earth with a bump. I had forgotten what it was like to live in a city of seventeen million people. The traffic sped frenetically along crowded thoroughfares, the noise from car horns was deafening, and people crossed the roads in a way that suggested their indifference toward protecting either life or limb. Brown dust lay over everything, and air conditioners clung to buildings like parasites. At dusk, the back streets and alleys became outdoor mosques as men laid out mats for evening prayers. As soon as these were concluded, the cafés were suddenly crowded with hungry people, nearly all of them men, eager to break their fast. TV screens glimmered with soap operas and football matches. Brightly lit shops and emporiums on each side of the avenues were filled with men's clothing, travel bags, women's fashion, headscarves and ties, belts, shoes, water pumps, perfume, underwear, electronic goods and power tools, guns and fishing tackle. Modern Cairo had been reduced to one huge bazaar into which a newly elevated middle class swarmed each evening until well after midnight.

I wandered about in a daze. Wishing to restore some sense of reality to my life, I decided to pay a visit to Mokattam Mountain, which overlooks Cairo. I had been told by the concierge at my hotel not only that this mountain had been moved to its present position by Saint Simeon, a tenth-century tanner from Babylon (Old Cairo), but also that an even more extraordinary miracle had occurred here back in 1974, when a trash collector by the name of Qiddees Al-Masseh managed to convince a senior government minister, whose trash he collected in uptown Shubra, to pay a visit to the Zaraayib area of town, a slum known as the "Pigsty." Al-Masseh urged the minister to help him build a church in this slum, believing it might provide hope among its benighted inhabitants.

The minister visited the Pigsty one day and was deeply moved by what he saw. He walked through the slum and climbed Mokattam Mountain along with his trash collector friend. There a voice told him to pray. On another visit to the same place three weeks later, the entire area was suddenly consumed by a whirlwind as he knelt in prayer. When the wind settled, the minister discovered a piece of paper at his feet upon which was written a verse from Saint Paul. It urged him not to be afraid but to build a church on the mountain, in accordance with his friend's request.

I took a taxi across town via the Citadel, an area through which, according to tradition, the Holy Family had passed on their way to Old Cairo from El-Matariyah, and then slowly negotiated the narrow streets of the suburb of Zaraayib up the hill to Mokattam. Scenes I had never thought possible greeted my gaze: the Pigsty was the place where Cairo's garbage was processed by hand, sorted into different categories of refuse, and then sold off to companies for recycling. Thousands of men, women, and children found themselves buried under the rubbish of a city. They were living in the intestine of Cairo, consumed by rotting food, plastic bottles and bags, junk, dead animals, and the sordid stench of decay that hung as a continuous odor over the area. Like vultures, the inhabitants of the quarter picked over piles of garbage dumped along the road. Pedestrians and cyclists threaded their way through this mélange of humanity, blood, and waste, struggling to escape from this cesspit.

As I looked at these people, dressed as they were in ragged clothes, I was less shocked by their predicament than I had expected to be. I began to see them as the noblest people on earth. Their grimy faces seemed radiant, their smiles ever present. It was as if the inhabitants of the Pigsty did not see what I saw. Their main street, their piles of garbage, their miserable teahouses and grocery shops, their sores and crippled limbs—all these had combined in a macabre representation of a celestial city and its inhabitants. People living here had overcome the taint of ugliness and unmitigated filth because of one thing only—the construction of their new church dedicated to Saint Simeon the Tanner carved out of Mokattam Mountain above. A miracle had allowed them to transcend their predicament, thanks to the intervention of a trash collector and a government minister. Now the streets of Zaraayib were the vestibule of heaven, and its people had discovered a reason to live.

My taxi passed through Zaraayib and on up to a gate into a compound on the side of the mountain, which was the site of the newly constructed outdoor church and monastery of Saint Simeon. Entering this sanctuary with its paved street, pathways, gardens, and overhanging cliff was almost as strange as entering the streets of the Pigsty. I was overwhelmed by the energy and vision that had made the construction of the monastery possible. In an age of spiritual decline it seemed unusual to visit an open-air church dug out from the face of a cliff and capable of seating many thousands of people. More importantly, I was struck by the cliff itself: sculpted in relief across its entire length was a series of large compositions and quotations from the Bible, all of which left me in no doubt that a sculptor of unusual talent must work here. He may not have been a Michelangelo, but certainly the man had been able to transform the overhang into one vast tableau of biblical events.

Most of the scenes depicted incidents from the New Testament, such as the birth of Christ with the Magi in attendance, Christ's ascension from the tomb, Christ walking on water toward his disciples in their fishing boat, the Samaritan women at the well, and the Savior turning water into wine. I was amazed at how difficult it must have been to haul oneself up the rock face in order to sculpt these reliefs. The risk to life and limb would have been acute.

Resolving to find out who the sculptor might be, I inquired in one of the shops selling icons and religious literature. The assistant informed me that if I followed a path off to the left I would find the compound where the workmen gathered in the morning. There I might run into Father Saman, the priest and overseer of the project, if he happened to be on hand. I was in luck; I found the good father sitting under a canvas awning behind some flower-pots, taking tea with a wiry, well-muscled man in his early forties, presumably one of the workmen. I walked over and introduced myself, informing them both how impressed I was by this edifice. Could I meet the sculptor, I asked, if only to congratulate him on his achievement?

"Here he is," Father Saman replied, turning and nodding toward the man seated beside him. "This is Mariusz Dybich, from Poland. It is he who has created the wonder that is Saint Simeon."

I looked at the rather small man sipping his tea. He had not understood a word of our conversation. He reminded me of a garden gnome, so robust and composed was his demeanor. Wispy blond hair fell across his forehead. His hands were gnarled, like bowls on a tree.

"What inspired Mr. Dybich to create such a masterpiece?" I asked.

Father Saman replied on Mr. Dybich's behalf: "Why, God, of course. Mariusz came here nearly ten years ago to work as a mechanic. I saw that he was good with his hands. And deeply pious too; he respected the miracle that had made Saint Simeon Monastery possible. If a simple tanner in the tenth century could move a mountain to this spot, then surely, I said to Mariusz, a mechanic such as he could turn his hand to anything."

"Mr. Dybich has had no previous experience as a sculptor?" I asked.

"None whatsoever. He is self-taught. Or should I say this cliff"—Father Saman looked up at the massive overhang in order to emphasize his point—"drew from him all the beauty it had harbored these past millennia? It was a marriage between faith and stone, between a desire to serve God and the need to make this mountain into an icon. It is a miracle."

I gazed at Mr. Dybich, trying to fathom his intent. It turned out that he had worked almost continuously during the first two years of the project in a bid to complete some of the reliefs. In those years he worked for food and board. Nothing, it seemed, could deter him from hauling himself up the rock face each morning, using a system of pulleys and rope. He would hang suspended against the cliff like a spider weaving its web throughout summer and winter, patiently chipping away stone with mallet and chisel. Sweat poured from his brow as he slowly translated images from the Bible onto this unyielding surface.

How he was able to achieve such a feat even Mr. Dybich was unable to explain. When asked, he simply replied, "God helps me: I am in his hands." I was looking at a man whose faith was so complete that nothing, not even the complex craft of a sculptor, could stand in the way of realizing his vision. This partnership between a priest and a mechanic, like that of a minister and a trash collector, had made it possible for Mokattam Mountain to become an icon for the faithful.

"You see, Mr. James," Father Saman said, translating Mariusz's remarks for me, "all we are doing is honoring the miracle of Saint Simeon. He was a lowly tanner, yet he was able to achieve the impossible. If he could move a mountain through the power of his faith, surely it is possible for a man like me to try to do the same."

Father Saman nodded approvingly.

"The event he is referring to occurred when a Jew attached to the Fatamid caliph's court of A-Mu'izz [ca. AD 975], a man named

Moses, chose to debate with the Christian patriarch Ephrem the superiority of Islam over Christianity, in the hope of ingratiating himself with his lord," he explained. "The debate ended in defeat for Moses, who was shown to be a fool. He immediately decided to test the patriarch's faith by challenging him to put into practice one of the verses from the Bible. It seems he wanted to humiliate the man who had done the same to him."

"What was the verse, Father?" I asked.

"Matthew 17:20. 'If you have faith as small as a mustard seed, you can say to this mountain, "move from here to there," and it will move. Nothing will be impossible for you.'"

"Which is exactly what the patriarch tried to do, I presume," I said.

"Not at all. He did not have such faith. After three days of prayer and fasting the patriarch was visited by the Virgin Mary in a dream. She told him to call upon the services of a one-eyed man he would find carrying a water jar outside the city gate."

"Who, I gather, turned out to be Simeon the Tanner?"

"A man of such lowly station, Mr. James. Imagine. A tanner, a man who deals in animal skins! But he was pure of heart and of great humility. His whole life was spent in prayer. And he was always helping others less fortunate than himself. He told the patriarch when he came into the presence of the caliph on the day of the test that he must raise his voice three times and call out 'Kyrie Eleison!'"

"Which he did, of course," I said.

"If Simeon said so, then he must, as he was a man of great virtue," replied Father Saman. "The Holy Virgin Mary had directed him to do so, too. When the earth started to shake at the sound of his voice, and the mountain suddenly began to move, great consternation and fear spread through the crowd that had come to watch. Then the miracle occurred: the mountain moved to where it stands now, and the truth of the Bible was vindicated for all to see, including the caliph."[81]

"What happened to Simeon?" I asked.

"Ah, that is the great mystery. When the patriarch cast about to find his benefactor in order to thank him, the man was nowhere to be found. Simeon had quietly disappeared, never to be seen again. To this day, no one knows what happened to him. Perhaps he was an angel."

"And now he has performed another miracle," I remarked, gazing at Mr. Dybich.

"It is the tanner's wish. He perceived the people of this benighted quarter needed something to help them renew their faith. It was he, I'm sure, who approached the minister in the guise of the trash collector, and asked him to facilitate the construction of the sanctuary."

"Has he disappeared also, Father?"

Father Saman smiled. "He is no longer with us, sadly, this much I can tell you!"[82]

Back at my hotel that evening, I went to bed rather late. Although I was tired, I couldn't sleep. I found myself lying half-awake in bed, tossing and turning, my mind in overdrive. I saw myself descending the mountain that afternoon through the streets of the Pigsty, trying to reconcile images of utter degradation with those of a mountain crammed with biblical scenes. It didn't make sense. Could it be that when human beings are reduced to their lowest ebb in life, miracles do occur? Was it possible for a lowly tanner to move a mountain through faith alone? How does a mechanic suddenly become a sculptor without any previous experience? Why does a government minister allow himself to be influenced by a whirlwind?

Each of these questions pressed themselves upon me as a jumble of images in my mind. Grimy faces mingled with verses in stone, biblical scenes rubbed against an animal's carcass hanging in a doorway of a butcher's shop, a child seated beside a pile of plastic bottles faded before a Samaritan woman standing by a well. I was transfixed. I blamed the coffee, the whisky I'd drunk, something

I might have eaten at dinner. Nothing could erase my sense of drowning in a dark pit of disorder. I had been thrown up against the cliff face. I was dangling there, far above the road, the sculptured relief before me a mass of chisel marks and chipped stone.

Finally I drifted off to sleep. Deep into the night I wandered, my dreams removing me to another place. I could feel myself floating, caught up in gusts of wind. Then, early in the morning, with dawn not yet upon me, I found myself in a dream unlike any I had experienced before.

I was standing in a village hall, one built of timber a hundred years ago. About its walls hung vaguely hieroglyphic plaques. I was in a familiar place, in my hometown possibly, but in a strange place as well. Clearly I had just returned from Egypt, as I was in the company of Father Abadir from Saint Bishoy. It was strange to see him by my side, his eyes blinking slowly in harmony with the sound of unheard music.

Below the stage I noticed a group of musicians sitting cross-legged in rows, almost filling the hall. They were dressed in black with shiny black turbans on their heads. Gold brocade featured on the sleeves of their clothing, with belts made of gold buckled around their waists. Each of them was playing a strange instrument like those used by wandering musicians in India.

I soon found myself gazing about the room. It was then that I noticed a number of pairs of dancers, each performing in perfect unison, as if they were attached to one another by invisible thread. On closer inspection, I realized they were not dancers but creatures, sylphs perhaps, dressed in black, skin-tight costumes.

I gazed in awe at this apparition. The creatures wore slender masks that were angular yet unrevealing. They didn't possess eyes as such, but rather a glowing, triangular space occupied what presumably were their eyes. I had the constant sensation that I was gazing upon individual pairs of gazelles, even though they possessed the physiology of humans. Their form was perfect in every way. When they moved about the room to the rhythm of the music they did so with supreme elegance, flightiness, defying gravity. Nor did they remain on the floor, where the musicians sat. Instead, they flitted from wall to ceiling, across the room, up and down, always in combination. Their behavior reminded me of what I had always imagined the trajectory of atoms might look like. Was I looking at the invisible structure of the world?

I could not drag my eyes away from the performance. These beautiful creatures, which seemed so celestial and elusive, had seduced me with their movement. Finally, with great effort, I managed to break away from the performance and go backstage to find Father Abadir. He and I were about to give a lecture, although the subject had not yet been announced. I asked him to come on stage quickly, in case the creatures might disappear before he had time to see them for himself. I was conscious that their actions, their atomic dance, had in some way "interrupted" our lecture. I turned to Father Abadir and told him so, hoping he might provide a solution to our problem.

"Let them continue the dance," he said to me. "My appearance, and our lecture, is not important at this stage. These creatures are giving us a taste."

At that point I awoke to the first signs of dawn coming through my window. It was five o'clock in the morning.

I sat on the edge of the bed and buried my head in my hands. I could not fathom what I had just dreamed. So vivid were the images, and so powerful was their effect upon me, that I felt as if I had been acting in a film with no beginning or end. The entire dream had been one continuous sequence of events orchestrated by a director who was nowhere to be seen. I knew that neither Father Abadir nor I had been responsible for the performance in the hall that night. We were onlookers only.

I switched on the light and went to the washbasin in the corner of my room. I turned on the tap and splashed cold water over my face. Then I gazed at myself in the mirror. I looked like I had gone a couple of rounds with a professional boxer. My face was puffy, with dark rings under my eyes. Yet, when I studied my face more closely, I detected a light emanating from my glance. It was as if I had witnessed something special, and indeed experienced a revelation that morning. I didn't know what the nature of this revelation might be, nor did I care. I simply felt different, knowing that I had encountered a startling new piece of information during the course of my dream. It had bestowed on me an unexpected sense of well-being.

I had no idea of what the day might bring, but I felt that from this moment onward I had crossed a Rubicon. That I had intended to resume my journey in the footsteps of the Holy Family seemed to me to be entirely appropriate. They were celestial entities too, I thought. They had danced throughout all the many spheres of the world, each a perfect unity, transporting everyone in their wake. I was just another one of their acolytes. If I had hesitated to speak more personally to them in the past, it was because I was unsure as to how I should accumulate those silent things we might have already experienced together. The Nile River, with its countless layers of history, and the suffering of these exiles who had traveled its length, had finally taught me how to listen. Now was the time to place my ear to their breasts and hear the heartbeat of the universe. Father Abadir, I realized, had made all this possible.

Heart of a City 14

THAT MORNING, I HAD INTENDED to visit the ancient churches clustered around the fortress in Old Cairo, one of which was associated with a visit from the Holy Family. I decided instead to wander through the alleys in the El-Gemaliya quarter of the city, south of El-Azhar Mosque. The Holy Family would have passed through this part of town anyway, as it represented the shortest distance between the Church of the Blessed Virgin in the Harat Zuwaila district and Babylon, once a camp for Chaldean workers during Pharaonic times.[83]

Tradition says that they stayed in Harat Zuwaila for three days, and that the infant Jesus blessed a well there. The country, of course, would have been an open field in their time, rather than the maze of streets that makes up what is now the Islamic district of Cairo. The Holy Family, according to tradition, was intent on traveling south along the Nile from this point, which probably indicates that they no longer felt safe in the delta region. Herod's soldiers were ever pressing, if not physically, then as rumor.

I took a taxi to El-Azhar Mosque, and from there started into the old quarter. My mind was in such an unsettled state after my dream early that morning that I needed to walk for as long as I could. It did not matter where I ended up; the important thing was to allow my legs to show some sign of resolution. Everything about my dream seemed unreal, and I was firmly of the opinion that it represented much more than a haphazard encounter with a group of gravity-defying dancers. My dream, I knew, must be filled with portent, but I did not possess a key to unlock its secrets. Probably the best thing to do was to return to Saint Bishoy and ask Father Abadir to interpret it for me. But I realized that this was too easy a solution. What I needed, instead, was to take responsibility for the conduct of my own thoughts, however unsettling they might be.

At one point on my wanderings I was invited into an antique shop by a gentleman eager to sell his wares. It was barely big enough for the two of us to sit down in. He produced one inlaid box after another, each one decorated with mother-of-pearl shell, laying them out on the table for me to enjoy. In my highly charged state of mind I imagined myself scuttling about on the ocean floor like a crab. In the end, I was saved by the perfect geometry of their designs, with their discreet angles and intersections evolving from the emptiness of a center. I began to calm down. This was the Islam I knew so well: of carefully crafted and vacuous spaces that coalesce to form an image of the stable nature of belief known to every Muslim. Though I did not buy one of the gentleman's boxes, I took away from his studio a sense that the disorder of my thoughts could be managed.

I passed a herd of goats grazing on refuse in an alley. Cats were on the prowl as vendors began to open their shops. I peered into deserted hairdresser salons where old-style pneumatic chairs stood empty yet attentive before mirrors. The early morning wash hung across the street overhead, while men began to congregate in cafés and sip tea. In another antique shop I spotted an old Bakelite telephone, some rusty flatirons, a pile of seventy-eight records and a Singer sewing machine. These objects reflected a period when Egypt was a protectorate of the British. But that too lay in the past, and now its artifacts lingered on in shop windows, unwanted, gathering dust. The city I was wandering through had lost contact with the present.

In an atelier where books were handcrafted from Moroccan leather I stopped and took tea with the proprietor, Mr. Abd el Zaher. He informed me his shop had been in the family for generations, and that its clients lived all over the world. People sent their precious tomes to him for restoration, as well as other items to be covered with leather, and their spines engraved with gold lettering. Here I felt at home. The sight of these individually crafted books made me realize how precious the word is. The book would always be a marker by the roadside, I decided, announcing the distance we have traveled from our state of ignorance.

I began to drift ever southward through the El-Saiyida Zinab district below the old wall of El-Fustat. I did not know where I was going, except when I consulted my map. I walked past Marmeluke palaces, their upper floors dominated by windows known as *mashrabiyas*, which permitted ladies to gaze into the street below unseen by passersby. Shops selling appliqué and leatherwork were dispersed between outdoor vendors selling dates. In a bird market I paused to gaze at the plumage of hundreds of caged avians. On the edge of the El-Abdin quarter I stumbled upon a market dedicated to the sale of spare vehicle parts. Next to its mosque was the Brooke Hospital for Animals, an institution founded by the Scottish-born Dorothy Brooke in 1934 to care for donkeys and other beasts of burden. Passing by the Southern Cemetery, where some 300,000 people are buried, I slowly made my way toward the Misa el-Qadima quarter of Old Cairo.

Why I should have gravitated to this quarter was a mystery, though I sensed that it was important to the Holy Family's journey through Egypt. After another glass of tea, kindly offered to me by a merchant in his shop, I soon revived enough to begin my tour of the ancient Christian churches in the area. First I paid a visit to the Hanging Church of the Holy Virgin (*al-Muallaqa*), which was built over the old atrium entrance to the Roman fortress of Babylon, not far from the cemetery. The church derives its name from the fact that it is suspended on Roman columns. A center of theology and philosophy since the ninth century, the church has a basilican plan but without cupolas. I pressed my way through the crowd at the entrance in order to climb a flight of steps leading to the doorway to the church.

Inside, I was struck by the marble panels on the pulpit and, at the end of the nave, the three cedar iconostases made up of numerous small, finely carved panels inlaid with ivory and ebony designs. Their interlocking mandalas were reminiscent of a celestial explosion, a star-burst, which seemed perfectly in keeping with the mystical nature of Christ's conception and birth. Behind the central haikal stood the sanctuary dedicated to the Holy Virgin, surmounted by a wooden bal-dachin on four columns. Across the uppermost part of the screen, with icons of Christ Enthroned, the Holy Virgin, the archangel Gabriel, Saint Peter, John the Baptist, and the archangel Michael gazed down at the congregation with the subdued brilliance of gods. For all its eclecticism, this church lies at the very heart of Coptic Christianity. It is a cathedral of the spirit.

I sat in a pew for a time to gather my thoughts after my long walk that day. Pilgrims and tourists milled around me, many of them standing in front of the iconostasis and offering up their prayers. A peculiar energy permeated the church. Were all these people pressing forward not its heart and lungs? Were they not its blood and breath? I began to wonder then whether my dream that morning was not affecting the way I saw things. The church had become a palace filled with the memories of Ethiopian kings and saints' relics. On the sidewalls icons shimmered. The wooden, barrel-vaulted roof reminded me that I was but ballast in a celestial ship. Chandeliers hanging along the central aisle could have been tiny meteorites blazing through the atmosphere. I bowed my head.

Gradually I became aware of an elderly, well-groomed gentleman sitting a short distance from me on the pew. He was dressed in a suit, his thin hair carefully combed across his head. His hands were clasped in front of him as he gazed up at the iconostasis. I was strangely drawn to him, sensing that his piety was heartfelt rather than merely an expression of his faith. At the same time, I felt he might be suffering from loneliness. Without realizing it at first, I turned to the man and made my presence known. I smiled and said "good morning," as if we were strollers passing one another on a path. He responded in quaint, Old-World English that charmed me at once. It had been ages since I had heard the language used in this manner.

We introduced ourselves. His name was Saad Fahmy. We spoke, partly in whispers, he informing me that he was a retired engineer from Heliopolis. That morning, like me perhaps, he had awoken from a dream that had urged him to make the trip to Old Cairo to say a prayer to the Holy Virgin. It had been a long time since his last visit, he said, and her voice implored him to venture forth.

"The morning air was so fresh," he half whispered. "When I awoke, I thought I had heard her voice. It rang like a bell in my thoughts. I was utterly taken aback."

I agreed with him about the power of dreams and their capacity to entreat. I told him how my most recent dream had sent me across town in the footsteps of the Holy Family—aimlessly perhaps, but in the end toward my ultimate destination.

"Is it not strange?" he replied. "We live such ordinary lives, most of us, that when we hear a voice telling us to do something, we are unsure as to whether it is not a product of our state of boredom or anxiety. Our Holy Mother, I am sure, sensed that I needed to break with certain habits this morning. She wanted me to come to her house here in Old Cairo and renew our communication."

Mr. Fahmy uttered the word *communication* as if it implied a long-distance phone call, not the words of a prayer. I was touched by his unquestioned faith in the otherworld. He reminded me of how important it is to pay attention to those urgings that some-times enter our thoughts unannounced.

"Would you like to join me today, Mr. Fahmy?" I asked. "You of all people will know where to find the various churches and sanc-tuaries associated with the Holy Family."

"It would be a pleasure, Mr. James. I am at your service."

Together we left the Hanging Church and made our way down the road, through the back alleys behind the Greek Orthodox Church, until we had reached a set of steps leading down to the entrance to the Church of Saint Sergius, Cairo's oldest. Saad informed me that "Abu Sarga," or Sergius, had been the servant of Bacchus, a saddler at Emperor Maximian's court. Both men endured martyrdom for their beliefs in AD 296 in Syria. The church itself was built over a cave in which the Holy Family rested a few days prior to boarding a boat on their voyage upriver. Saad informed me that I could visit the crypt, which was under the sanctuary, by descending a set of stairs behind the iconostasis.

"It is a beautiful chapel, Mr. James," he said, as I joined him in paying my respects in front of the haikal.

I followed Saad through a doorway on the left aisle that led into a room above the stairway to the crypt. A group of Japanese Christians stood around the entrance as we approached. Taking advantage of their meditation, we hurried down the steps into the crypt. There before us lay a tiny chapel, about six by five meters wide, carved out of stone. A stone altar stood at the far end, beyond which was a niche in the wall. Three Roman columns separated this space from a baptistery on the southern side. For some moments Saad and I stood there, absorbing the atmosphere of this ancient chapel. The air smelled of incense.

"It is strange to think the Holy Virgin Mary slept here with her child," Saad remarked.

"Indeed it is, Mr. Fahmy. Of all the places associated with the life of Christ, this chapel must surely rate as one of the simplest yet most real," I said in a half whisper.

"It is true. We are always looking for some tangible link with Our Lord's existence. Without it, I fear we become disheartened. Life is an empty thing when we grow distant from his holy presence."

"Perhaps our dreams this morning were urging us to resume our journey. Though, for my part, I had not felt the need to do so before," I said.

"You started out on a walk through Islamic Cairo, only to end up here in Babylon among Christians! Isn't that a miracle, Mr. James?"

"My compass must have been working overtime," I countered.

Mr. Fahmy then suggested we take a short taxi ride to the nearby monastery of Abu Seifein, or Saint Mercurius. Founded in the seventh century and dedicated to a Roman officer belonging to a noble family, who underwent martyrdom for having vigorously defended the Christian religion, the church possessed a beautiful curved apse decorated with icons of the twelve apostles and Christ Enthroned. Saad wanted me to visit this church, if only to see the paintings decorating a wooden ciborium, as well as two marble columns painted with images of Mary and the infant Jesus, and Christ bestowing his blessing. Both of these paintings, he maintained, were mature examples of Coptic art.

"Most of all," he added, "I would like to introduce you to Mother Lolita, who lives there. She has a story to tell."

Arriving at the convent gate, I asked the taxi driver to wait outside until we had concluded our visit. Inside the convent, we soon found ourselves walking around a cloister toward the main church. According to Saad the convent presently housed over eighty nuns, a large congregation for these times. A part of the reason for the convent's popularity among young Coptic women, he said, was the fact that one of the churches in the complex was dedicated to the forty martyrs of Saint Damiana. For some reason, he said, young women were drawn by their example. Their love for Our Lord transcended all other loves—surely an important gesture for women who have given up the prospect of motherhood.

As it was late in the afternoon, Saad spoke with one of the nuns, who immediately invited us to relax in the reception room, while another went off in search of refreshments. I was hungry and by now quite fatigued, given the hours of walking I had done that day. My bones were beginning to ache.

Presently an older nun appeared, followed by a tray of food. The nun wore glasses, which made her appear older than she really was. But her voice was strong and well modulated, indicating how secure she felt in her monastic life. The nun introduced herself as Mother Lolita, and asked us to take refreshments at our leisure. The freshly baked bread and hummus were more than enough. And the olives: their flesh broke in my mouth with the ease of food full of sustaining nutriment.

"Our present abbess, Ummina Ireny, was responsible for the rebirth of this convent," Mother Lolita said.

"Sometimes one needs an able administrator to help things along, Sister," I replied, my mouth already filled with slices of carrot.

"It seems," Saad interposed, "that Abbess Ireny also entertained a dream, like you and I."

I glanced at Saad to assure myself he was not trying to pull my leg.

"Abbess Ireny was informed in a dream that the Holy Family rested here on their way to Al-Maadi," Mother Lolita elaborated. "It was from there they set sail for Upper Egypt."

"The good abbess was fortunate enough to meet with the Virgin Mary in the monastery garden one evening in 1968," added Saad.

I looked toward Mother Lolita, wondering how on earth one meets the Virgin Mary on an evening stroll in a garden.

"Is it true, Sister?" I asked.

Mother Lolita nodded, then poured us both a soft drink.

"It was her secret that they had met," she said. "For many years, Abbess Ireny would not divulge it to anyone."

"Why not, I wonder?" I said.

"Dreams are like a garden, Mr. James. They contain plants whose blossoms are for the eyes of their owners only. A true garden is a very private place because it is often a very personal creation. What we plant in that garden is a reflection of ourselves, you see. I suspect Abbess Ireny felt that her encounter with the holy Virgin Mary was in the nature of a private blossom. To show it to anyone would have diminished its fragrance."

"How did her secret become common knowledge, Sister?" I asked.

"Through the intercession of Pope Cyril, the previous pope but one to our beloved Pope Shenouda," Mother Lolita responded. "He was visiting the monastery one night in order to consecrate a newly built chapel when he, too, had a sudden insight, a flash of inspiration. He realized the grotto where the chapel was constructed stood above the exact place where the Holy Family had rested. At the ceremony that evening Pope Cyril shared with the congregation his thoughts on the matter, only to hear Abbess Ireny confess her secret about her meeting with the Holy Virgin Mary. The pope, of course, was dumbfounded. He could not believe such a miracle had occurred. Two people dreaming the same dream was more than enough for him."

"Since then," Saad began, "our Holy Virgin Mary has appeared to this congregation each Easter Saturday—"

"—Dressed in a silver garment," Mother Lolita said, finishing his sentence with authority, as though she had witnessed the apparition on a number of occasions.

"Is this possible?" I asked.

Mother Lolita looked at me over the rim of her glasses.

"Why not? Are not all our dreams filled with similar encounters?"

Recalling my dream of that morning, it was my turn to nod.

"We must assume," she continued, adjusting her glasses as a teacher might, "that the Spirit manifests itself in accordance with its secret intentions, which are invariably of a divine origin. Our convent was the home to a secret. Such was the faith of the nuns during the early years of the convent's revival that it was relatively safe for Abbess Ireny to keep her secret. Miracles occur in time, as you know. This is why they reveal themselves in the first place: to reinforce and to encourage our faltering faith. It is only natural for our beloved Virgin Mary to come to our rescue occasionally when she senses our need, do you not agree? She is conscious of the years that separate us from the events of her life, and wishes us to participate in them as much as we are capable. Thus, while a miracle occurs in time as I have said, it is also able to transport us back *through* time. When we experience a miracle, it is our one opportunity to partake of the retrospective moment. Through miracles we are able to glimpse eternity."

"And Abbess Ireny did just this, I presume," I said. "She saw Saint Mary clad in silver garments, and guessed her secret."

Again Mother Lolita nodded.

"Miracles are not always so easy to interpret as hers, however," she admitted.

"It is because Abbess Ireny is a woman of much sanctity, Mr. James," Saad informed me. "Her dreams are more composed than most."

My energy renewed after eating the food, and sensing it was time to leave, I asked Mother Lolita for her blessing. Together, Saad and I made a gesture of kissing her hand, though she managed to withdraw from our lips before we had touched it. Meanwhile, she gave us both a phial of holy oil as a parting gift. Passing through the gate, Saad and I walked over to our taxi on the opposite side of the road. As we sat back in the seat, I noticed that Saad seemed to be almost tearful. Finally I asked him what was wrong.

"It is a miracle, Mr. James, truly it is," he confessed. "This morning I left home feeling very sad. It was to do with a decision by my second daughter, who has chosen to enter a convent here in Cairo. Of course I should be delighted that a member of my own family wishes to dedicate her life to God. You see, my first daughter is also a nun in the same convent. I was saddened to think, however, that as a widower I would never experience the joys of becoming a grandfather. I have waited so patiently for this to happen, as you can imagine."

"You feel you had lost two daughters to the church, and now you are alone, Mr. Fahmy."

He nodded. "Spending this day with you has made me realize how miraculous can be the joys of life when one expects so little from it. You invited me to join you in discovering the churches of Old Cairo. It has given me immense pleasure to show you the wonders of our past. And to think now that I have been able to share with you Abbess Ireny's miracle; this makes me realize what gifts I have been fortunate enough to have received from our beloved Virgin Mary. I begin to realize she hasn't taken away from me my daughters, but that she has allowed me the privilege of offering up to her my own flesh and blood. I should be more than thankful. Through your intercession today, I have been able to come to terms with my loss. Again, I thank you, Mr. James. This is indeed a miracle that you have bestowed upon an old man."

"Or perhaps, Mr. Fahmy, it is as a result of our dreams this morning," I said, hoping to ease his feeling of sadness. "In the future, I for one will be more than willing to grant dreams their status of oracles, as you suggest."

Mr. Fahmy's face brightened. "We are living proof that the Spirit works through us!"

I could not argue with Saad's logic, so I said: "Tomorrow, Mr. Fahmy, I plan to visit the church at Al-Maadi, from where the Holy Family embarked on their voyage up the Nile. I would count it a great honor if you might join my on this excursion."

Again Saad's face beamed. His tears had all but vanished.

"I assure you, Mr. James, that being in your company has made me realize how fortunate an old man can be. You have given me strength to face what few years remain to me without the comfort of my daughters. I can now dedicate myself to understanding the depth of their faith and love for God by making these excursions with you. Are these not of my intention and need also?"

He looked at me inquiringly, hoping I might agree.

"I've come to the conclusion, Mr. Fahmy," I replied, as the taxi sped past Garden City on our way downtown, "that everything about our lives becomes enriched by reverie and dreams. Abbess Ireny's story has proved as much."

"It must be the way the good Lord communicates with us," Saad said, placing the same emphasis on the word *communicate* as he had done earlier that day. He was silent for the rest of the journey.

Voyage on the Nile 15

ON AN EARLY SPRING DAY IN MARCH 1976, when many parishioners were gathered in the fore-court of the Church of the Virgin Mary at Al-Maadi, by the Nile River, after hearing Mass, an extraordinary event unfolded before them. A deacon, who was gazing down at the waters of the Nile while he conversed, suddenly recognized what looked like a half-submerged book floating past. He hurried down to the banks of the river and dragged out of the current what turned out to be a Protestant pulpit Bible opened to a particular page.[84] The parishioners who had gathered around to observe the event could not believe what they were witnessing, for the book was open at the prophecy of Isaiah in the verses that confirmed Theophilus's *Vision* locating the now legendary "Altar of the Lord" at Al-Muharraq in Upper Egypt.[85] Once again a seemingly miraculous event had come to the rescue of a waning tradition. As a result, the church at Al-Maadi was restored to its full splendor at the instigation of Pope Shenouda in 1983.

It was a significant event for a variety of reasons. The Coptic Church relies a great deal on the written word to justify its position with regard to many events in history. Naturally the Gospels were accepted without question; and the Old Testament, with its special emphasis on Egypt, was also held in reverence. Unlike other

Christian denominations, which mark the entrance of the religion to sometime during the centuries after Christ's death, the Copts regard themselves as keepers of the original tradition. Not only did they offer a haven to the Holy Family during their time of persecution, but it was they who gave to Christianity its intellectual foundation through the work of its early theologians. Egypt and the Copts are therefore synonymous with the birth of Christianity as a world religion. Between them, they welded all the disparate events of Jewish history into a model of transcendent life. This was their genius: they made prophecy, revelation, and history cohesive. Furthermore, they managed to translate the character and life of Christ into a rule by creating the monastic tradition. No Roman, Byzantine, or Cappadocian had been able to do it in the past. In fact, these people had come to Egypt to learn the principles of asceticism from the anchorites, much as their philosophic forebears had come to sit at the feet of temple priests in Heliopolis.

The Coptic Church employed biblical exegesis in order to enhance its ascendancy over other churches in the Levant. What had begun as an encounter with the life, death, and resurrection of a God-man, ended in a gradual accumulation of words and thoughts to describe the miracles of this divine life. It is no accident that Christ identified himself with the Logos, and thus with the power of the word. Language was inherent to his being—and it was language he resorted to in order to spread his message. Neither is it an accident that the Greeks of Alexandria were the first to recognize the power of his example, given their allegiance to language. They, more than any other people, understood that the idea of transcendence lay buried in the word itself. Language held the key to unraveling the mystical nature of Godhead. It ensured that revelation might be made comprehensible for a people long familiar with the language of its philosophers.

Christ was committed to the value of language from an early age. We are told in a number of apocryphal sources that he became embroiled in argument over the value and symbolism of the

Hebrew alphabet.[86] The different versions of the story are consistent. At around the age of six, Joseph brought his son to a teacher named Zacchaeus of Jerusalem to be taught how to read and write. The teacher proceeded to write on a board all the letters of the alphabet, beginning with *aleph*. He ordered the young Jesus to pronounce them in parrot fashion, commencing first with *aleph* and then *beth*. The *Arabic Infancy Gospel* suggests that Christ already knew these letters, and was able to continue reciting the alphabet, pronouncing in turn *gimel*, *daleth*, and so on to *tav*. Zacchaeus was astounded at the child's precociousness—even more so when Jesus reprimanded him for *not* teaching him the meaning of these letters.

"If you do not know the *aleph* according to its nature, how can you teach others the *beth*?" he argued.

Jesus then went on to explain the meaning of the letters, and the significance of their individual forms. It became clear to Zacchaeus that the child knew letters to contain an esoteric meaning that he, as his teacher, did not. He was "confounded" by the child's knowledge and requested that Joseph take the child away, as there was nothing he could do for him.

Zacchaeus made a remark to Joseph that summed up his confusion in the presence of the child: "Take him away, my brother Joseph, for I cannot endure the severity of his look. Nor can I once make clear my words. This young boy is not earthly born: he is one that can tame fire. He is like one begotten before the creation of the world. What womb nurtured him? O my friend, he confuses me completely. Nor can I follow his understanding. I tried to teach him as the master, but now I find myself his student. I am overcome by your child and am ready to faint. This is because *I am unable to look him in the eye.*"[87]

Reading the statement by Zacchaeus, one is overcome by a sense of prefiguring power. What is not said in the text is that the young boy became aware of his essential nature. The *aleph* stands for *en soph* and represents the pure and boundless Godhead. It is said to take the form of a man pointing to both heaven and earth in order to show that the lower world is the map and mirror of the higher. The young Jesus obviously saw himself as embodying the qualities of the *aleph*, as he alone was to become the map and mirror of the higher world. The teacher, however, had received intimation of who Christ was in that he was unable to look him in the eye. As the "tamer of fire" and someone "begotten before the creation of the world," the young Jesus had finally decided to reveal who he was. One senses the predicament both Zacchaeus and Joseph found themselves in when the child remarked: "I come from above, and I call all to the things that are above."[88]

How does one deal with a child whose self-awareness is conditioned by another premise entirely?

Language thus became the embodiment of Jesus. He was immersed in the *aleph*, in the alpha of supramundane existence. One tends to forget how important words are to the configuration of deity in that they alone make palpable what is perennially absent. The sixth-century Neoplatonist Dionysius the Areopagite was aware of both the need and limitation of language when it came to determining what the hidden nature of Godhead was. "We must not then dare to speak, or indeed to form any conception, of the hidden super-essential Godhead, except those things that are revealed to us from Holy Scriptures," he wrote.[89]

By identifying himself with the *aleph*, and by implication with the power of language, Christ recognized the importance of both the written word and speech as the method by which sacred knowledge might be realized. Because of his deific nature, he knew that in order to understand the essence of Godhead, it was necessary to accept that the divine Word preceded the word. Human language became the garb that clothed the Word. In a Gnostic text dated from the early second century AD, taken from the *Acts of John* discovered in Upper Egypt in 1945 and known as the "Mystic Cross," we hear an echo of this same message:

Now what those things are I signify unto thee, for I know
that thou wilt understand. Perceive thou therefore in me the
rest of the Word (Logos), the piercing of the Word, the blood
of the Word, the wound of the Word, the hanging up of the
Word, the suffering of the Word, the nailing of the Word, the
death of the Word. And so I speak, separating myself off my
manhood. Be aware therefore in the first place of the Word;
then shall thou recognize the Lord, and in the third place the
man, and what he hath suffered.[90]

At the Church of Holy Virgin at Al-Maadi that morning, while
waiting for Saad to arrive, I became aware of how important language was to the Copts. I was also aware that the departure of the
Holy Family from this point implicated them in a move away from
the dialectical embrace of Alexandria and the ancient temples of the
delta toward a region of Egypt less hidebound by language. Not only
had they spent some two years or so in the heartland of Pharaonic
culture, traveling from one city to another, but they must also have
felt the proximity of Alexandria in the sense of both its philosophic
inheritance and its rich Jewish tradition.

What must it have been like for Joseph and Mary to encounter
this world? First, they would not have spoken Egyptian or Greek.
Aramaic was their language, so the prospect of talking to people
other than fellow Jews recently migrated from Israel was remote.
The cosmopolitan culture of cities such as Heliopolis, Sais, and
Tanis would have been alien to them. Rather than experiencing a
sense of freedom in their country of exile, one must assume they
had become imprisoned there in their own language. It may have
been one reason why they were badly treated in certain places; they
found it difficult to communicate.

For a book, therefore, to float downriver twenty centuries
later in front of the church was to remind all of how important
language is to their story. It reiterated the presence of an altar at

the center of the world somewhere in Upper Egypt, away from the more disciplined thought of the delta. Only by quitting this region would they have been able to become themselves. Their clandestine existence in Lower Egypt is made more poignant by the fact that they had no recourse to friends or relatives. Did they ever send a note to their families back in Nazareth? This is unlikely, given that it could have been opened en route. So they were most likely forced to live in a vacuum, isolated not only by language but also by their situation. They were a family on the run, a family sought after by someone intent on their death. As a result, they would have found themselves lost among a jumble of hieroglyphs and empty tombs.

Nonetheless, they chose to make their departure from Al-Maadi, reputedly the place where Moses was discovered among the bulrushes. At every stage along the way, it seems, the Holy Family wished to identify with seminal moments in Jewish history or Pharaonic culture. In spite of the infant Jesus being a herald of the new dispensation, they were still intent on remaining within the preserve of Judaism. Herod, for all his desire to eliminate them, could not separate them from their origins. They were, in every sense, the first Jewish family exiled *from* Israel into Egypt.

Meanwhile, I stood in the forecourt of the church overlooking the Nile. A few minutes passed before Mr. Fahmy arrived, breathless after his trip on the subway from Heliopolis. He seemed more than glad to see me again. Together we entered the church to look at its treasures. These included the water-stained Bible opened at the relevant page, now housed in a glass case near the entrance.

"You see the stains on it, Mr. James," Saad remarked.

"Yet somehow it survived immersion in the river," I commented. "Amazing."

"When it was first photographed, and the negative developed, something strange appeared on the print," Saad went on. "I have seen it for myself. An image of the Holy Family and their donkey emerged from the left-hand page of the Bible. There," Saad said, pointing to the book. "It was as if the photograph wished to reaffirm what we have always believed: that the Holy Family left these shores onboard a papyrus boat bound for Upper Egypt."

"Not only did this Bible quote chapter and verse from Isaiah's prophecy to authenticate their journey, but it also depicted an image of their flight. Does it not say something to you, Mr. Fahmy?"

"I don't think I follow you," Saad responded.

"The fact is that the Holy Family transcends words," I said. "They speak to us in a way that helps us to understand with our hearts as well as our minds. They have become, since you have seen the photograph of them on the page, a kind of sign."

Mr. Fahmy looked confused. "Are you saying that the Holy Family is a hieroglyphic?" he asked.

"Try to imagine them symbolically," I replied. "An old man, Joseph—that is, a sage; Mary a virgin woman—that is, an aspect of purity; and a divine child who represents all we imagine deity to be in its precursory state: these make up what we know as the Holy Family."

"Precursory state? Forgive me, but my English begins to suffer at this point, Mr. James."

"It is the condition of deity *before* it has had time to realize itself in our lives as the saving grace of the world," I explained.

"We are therefore talking about the very beginning of the Christian religion, when the infant Jesus was not yet the Christ we have come to know and love," Saad responded.

"It makes it possible for us to identify with the Holy Family, because they too once suffered," I suggested.

"Now I begin to follow you." Saad's eyes brightened as he gazed once more at the water-stained Bible in the case. "The flight of Mary and Joseph has given us something humble, ordinary, yet exalted with which we can identify. Remarkable, indeed, Mr. James. In the future, I shall never return to this church without recalling our conversation. You have made me very proud to be Egyptian. I never imagined that we might have had such a contribution to make to the clarification of the Christian message."

Later, after we had toured the church and studied its gallery of precious icons, Saad and I walked out onto the forecourt to watch the sailboats on the river. They glided past, their lateen sails agelessly geometrical in shape. He then led me down a set of steps along a narrow, arched passageway leading to yet another set of steps underground. These finally opened onto a landing by the water's edge. However, a grill with a Coptic cross at its center prevented us from going any further.

"Here is the precise spot from where the Holy Family embarked for Upper Egypt," Saad explained, his voice assuming a reverential tone. "From this point onward, you too will be following the Nile toward its unknown origin."

"Do you think Joseph and Mary might have had second thoughts when they stood here, Mr. Fahmy?" I asked. "After all, once they had boarded a boat, they were about to travel even further from their homeland into Africa. They must have asked themselves where all this might end."

"I'm sure they did, Mr. James. It's not easy to leave your own country in fear of your life, and then find yourself voyaging on a river that seems to have no end."

"Christianity has always been a religion of exile," I said. "It calls no place its home, even here in Egypt."

Standing there at the top of the steps, I felt I was waiting for an alternative text to wash up on the landing. Only this time I hoped it would announce some new insight into the mystery surrounding the miracle of language. I would then be able to embark on my own voyage up the Nile, knowing that each step I made was toward understanding what Dionysius the Areopagite called the "Super-Unity of Differentiation."[91] Surely this was worth making a journey to an unknown place in search of something that could never be properly expressed. Exile could not be *all* bad, I thought. It must have something to say to us, even if this turned out to be more inscrutable than hieroglyphics.

Toward Memphis 16

SOUTH OF CAIRO THE COUNTRY along the Nile becomes a confused network of roads, which in places are reduced to little more than goat tracks skirting the edge of the desert. As many of the monasteries that I intended to visit were located in the desert, I could not simply rely on a map. I needed a guide who knew where the Coptic sites were located.

On the recommendation of the concierge at the Windsor Hotel, I invited a retired oil engineer named Mounir Bedwani to join me. Though Mr. Bedwani had spent most of his life working in the Middle East overseeing the construction of oil refineries, he had always remained true to his Christian faith. Now living in semiretirement working as a consultant, he made it his business to visit almost every Coptic church, monastery, and archaeological site in the country during his spare time. Moreover, he knew as much as anyone about the Holy Family's journey along the Nile. That most of the monks in the monasteries were friends of his was an added bonus: it meant we would always be welcomed as guests when we arrived. From here on, I realized, we would be staying in monasteries rather than hotels, and we would be dependent upon their hospitality.

Our first stop was at the ruins of Saqqara, some thirty kilometers south of Cairo. It is the largest necropolis in Egypt, and famed as the burial place of the nobility from nearby Memphis. Lying on the western escarpment of the Nile, the side of the river traditionally associated with the land of the dead, the site is home to a number of smaller pyramids, a funerary complex dedicated to King Zoser (2700 BC), and the legendary Step Pyramid regarded as the prototype of all others, including those at Giza. Just north of Zoser's pyramid lies a tilted masonry box containing a life-size statue of Zoser gazing toward Sirius, the star used by the ancient Egyptians to compute the number of days in the year. Known as the "Great Provider," Sirius played the role of the central fire to the sun, the sun behind the sun, and so was all-powerful in cosmological terms, given that its heliacal rising heralded the day when the Nile waters began to rise each year. It was Sirius who inseminated Isis through Osiris, and so produced the divine child-on-earth, Horus.[92] Zoser's gaze was therefore the gaze of regnal man toward the spirit that nourished him.

Among the mastabas at Saqqara lay the ruins of a monastery located on a spot reputedly linked to the Holy Family's journey. Again I was struck by the way the Holy Family always seemed to pass by places of great religious significance to the ancient Egyptians—at least, from Theophilus's point of view. An act of expropriation on his part? Perhaps. Memphis, meanwhile, the capital of the Old Kingdom prior to the ascendancy of Thebes (Luxor), was home to another version of the sun-god in the form of Ptah, the divine "Opener" of the day like that of his counterpart Tem in the delta, who was often seen as the "Closer" of the day. Ptah's epithets are indicative of his primeval role; "The very god who came into being at the earliest time," "Father of father, Power of powers," "Illuminer of the two lands with the fire of his two eyes."

As a guest of the villagers at Memphis, the infant Jesus must have felt the proximity of his own divine Father as he traversed the path through the hypostyle hall beside Zoser's pyramid with his parents. For here indeed was the "workshop of Ptah," the master architect and designer of everything that exists in the world. Did he at all feel at home? One wonders.

The ruins of the monastery of Saint Jeremiah were situated in the southern area of the excavations of Saqqara, now a popular tourist destination. This was my first encounter with such a large group of foreign tourists in buses, and I found it difficult to come to terms with the hordes of brightly dressed people, all wearing peaked caps and running shoes, ambling aimlessly behind their tour guides. The tawny hills and desert sand surrounding the site seemed oddly subdued by this inundation of color. My first instinct was to retreat. In the end, I was carried away by Mounir's enthusiasm. He seemed oblivious to the crowds as we threaded our way through archaeological debris and fallen columns. Mr. Bedwani was like a terrier in his ability to sniff out ruined monasteries or village churches buried in back streets.

Eventually we climbed onto high ground overlooking the monastery ruins. Before us lay the foundations of a church, a refectory, a number of cells, and a funerary chapel, their mud bricks worn by erosion and already subsiding into the sand. The air of dilapidation starkly contrasted the nearby pyramids and hypostyle of Saqqara. Yet it had been home to a community of monks, not a covey of temple priests whose task was to serve innumerable gods and to augment the godlike status of the Pharaoh by performing sacred rites.

"Does it seem reasonable to you that the Holy Family might have come so far inland from the Nile?" I asked politely. As I did not yet know Mr. Bedwani very well, I thought it best I tread carefully.

"We must assume the course of the river passed closer to Memphis than it does today, Mr. James," he replied, producing an antiquated camera from his shoulder bag and pointing it toward the ruins. "In any event, Saqqara would have largely been buried under sand at the time of their visit. Perhaps they came ashore and sought refuge in the protruding remnants of the hypostyle, as this would have offered them some shelter. Such ruins were always popular with hermits because they offered them a readymade 'cave' to live in. The great Saint Anthony, our first anchorite as you know, lived in an old fort at Maimum not far from Beni Suef, before he chose to retreat to Mount Colzim in the eastern desert. It is not unimaginable to think of the Holy Family laying down their sleeping mats and building a small fire, somewhere among these ruins."

"Presumably, then, Jeremiah was a hermit also."

"It is said that he was from Alexandria and arrived here in the early part of the sixth century," replied Mounir. "But we know little about him. He probably came upon these ruins and built a rough hut among the debris. In time others joined him, and so a community was born. According to what I have read, the monastery was constructed in the seventh century. That the Holy Family passed by here may have also inspired the monks to identify with their passage through the region."

"By then, of course, Theophilus's *Vision* would have been widely known and read."

"It's possible, yes. It was a time of great excitement for many monastic communities. Everything was so new at that time. Christianity was little more than in its infancy. Every word written down by theologians and visionaries was consumed by monk and hermit alike. Men couldn't get enough of their new religion. Everyone wanted to share in the experience of realizing this new life for themselves. I fear it is not the same today," Mounir added, as he slipped his camera back into his shoulder bag.

We wandered among the ruins of the monastery, away from the tourists, who preferred to congregate near Zoser's Pyramid. There was a long queue of tourists who wished to see the figure of Zoser gazing up into the sky where Sirius might be, had it been night. My thoughts drifted back in time as I tried to unravel the unusual nature of monastic life. Those men who had lived on the edge of the desert all their lives, their view of the world confined to arid reaches of sand and little more than a glimpse of the Nile in the distance, they must have been strange people indeed. Everything they thought or did was defined by limits; by deliberately imposing constraints on their physical life, these men had sought to open up their minds to another dispensation. The monastery was not a self-imposed prison but a deliberate attempt to exclude the mundane. This may have been a form of exile for them, extreme perhaps, but fruitful nonetheless.

Meanwhile, Mounir suggested we drive on to nearby Saint Mercurius monastery, which he told me stood on the shores of the Nile River. He felt that Father Saleb would welcome us, as well as offer us a bed for the night. The monastery was located in the spot where Jacob's son Joseph had built his palace at the time of the Jewish exile in Egypt. Joseph had been Pharaoh's chief minister, and so exempt from any restrictions determining where he might choose to live. Furthermore, there was an ancient tree in the forecourt of the monastery known as the Moses Tree. This was the spot, Mounir told me, where Pharaoh's daughter had discovered Moses while he was drifting past on the river.

"I thought Moses had been rescued by the princess at Al-Maadi," I reminded Mounir.

Mounir adjusted his shoulder bag as we walked back to the car.

"Does it really matter, Mr. James? The important thing to know is that the Holy Family embarked from here, just as they did from Al-Maadi. Both places claim Moses as their own."

We drove back through the fields by the Nile in order to reach the main road heading south. To our right, I could still make out a line of pyramids along the limestone ridge through the heat haze. Groves of palms shaded the earth beside the irrigated land on each side of the road as we sped past. White herons stood guard on the levee banks or waded in the shallows, seeking out insects. We overtook a horse-drawn cart piled high with freshly harvested carrots. Date fronds lay in clumps on the road, making the trip rather bumpy. With Mounir as my translator, I asked the driver why these fronds had been deliberately laid out on the road like this.

"The cars soften up the fiber with their wheels," Mounir translated. "It can then be used to make household brooms."

Finally we arrived outside the gate of the Church of Saint Mercurius. A watchman opened it in order that we might enter the forecourt. There was no sign of life other than a dog that struggled to its feet as we parked the car. While the watchman walked off to find Father Saleb, I gazed about the monastery grounds. In the left-hand corner of the compound I recognized a very old balsam tree, not far from the riverbank. It was the so-called Moses Tree Mounir had mentioned earlier.

Presently a priest appeared and walked over to greet us. Mounir introduced me to Father Saleb, who offered his hand for me to kiss. He was a man in his midfifties, gray-haired, and rather lean. He told me that he had commenced life as a monk at Saint Simeon Monastery in Upper Egypt at the age of twenty-nine, and had lived there for twenty-four years until called upon by the local bishop to become the priest at Saint Mercurius. Before becoming a monk, he had been an agricultural engineer working for a government agency. When I asked him the whereabouts of his fellow monks, he shrugged. Evidently he lived alone in the monastery.

"It must be lonely at times, Father," I said.

"It is my life," Father Saleb replied. "There is a small Coptic community living in the nearby village. I am here to serve them."

"Do these people ever experience prejudice and ostracism by their Muslim neighbors?"

"When people grow up together, there is rarely much room for animosity or hate. These only become inflamed by outsiders seeking advantage, or if the government chooses to accuse certain bishops of engaging in politics," explained Father Saleb.

"As it happened to Pope Shenouda during the time of President Sadat, when he was imprisoned," I suggested.

"Even the president was under pressure from fundamentalist elements within his own party. I do not think he wanted to act against Pope Shenouda, or order his imprisonment. Sometimes a tree must bend when the wind blows too hard, do you not agree?"

"Joseph had the same difficulties leading his people during the time of Pharaoh," Mounir remarked. "He was always treading a narrow path, just as Pope Shenouda does in our time."

"When politics mixes with religion, the water grows muddy," Father Saleb observed.

"Whether one is a Jew or Christian in this land," I suggested, "the task of reconciling oneself with ancient and unresolved animosities can be difficult."

"It is true," Mounir agreed. "Islam today has merely replaced the old Pharaonic culture of the past. Whether we are Jew or Christian, we will always be a minority in our own land, and therefore subject to periods of oppression. Fortunately for the Jewish community, it no longer exists in Egypt any more. We Copts, however, have replaced them in the eyes of certain fundamentalist Islamic groups. They see us as a convenient scapegoat, particularly when issues arise with the state of Israel."

"Nothing really changes," Father Saleb responded. "Those committed to strong religious belief, and who continue to resist the jurisdiction of government authorities, will always find themselves open to oppression. Our strength is also our undoing. It is perhaps why our monastic tradition is so inward looking. It has had to build high walls around itself since the fifth century. Men who choose to live exclusively the life of the Spirit will invariably become the target of those who are afraid of its power, I'm afraid. Often, in the past, the monastery was seen as a hotbed of political intrigue, whether because of heretical disputation or social resistance. The truth is, the life of a monk is a life dedicated to God, not to some man who happens to be a Pharaoh or president. Men in power always feel uncomfortable in the presence of men of the cloth, for they know they harbor some inner power denied to them."

"Will you survive, Father, in this era that is ever pressing us toward cultural conformity?" I asked.

Father Saleb smiled.

"Of course," he said. "We Christians have been a part of Egypt for nearly two thousand years, and have overcome all obstacles. Our strength lies in the knowledge that we have built up a tradition and a body of doctrine out of the land of Egypt itself. All our thought and monastic practices are indigenous to this country. They cannot be separated from it, or transported elsewhere, as they have by men like John Cassian, the founder of monasticism in Europe. Every Muslim knows this, because every Muslim is also, at heart, an Egyptian, just as we are. We did not come here as exiles like Joseph, sold into bondage. Or Moses, who desired to return to Canaan, or the Holy Family fleeing Herod. We are born here, and claim our inheritance from antiquity. This makes us strong—stronger than most people, Mr. James."

"It is true. We Copts are stubborn," Mounir added with a certain pride.

"And courageous, it seems," I replied.

During our discussion, sitting under the Moses Tree with the afternoon sun at our backs, the watchman, who obviously doubled up as a personal servant to Father Saleb, soon brought tea to us. The river itself had intervened, overflowing its banks, submerging us in its gentle wash. Where did it come from? To speak of Nubia, Lake Victoria, or Ethiopia was to speak of its geographical origin, not its true source. The Nile was more than a body of water threading its way toward the sea. It was a wide stream of thought capable of being tapped into by countless generations. Every utterance written on papyrus, every ceremonial pronouncement carved on obelisk or stele, every pronouncement by temple priest, philosopher, or theologian was ultimately derived from the ageless perturbations of the Nile itself.

Dusk by the river was a memorable experience. Noiselessly it flowed past, weed and flotsam bobbing gently in the current. Father Saleb did not feel so lonely after all. He had the voices of the Nile to keep him company. They spoke to him of gods and Pharaohs, of solar barges bathed in flares and richly ornamented, of farmers, merchants, apothecaries, scribes, embalming experts, millers, papyrus makers, masons, carpenters, geometers, teachers, priests, monks, bishops—indeed, all variety of men and women who had helped to make up ancient society in this land. The river was his friend, his floating Bible.

Meanwhile, Father Saleb had kindly made available to us both two small rooms in the monastery compound. If I did not dream that night, it was not because I felt overly tired. Rather, the river's current washed against me as it might a papyrus boat, cleansing me of all memory. Tomorrow, I knew, we would be heading south to Beni Suef, the river town closest to where Saint Anthony had lived on Mount Colzim.

17

Sailing South

I SAT ON THE BALCONY OFF MY ROOM in Bayad al-Nasara monastery overlooking the Nile, home to the Daughters of the Holy Virgin since 1965. Across the river I could make out the skyline of Beni Suef and hear, distantly, the muezzin calling the faithful to evening prayer. An island lay in the foreground, splitting the river in two, and men were returning home with their livestock from the fields. A flock of sheep, their mouths muzzled to stop them grazing on the way home, dutifully followed their master. Neatly ordered gardens framed by irrigation canals greeted my gaze. Below, on the river, I noticed a fisherman drawing in his net. Such a panorama had varied little in the past three thousand years. This was the true history of Egypt—a land whose layers of habitation were like those on an antique lacquer jewelry box: each one helped to concentrate and intensify the unchanging movement and gesture of a people.

It was difficult to imagine how the Holy Family dealt with their exile in Egypt. Did they attend service in a synagogue when they came upon one in village or town? Joseph, we know, was a pious man, and tradition tells us Mary was a temple virgin in her earlier life. Surely they both felt the need to observe the feasts of the Jewish calendar and to atone, fast, and repent. Did they ever set up a tabernacle under a palm tree in order to pray? It was hard to imagine how they overcame their spiritual isolation in the midst of Egypt. Homesickness must have been an affliction that they could barely suppress. However rich and fertile Egypt was, their memories of Capernaum's olive trees growing on hillsides or the smell of freshly caught fish in Galilee's markets must have been difficult to erase. Pharaoh's wealth would have been no match for the simple pleasures of a wedding feast in Nazareth.

We met for dinner in the refectory of the monastery that evening. Mounir had arranged for Mother Yohanna to join us. When I walked into the cafeteria, which obviously catered to large groups of pilgrims on the occasion of its annual festival, I recognized Mounir seated at table with a nun dressed in full habit. They both stood up to greet me as I approached. Mother Yohanna smiled warmly when we shook hands. She was a woman in her early forties, although with an expression of fatigue on her face, as if she had not slept for some time. Her voice, however, was filled with energy. Mounir informed me that Mother Yohanna was a qualified doctor, as well as being the chief health superintendent in the monastery. Her task was to manage women's health among the villages throughout the Beni Suef region.

"Mr. Bedwani tells me you have been following in the footsteps of the Holy Family," she said as we began a meal of chicken and vegetables. "I hope it has proved to be inspiring for you."

I confessed that it had, though I added that I had not anticipated being diverted by so many other considerations I had encountered on the trip.

"Egypt has a way of encouraging us to wander, Mr. James," she agreed. "I think it is in the nature of the Nile to meander. It makes us do the same, I'm afraid."

"Do you think it had the same effect on the Holy Family?" I asked.

Mother Yohanna was a little taken aback by my question.

"I don't think I have ever thought about it," she admitted. "We Copts tend not to speculate on what the Holy Family did or thought as they made their way up the river. It is a fault of ours.

We should be more inquisitive about the difficulties they may have faced."

"Mr. James is more interested in their humanity than he is in their journey, I suspect," Mounir added.

"He is quite right to think this way. After all, do we not daily deal with the problems of humanity?" Mother Yohanna said.

"You especially, Sister," I replied. "Every day as a doctor you must assess the motives and afflictions of your patients. It is part of each diagnosis: to unravel how people think in order to know what might be ailing them."

Mother Yohanna laughed—relieved, I think, to be able to reflect upon her professional life as a doctor with someone like myself.

"My greatest challenge is to confront Egyptian women and help them to see themselves as they are. They find it hard to abandon age-old practices dealing with health and contraception. Can you imagine that I am still dealing with issues such as female circumcision in this day and age? In our society, unfortunately, women do not own their lives or their bodies; they are still the chattels of men."

"How do you change their way of thinking?" I said.

"I try to find a woman in a community who has resisted the pressure to allow her child to be mutilated like this," Mother Yohanna explained. "If such a woman is able to stand up and say no, then I am halfway there. Other women will come forward, and still others begin to listen to their experience. We call this method of mentoring 'positive deviancy,' when a woman chooses to go against tradition and answer for herself."

"Does it work?"

"We have had some significant successes, yes. Slowly we are beginning to educate villagers into recognizing the value of girl children. But it is hard. Muslim cultural practices can be very confronting at times."

"Which is what the Holy Family must have encountered too," I suggested. "Not female circumcision so much as other ways of doing things. I am thinking, for example, of mummification.

Preparing a body for eternal life, at least in a physical sense, this must have seemed odd to them, don't you think?"

"Ancient Egypt would surely have been foreign to the Holy Family, Mr. James, as you suggest. Mary, in particular, would have viewed the elaborate rituals of the temple priests as strange and rather confronting. While she had lived some years in the Jewish temple herself, she would never have seen such elaborate parades and funeral regattas that were a part of a Pharaoh's journey to the otherworld."

"And the infant Jesus: what do you think he made of Egypt?" I asked.

Mounir glanced at Mother Yohanna. I sensed that he was uncomfortable about where the conversation might be heading.

"He was only a child, Mr. James," she said.

"Yes, but he was also a divine child," I countered. "We already know how advanced he was intellectually at the age of twelve, when he discussed points of Jewish doctrine with the Pharisees in Jerusalem. He knew then that he was attending to his father's business. Surely, even as an infant, he was absorbing the mystery that was Egypt."

"We have an obligation to see Jesus as more than simply someone we revere. What do you think, Mr. Bedwani?" Mother Yohanna said, attempting to draw Mounir back into the discussion.

"Christ is our mentor, Mother Yohanna," Mounir admitted. "By his actions, he showed us another way of dealing with our individual predicament. His transfiguration alone is proof that this 'positive deviancy' of yours really works."

"Goodness!" Mother Yohanna almost laughed. "Had I known that we would end up using medical jargon to account for the life of Christ, I would have been reluctant to believe it."

The next morning, we set out for the Church of the Holy Virgin at Dair al-Garnus in Ishnin, and on to nearby Al-Bahnasa. The first place was home to a well where the Holy Family had stopped to drink on their way to Al-Muharraq, the site where the Altar of the Lord was located. Al-Bahnasa interested me for other reasons, one of which was to do with the fact that a number of important Gnostic texts were discovered at nearby Oxyrhynchus in the late nineteenth century by two English archaeologists, B. P. Grenfell and A. S. Hunt. A chance find near what must have been the ancient city's rubbish dump produced some forty thousand documents and scraps of papyrus written mostly in Greek and Latin, but also in demotic Egyptian, Coptic, Hebrew, Syriac, and Arabic. These fragments date from between 250 BC and AD 700. I had always wanted to visit Oxyrhynchus, if only because it represented the first major discovery of the earliest "unauthorized" sayings of Christ.[93]

We said goodbye to Mother Yohanna that morning after breakfast. She was about to set off on her calls in a neighboring town to check on the health of a number of newly pregnant women. "They need me!" she cried, as she climbed into her driver's vehicle. "Say a prayer to give me strength when you reach Al-Garnus, Mr. James. The sacred water from its well does a better job than I do."

"I wonder whether this is true," I replied, waving to her as the car disappeared through the monastery gate.

We drove south toward Maghagha on the Nile. The traffic was heavy that morning, so the going was slow. If it were not trucks laden with farm produce, then it was men on donkeys. We overtook one vehicle overloaded with eggs. Eventually, in one of the backstreets of Ishnin, Mounir signaled to me that we had reached the monastery gate.

We were met by the village priest, Father Bishoy, named after the legendary fourth-century ascetic of the Nitrea Desert. He agreed to show us around his church where, each year in June, pilgrims gather to celebrate the Holy Family's visit to the village, and to draw water from the well. "On the night of 25th Bashans (1st June)," wrote the historian al-Maqrizi in the fifteenth century, "a spring in the name of Jesus is closed; and in the sixth hour people collect and take away the stone from the well, and find that the water within it had risen. . . . From this they reckon how high the

Nile will be that year." Father Bishoy told me his parish consisted of over six hundred families, nearly half the population of Ishnin.

After visiting the well in the courtyard, we decided to push on to Dair al-Garnus, another spot where the family had rested. Dedicated to the Virgin Mary, the church was built in the late nineteenth century as a domed structure, which is presently painted in green throughout. Arriving there, I felt that I had entered a grotto. While I spent some minutes studying the newly painted icons by Massir Kirolus around the walls, a steady stream of village women entering the church suddenly confronted me. I asked Father Bishoy what had precipitated such an event.

"They come once a week to sing psalms, Mr. James," he told me. "It is their one opportunity to come together as women."

The sight of these women sitting in pews in the bluish light of the church, nearly all of them dressed in black, struck a chord. They reminded me of women in a Greek chorus. The sound of their voices was both tuneful and somber. Was it the sound of the wind brushing against sand? If the desert could sing, then this was what one might hear: words barely attached to sound, mournful, each one of them the articulation of humanity's feeling of awe in the presence of the infinite. Such was the plaint of these women that morning as they attempted to bridge the gap between themselves and God.

"What you are hearing, Mr. James," Mounir whispered to me, "is the sound of ancient Egypt. The chords these women are singing go back to Pharaonic times."

"What is Christian for you and me is Pharaonic for these women, it seems."

"Much of what we believe to be Christian in our rituals and beliefs comes from our ancient inheritance," Mounir finally admitted.

"Let us hope, Mounir," I added, "that before we finish this trip, we might begin to know what it means to be Egyptian, Christian, and Muslim all in one."

"It will be difficult for me. But I will try, Mr. James."

Mounir and I said our farewells to Father Bishoy, and climbed into our car. Where we planned to visit next would take us into the very heartland of heresy as viewed by the church, buried as it once was among the stones at Oxyrhynchus. We headed inland from Beni Mazar on the Nile toward the ruins of one of the most important provincial cities in ancient Egypt. Oxyrhynchus, after all, held secrets that were destined to shake the pillars of the world.

$\mathcal{A}$ *Heavenly City* 18

AFTER THE HOLY FAMILY DOCKED
at the village of Deir al-Garnus on their sailboat, they proceeded on foot to a spot later named *Abai Issous,* "the Home of
Jesus," now the site of present-day Sandafa village on the Baher
Yusef Canal. This body of water lies east of Al-Bahnasa where the
ruins of Oxyrhynchus are located.

Named Oxyrhynchus by the Romans after a fish of the region,
it was the capital of the nineteenth nome during the Pharaonic
period, being the third largest city in Egypt at that time. The city
occupied an area of two square kilometers in its heyday, and was
home to many public buildings and temples. It possessed a theater
for eleven thousand spectators, a hippodrome, four public baths,
and a gymnasium. It is also probable that Oxyrhynchus supported
a large military garrison during the Roman and Byzantine periods.
At the time of the Ptolemies there were temples dedicated to
Serapis, Amun, Isis, and Osiris, as well as a number of Greek
deities such as Hermes and Apollo. At its peak the population was
estimated to be around thirty thousand. From the fourth century
onward it became one of the leading centers of Christianity in
Egypt after scores of monasteries and churches were built here.
The anonymous author of the *Historia Monachorum in Aegypto*
regarded Oxyrhynchus as a genuine "heavenly city," a haven for
Christians from all over Egypt:

> Eventually we came to a certain city of the Thebaid [Middle
> Egypt] called Oxyrhynchus, which was so famous for good
> religious activities that no description could possibly do jus-
> tice to them all. We found monks everywhere inside the city,
> and also in the countryside around. What had been the pub-
> lic buildings and temples of a former superstitious age were
> now occupied by monks. Throughout the whole city there
> were more monasteries than houses. From the very gates
> with its battlements, to the tiniest corner of the city, there is
> no place without its monks who, night and day, in every part
> of the city, offer up hymns and praises to God, thus making
> the whole city into one great church of God.[94]

Today, little remains of that monastic dream. After it was
abandoned in the late seventh century, what was left of the city's
walls and gates, its main street flanked by elegant colonnades, and
its numerous churches and temples, have long since disappeared.
All that remains are a few crumbling foundations and the usual
collection of pillars and pediments lying on the ground. It is hard
to imagine that in this once-thriving metropolis an important
discovery would be made by the English Egyptologist B. P.
Grenfell and his colleague, the English papyrologist A. S. Hunt, in
1896. Could these two men have imagined when they unearthed
fragments of papyri from the city's dump that their find would
transform our current view of orthodox Christianity, not to
mention the opinion of its early theologians as to what Christ did
and said during the period of his ministry? The uncial fragments
they unearthed included most of the first chapter of Matthew, as
well as another remarkable document known today as the *Gospel of
Thomas*, a text regarded by many as one of the most important of
the Gnostic writings so far uncovered.[95]

The Gnostic writings of Egypt are a window onto the minds of
early Christian thinkers struggling to find a language to express

Christ's message at a time when Greek dialectic was very much in vogue. Though many of the theologians in Alexandria and in Byzantium generally condemned these writings as heretical—men such as Tertullian, Irenaeus, Justin, Hyppolytus, and even Athanasius himself—their arguments did not prevent many people from regarding these writings as important additions to the corpus of Christian thought.

During the first centuries after the death of Christ there arose a body of men, most of whom were churchmen, who between them formulated every detail of holy doctrine. Under the aegis of various ecumenical councils, from the first in Nicaea (AD 325) to the seventh in AD 787, emperors, theologians, and priests set about determining the principles of faith for the Christian church. The evolution of Christian doctrine became an intellectual exercise that could only be authenticated through adherence to holy tradition and the teachings of the early Fathers. Christ's revolutionary utterance was in time determined by men primarily interested in building formal theological structures within the newly emerging universal church. The voice of ordinary people was thus excluded from any dialogue pertaining to the mystery of Christ. Interest was centered on developing a singular, consensual view that was to henceforth remain the bulwark of orthodoxy. It is this fact alone that makes Hunt and Grenfell's discovery so interesting.

One must place the discovery in its proper context. Until the Oxyrhynchus and Nag Hammadi discoveries, little was known about Gnosticism or its writings, other than through the work of Christian apologists who strove to refute and sometimes ridicule what the Gnostics authors had written. Their arguments were negative, portraying Gnosticism as a deviant faith incapable of bearing the full revelation of Christ. Moreover, they argued that is was dualist and subscribed to a view of the world that gave equal rank to the demiurgic principle of darkness over light. Gnostics were seen as cultic and elitist by disposition, regarding themselves as possessors of divine truth in the form of an esoteric doctrine not available to ordinary Christians. "He [Basilides] says that his followers should reveal the teaching about the Father and his cult to no one at all," wrote Epiphanius in the fourth century, "but keep it in silence in themselves, revealing it to no one out of a thousand and two out of ten thousand. He lays down a principle for his disciples: 'Know everyone, but let no one know you.'"[96] It was this kind of attack leveled by orthodox theologians at Gnostics and their writings that often forced its proponents to flee cities like Alexandria and Antioch for their own safety. When it came to heresy, it seems, the milk of human kindness quickly dried up.

Gnostic cosmology was essentially mythological. It thrived upon elaborate systems of hierarchies designed to make it both impenetrable yet ordered at the same time. If initiates understood the system, performed the correct rituals, then they were offered the chance to rise above the material limitations that bound them to the eternal cycle of incarnations associated with the gloomy world in which they lived. They could then become perfect, and therefore able to escape once and for all into the intermediary world of the pleroma. Throwing off the opacity of material existence in order to attain to a state that was, so to speak, "weightless" became the principal aim of the Gnostic. This vision of the world and of life was in large part pessimistic, given the understanding of the corrupt nature of late classical society and its inability to nourish the soul. Many Gnostics put their faith in Sirius, since this remote star implied a detachment not achievable except by realizing *gnosis*, or divine wisdom, often through the practice of an extreme form of asceticism. Though evil existed in its own right, humanity had a responsibility to defeat it by way of total physical abstinence. They could not become a true Gnostic, and so defeat the primary powers of the Demiurge, unless they detached themselves from material existence. The Gnostic had to learn how to die *in this world* if he or she were ever going to escape it.

For the orthodox Christian, this path represented a flight from reality. It demeaned the significance of Christ as both God *and* man in that it demeaned the importance of the physical nature of people generally. Christ died on the cross as a man, not as a divine being without substance. He suffered in himself and for humankind, not in any illusory way, as certain Gnostics maintained. He was no shade who had mysteriously "appeared" among us, only to disappear at an importunate moment. Though his message was a divine one, and therefore relevant to human existence in the world, he did not advocate an escape into the pleroma as a perfected being. Rather, at least according to orthodox Christians, one had a responsibility to work out one's salvation with diligence in this world, and not hope to escape it by way of an act of severance.

The Gnostic way was the way of psychic dispossession, and thus the Gnostic was the true Stranger (*Xeniteia*), the man alone, an autarch whose ultimate aim was to disengage from society. Unlike the anchorite, who also practiced autarchy, the Gnostics' aim was to destroy society rather than renew it. They wanted to establish isolated cells of elite beings able to overcome the messianic prophecy of the "End of the World" and so live eternally. Gnostics, because of this innate gnosis, set themselves up as the Chosen Ones, and therefore Christ's true emissaries on earth.

No wonder orthodox Christians feared them. The Gnostics proposed a spiritual disengagement from the mass of other humans in favor of an enclosed order of disembodied intellects masquerading as perfect people. The historicity of Christ became a metaphor for resistance against church hierarchy and the imposition of officially sanctioned dogma, as witnessed much later among the Cathars in southwest France. From a Gnostic's point of view, once Constantine had proclaimed toleration of the Christian religion early in the fourth century AD, a new form of religious oppression was enacted to replace that of the cult of the emperor. Christianity was now a weapon in the emperor's armory that he could use to mold minds in conformity with imperial edict. The bishops and theologians became the new centurions of a religious army sent to pacify the people on the borders of empire in a bid to weaken their resistance. It is no accident that various emperors personally involved themselves in doctrinal issues in order to ensure Roman political authority. As an imperial religion, Christianity finally put an end to the sheer anarchy of belief that had been a feature of a Roman society previously interested in catering to the diverse beliefs of its citizens. Christianity homogenized belief and made all other religions redundant.

The Gnostics, however, represented freedom of and from belief. They refused to allow themselves to become subject to Christian authority or its doctrine. If they were not constructing elaborate structures of their own to account for world-creation, they were busy meeting in secret with other like-minded individuals in order to undermine Church authority. They were accused of subverting holy doctrine by introducing ideas from pagan philosophers, engaging in unseemly sexual orgies with fellow parishioners, promoting the idea of two gods rather than one, and generally portraying Jesus Christ as a revolutionary and not a genuine God-man.

Yet the Oxyrhynchus *Gospel of Thomas* gives us an entirely different picture of the Gnostic vision of life, as do many other texts discovered later at Nag Hammadi, further south along the Nile. As a collection of traditional sayings attributed to Christ, many of its proverbs and parables are similar to those expressed in the canonical Gospels. A superficial reading of them may not suggest anything that is heretical or particularly "Gnostic." The prologue to the *Sayings*, notably in the Oxyrhynchus version, alerts us to the exclusive nature of their contents, however. They are "hidden sayings," and are not to be shown to all and sundry. "These are hidden sayings that the living Jesus spoke, and Judas who is Thomas recorded. He [Christ] said, 'Whoever finds the interpretation of [understands] these sayings will not experience death.'"[97] This is a classic Gnostic injunction: that the individual must interpret what Christ said according to his own understanding of the Master's motives. The individual is enjoined to escape death—that is, attain immortality—by way of such knowledge. Gnosis is about making an individual claim to esoteric knowledge that will help to release a person from material constraints.

Gnosticism promotes a subjective stance not apparent in the visionary literature of the age, least of all in the Gospels themselves. It asks Christians to be more discerning about received doctrine as espoused by the priest, and to understand one's inner relationship with God as something generated by oneself, not as something handed down by way of holy tradition. *Thomas* betrays an antitraditional stance, while appealing to individuals to reduce the distance between themselves and God, as it is described in the following passage:

> Jesus said, "If those who lead you say to you, 'See, the kingdom is in the sky,' then the birds of the sky will precede you. If they say to you, 'It is in the sea,' then the fish will precede you. Rather, the kingdom is *inside* you, and it is outside of you. When you come to know yourselves, then you will become known, and you will realize that it is you who are the sons of the living father. But if you will not know yourselves, you dwell in poverty, and it is you who are that poverty."[98]

Jesus is referring here to the illusion of the spatial nature of heaven, where birds and fish will always take precedence over our entry, so long as we insist on viewing it in such terms. Rather, the kingdom of heaven is inside us, and pervades all things when we begin to realize our relationship with the "living father." To suggest that we are *all* the sons of God, a condition previously only attributed to the Savior, and that we merely have to know ourselves—that is, understand our primordial nature—if we wish to dwell in a state contrary to that of spiritual impoverishment, is to embark upon a path toward a form of spiritual realization the church vehemently condemned. It was, after all, taking away from its priests the role of intermediary between God and his flock.

In this one respect, Gnosticism displays similarities to the ideas of Martin Luther in the sixteenth century, with their emphasis of individual encounter with the divine.

But the real difficulty lies in affirming the value of individual discernment as something that comes from within. "Jesus said, 'Recognize what is in your sight, and that which is hidden from you will become plain to you. For there is nothing hidden which will not become manifest.'"[99] In other words, personal insight counts for more than doctrinal explanation. That which is hidden is deliberately so; for the Gnostic, to cast pearls of wisdom before swine is the real sin. Esoteric knowledge of the Christian message, and the role of humankind in this world as ordered by God, can only be understood when one casts aside the material aspect of being in favor of a more subjective encounter with God. *Thomas* compares the Gnostic to a wise fisherman able to discern the difference between the doctrinal clutter of orthodox Christianity and the true message of Christ, that of "dwelling in the light."[100] Esoteric doctrine is thus the "big fish" as embodied by Christ: "And he said, 'The man is like a wise fisherman who casts his net into the sea and drew it up from the sea full of small fish. Among them, the wise fisherman found a fine large fish. He threw all the small fish back into the sea and chose the large fish without hesitation. Whoever has ears to hear, let him hear.'"[101]

The Gnostic message was subversive. It challenged both the state and society. It was not a doctrine for the timid, but for those who were willing to take upon themselves the task of rejecting conventional mores. Its image of Christ was that of an iconoclast who was not afraid to preach revolution for the sake of spiritual understanding. Gnosis could only be attained by a return to verities not subject to theological interpretation. The true Gnostic is he who came into being before he came into being. He was a man who acknowledged his Adamic self as taking precedence over that of his dialectical self. Only then could he heed the "message of the stones," which was another way of listening to the voice of nature itself.[102] As *Thomas* relates: "Jesus said, 'Men think, perhaps, that it is peace which I have come to cast upon the world. Know that it is dissension that I have come to cast upon the earth: fire, sword, and war. For there will be five in a house; three will be against two, and two against three, the father against the son, and the son against the father. And they will stand solitary.'"[103]

The Gnostic influence on early Christianity, and the controversies it subsequently invoked, was all in the future as far as the Holy Family was concerned as they journeyed deep into ancient Egypt. In the meantime, Muhammad al-Baqir (AD 676–731), an early Muslim historian, informs us that Mary enrolled Jesus in school in Al-Bahnasa for a short time. The teacher ordered the boy to recite the alphabet, to which he again enjoined the teacher to account for its symbolic meaning. Unlike the version of this story recounted earlier, Jesus proceeded to tell the teacher all he knew about the esoteric meaning of the alphabet. But with added emphasis: he insisted this time on replacing the teacher at the head of the class, ordering him to sit with his pupils. "The *Alef* stands for the good deeds of God," Jesus went on to explain. "The *Da* stands for the glory of God, the *Gim* for the splendor of God, the *Dal* for the religion of God, the *Ha* for the abyss of Hell, the *Wa* indicates the misery of those living in Hell. The *Ha* also means the remission of sins of all those who ask forgiveness, the *K* is the word of God which will never change, the *Sad* is the measure for a measure, the *Ta* stands for the serpents of Hell."[104]

In the context of this legend, the alphabet of Jesus's Judaism has suddenly become a form of Gnostic utterance in keeping with the tradition of exegesis associated with Oxyrhynchus and Nag Hammadi. Perhaps the Holy Family sought to knit together the many strands of an esoteric message that they encountered throughout their wanderings, as they were later to do when they honored Hermopolis with their presence at present-day Al-Ashmounein, further south. Hermopolis was the city dedicated to Thoth, the god of divine Mind and the heart and tongue of Ra.

As such, he was the god of writing. The infant Jesus was disposed to emphasize his links with the divine Word of the Logos. Clearly he had no hesitation in claiming for himself any tradition that might celebrate the living Word as the vital premise for his existence.

Is it any wonder that the church chose to expurgate such linguistic symbolism from its canon? Its theologians knew full well that esotericism could only lead to a diminution of their authority, and the subsequent increase in the value of personal interpretation as the basis of Christian belief.

Another Muslim narrator, Wahb ibn Munabbih (d. AD 728), tells us that the Holy Family stayed at a hospice for the poor while in Al-Bahnasa. A local nobleman who befriended Mary supported the hospice. One day he discovered that a part of his treasure had been stolen, and he related the incident to her. When the infant Jesus realized what had happened, he informed his mother not to worry. "Ask the nobleman to gather together all the villagers, and I will soon discover the culprits," he said. When this had been done Jesus approached two men in the crowd, one of whom was lame and the other blind. To the blind man he said: "Arise!" To which the blind man replied, "I can't." Jesus then asked him: "How then were you able to steal?" Immediately the crowd realized the man's guilt and began to strike him. The blind man finally admitted his crime, implicating the lame man in the plot as well. He eventually confessed that the lame man used his eyes to guide him to the nobleman's treasure, while he used his strength to make off with it.

This incident at Al-Bahnasa reveals the infant Jesus in his capacity as a seer. It is a part of his behavior that the church tends to dismiss as not in keeping with his God-manhood.[105] That the early chronicles celebrate his liking for linguistic games, as well as his ability to identify the stain of culpability in men, reveals him more as a magus than a healer.

Throughout Theophilus's *Vision* we see Jesus depicted as a miracle-worker, even when a child. The Christ of the Gospels is a different kind of wonder-worker; his task as an adult is to affirm the message of God rather than to perform acts of immediate benefit to the community. The miracle is no longer a sign of his theurgic power but of his messianic role. In Egypt, though, we see the infant Jesus becoming aware of his powers, playing with them, and using them in a childishly demonstrative way. The chronicles seem to be saying to us: here is the God-man in his chrysalis-like state. He is yet to emerge as the superlative being that we know through the Gospels. Take note of this child; where human suffering is, so is his caring presence. Under the sign of the *aleph* he renders miraculous deeds so that men and women might begin to wonder. *Da* is the awe of his glory, just as *ha* is a sign of his love.

For all the unorthodoxy of their views, the Gnostics were aware of these aspects of Christ's nature. They were more interested in his capacity for wholeness than his intention to draw people to him through fear of being excluded from the kingdom of heaven. The Christ they wished to believe in was able to resolve division in the human soul. As the *Gospel of Thomas* relates:

> When you make the two one, and when you make the inside like the outside and the outside like the inside, and the above like the below, and when you make the male and the female one and the same, so that the male is not male nor the female female; and when you fashion eyes in place of an eye, and a hand in place of a hand, and a foot in place of a foot, and a likeness in place of a likeness, then will you enter the kingdom.[106]

Such a resolution of opposites was central to the Gnostics' view of Christianity. Their religion was one where a person could be chosen "one out of a thousand" in order that he or she might stand as one in Christ. It was this kind of exclusivity that they saw as reflecting Christ's love for all people. He appeared on earth to "cause life in many," and so to intercede on their behalf with the Father.[107] Humanity's role was to return to the Father as purified "mental substance," in order that they might "exist in his thought" for evermore.[108] They were destined to become the "faultless ones" in possession of a "perfect idea of beneficence." This was the desired state of Gnostic Christians; their task was to purify matter so that it could finally return to its origin free of all taint of materiality.

As a haven for the Holy Family, Oxyrhynchus was truly a heavenly city. So many threads of belief, both heterodox and otherwise, came together in this ancient metropolis. Nothing was off limits in this remarkable country, where people throughout the millennia had chosen to wrestle with ideas in order to help them better understand themselves. If there is one message that reaches us from the discovery of the Gnostic texts there and in Nag Hammadi, it is the knowledge that religious belief was central to the evolution of consciousness.

I was reminded of this fact when I read a quotation in Greek on a sixth-century funeral shroud discovered in Oxyrhynchus sometime around 1953. It read: "Jesus said: 'nothing is buried, which will not be raised.'" Comparing this remark with a similar one from the *Gospel of Thomas* quoted earlier, one realizes that the current of Gnosticism ran deep in Upper Egypt during those early centuries of the Christian era, in spite of every attempt the Alexandrian church made to stamp it out. This revolutionary doctrine relating to the resurrection of the body could not be silenced. Today, it still speaks to us in a way that inspires our respect, if not our acceptance. For it is the voice of gnosis urging us to transcend our predicament, confined as we are by our limitations and material constraints: "Jesus says, 'Know what is before your face, and that which is hidden from you will be revealed to you. For there is nothing hidden that will not be made manifest, and nothing buried which will not be raised up.'"[109] This voice telling us that what lies "before our face" is none other than the Christian message emerging from its long-buried state into the realm of heterodox thought.

It was an argument that Gnostics laid claim to before they were hounded from their enclaves in Middle and Upper Egypt by men eager to silence their unique view of Christ.

19
Language of Stones

AS RECENTLY AS FORTY YEARS ago, it was only possible to reach the Monastery of the Holy Virgin at Gebel al-Tair, known affectionately as the "Monastery of the Birds" because of the thousands that nest in the cliff below, by taking a boat upriver from Minya. The Holy Family, according to tradition, embarked in a similar fashion from Cynopolis, once home to Anubis the overseer of the underworld, where the village of Al-Kais now stands. From Al-Kais they sailed south past Gebel al-Tair on the Nile.

The monastery is located on a high plateau that in turn follows the course of the river, and in the old days it was only accessible by way of a pulley lowered to visitors by the monks. The cliff that separates the Nile Valley from the plateau is filled with natural caves that the ancient Egyptians once used as rock temples and burial chambers. During the course of the fifth and sixth centuries, these caves became popular among Christian anchorites eager to follow the ascetic path. It is likely that the church on top of the cliff was once a Roman tomb. One can only imagine how difficult it must have been to ascend to the monastery, given the swirling current in the river and the uncertain nature of the wind.

Robert Curzon, the nineteenth-century English bibliophile and traveler, described his own attempt to reach the monastery in his pursuit of ancient codices as one fraught with danger: "There was a high wind," he writes, "which rendered the management of my immense boat, above 80 feet long, somewhat difficult; and we were afraid of being dashed against the rocks if we ventured too near to them in our attempt to land at the foot of the precipice." He then goes on to describe his unlikely saviors, none other than several "nude monks" who suddenly appeared from a cleft in the rock face and jumped in the water beside his boat.

"They swam like Newfoundland dogs," Curzon relates. Eventually, after numerous attempts to land, Curzon consented to be carried ashore on the shoulders of one of these naked monks and deposited at the foot of the rock. Under the guidance of the abbot, who meanwhile had resumed his robe, he climbed up a narrow fissure, losing his slippers in the process. These, apparently, hit the turbaned head of his skipper clinging to the escarpment below, much to the amusement of all concerned.

"We became lost in the gloom of a narrow cavern through which we were advancing," he writes, "the procession being led by these unrobed ecclesiastics." It is hard to imagine this scene without suppressing a smile: Curzon, the archstealer of books and codices, found himself at the mercy of men that he was about to divest of what few treasures they possessed.

Today, it is far easier to reach the monastery, on a newly macadamized road that skirts the eastern desert, through arid hills of sand and blasted stone, past lonely Muslim tombstones and abandoned border posts, until one finally passes the cement factory of Samalut on the right. After about an hour's drive, Mounir and I approached the monastery through a large Christian necropolis located halfway up a hillside. It reminded me of a deserted city. Its narrow roads, its thoroughfares, its myriad domes and padlocked tombs were reminiscent of a recently vacated metropolis. When I commented on this to Mounir, he shrugged, as if to say, "The dead are important to Copts, even as they were for our ancestors." The rock tombs along the Nile had found a new incarnation in these cities of the dead at Gebel al-Tair. Anubis, the god of the dead, was still in residence, it seemed.

When we arrived outside the church, it was locked. Three or four guards, bored beyond description, sat about near the entrance, their guns lazily cradled in their arms. When I asked Mounir why they were in this out-of-the-way place, he replied: "To protect travelers such as ourselves."

"But we're perfectly safe. What could possibly happen?"

"This area was considered a hotbed of Islamic extremists some years ago, Mr. James. A number of tourist buses were ambushed outside Qena, Assyut, and Dairut in the early 1990s. The government is still worried such incidents might reoccur. As a consequence, guards are posted at most archaeological sites throughout Middle Egypt."

"I will bear this in mind," I said.

"I really don't think these young men know how to use their guns, even if they were called upon to do so," Mounir said.

After Mounir negotiated a small "entrance fee" with the soldiers, a large key to the church was produced. Removing our shoes at the door, we entered one of the oldest churches in Egypt, said to have been built by Constantine's mother Helena in AD 328. It was dark inside, with patches of light entering small windows in the roof of the nave. Finally a switch was activated to help us see by the light of a chandelier.

I was immediately struck by the rustic simplicity of the church. Its walls were bare. Its eight encircling columns contained a nave, some steps leading to an altar, and a tiny apse framed by a haikal decorated with icons. In one of the pillars a baptismal font had been hollowed out, and in the center of the nave I noticed a *laccan*, or stone washbasin in the floor. This, Mounir informed me, was used to bathe the feet of the priest on ceremonial occasions.

To the right of the sanctuary was a cave-like chapel where the Holy Family is said to have rested. Mounir dutifully made the sign of the cross in front of the reliquary of Saint Mary inside, while I looked around the church. I noticed on one of the walls a painting of the Holy Family in a boat sailing on the Nile, as well as numerous tiny crosses daubed with henna on pillars. The painting was barely visible because of its age, but it nonetheless managed to convey a sense of presence. The Holy Family seemed to be there at that moment.

There was a subterranean feeling about the interior of this church: clearly it had been dug out of a quarry at some stage in its development. After making some notes in my field book, I joined Mounir, who was beckoning me, outside by a low wall on the edge of the cliff overlooking the Nile. There he had organized with the guards for tea to be served. I knew then that he must want to tell me important information about the monastery, as two chairs had been set up for us beside the wall.

The Nile lay below, framed by palm groves, its expanse of brown water threading its way northward as we watched. I could see a number of sailboats tacking against the current on their way south. The fields were well irrigated, and it was not hard to make out farmers and their livestock walking along levees. Once or twice I heard a donkey braying. Since Curzon's time, however, the course of the river had changed, and its bank no longer abutted the base of the cliff on which we sat. I had to imagine his boat attempting to tack against the wind on that February day in 1838 as he tried to make landfall. The farmers in the fields below, dressed as they were in long robes, could have easily been those monks about to throw off their vestments.

"Theophilus mentions a miracle occurring here at Gebel al-Tair in his *Vision*," I announced, pulling the document out of my shoulder bag so that we might reacquaint ourselves with his words.

"Could you read it to me, Mr. James?" Mounir asked, as he sipped his tea.

"He says, and I quote Mary's remarks in the *Vision*, 'As we repaired to the land of Egypt, the mountains, the animals and the stones honored my Son, and when we walked they walked with us.

And my Son turned to those mountains, stones and animals, and spoke to them. Then he laid his right hand on the eastern mountain and his left hand on the northern mountain and said: "Stop." And they stopped. And the traces of his two hands were impressed in the mountains as if in dough or wax. And lo! they are seen down to this day. And he said to them, "See this as a sign and a mark to all who are weak in faith concerning my coming, and do not believe that I came into the world. But let the cursed unbelieving Jews and Herod receive anathemas, together with all those who do not believe in my holy name.""""

"What is your opinion of these words, Mr. James?" Mounir asked.

"I find it a very strong statement indeed. It is almost a pronouncement. For the first time in the *Vision* it seems that the infant Jesus has uttered a truly adult remark."

Mounir agreed. "It is almost as if he has shed his childhood. We are seeing instead a man who is prepared to curse his enemies for what they have done to his family."

"Why does he address the mountains, I wonder? I presume the place is where we are sitting right at this moment."

"And the stones and the animals too. I am beginning to believe that he enjoyed a special kind of relationship with the things of this world."

"As if he spoke their language," I ventured.

"Yet stones and animals cannot talk," replied Mounir, a little nonplussed.

"Egypt has taught me one thing, Mr. Mounir: that the people of this land devised many languages over the course of history to express their relationship with it. The priests of Amun spoke one language; the Gnostics another; theologians a more complex language again. I have yet to mention the language of the ascetics or that of Akhenaton, the legendary king of Amarna who founded his own religion in the fourteenth century BC. Whether it is Akhenaton, Anthony, Arius, or Athanasius speaking, each man spoke to a different aspect of ourselves. They each wanted to make a point about humanity's relationship with the world."

"That's quite a pantheon of Egyptian heroes you have mentioned, Mr. James."

"And all of them had one thing in mind," I countered. "Like the infant Jesus, they were prepared to talk to mountains and stones. It's no accident that nearly all these men spent a good period of their lives in the desert, either as exiles, monks, heretics, or empire builders. Why did they do this if not because they felt they could not be heard by their contemporaries? People simply refused to understand them. They were prophets without a cause. All they could do was talk to stones, to mountains, to the animals."

"It sounds like madness," Mounir admitted. "But I think I understand what you mean. Nature accepts Jesus's entreaty more than we do."

"According to the *Vision*, this is so," I said. "Let me read a few more words that are even more explicit. 'And he said to the Mountains: "You have acknowledged me and believed in me even though you have neither soul nor body, yet those who have soul and body do not believe in me. And the kings that I have created in my likeness, and in my image, do not believe in me. Those for whom I have come into the world do not believe in me, nor do they honor me, but instead endeavor to kill me, until I reached this very place [Gebel al-Tair].""""

"The sequel to this story, it seems, is the way he impressed his hands on the mountains as in dough or wax."

"What does this mean, I wonder?" I asked.

"According to the historian Abu 'l-Makarim, when the Holy Family passed by this cliff as they sailed up the Nile, a large rock threatened to dislodge and swamp them," Mounir informed me. "Needless to say Mary was extremely frightened, and pleaded with her son to intervene."

"Jesus, we now know, extended his hand and stopped the rock from falling on their boat," I remarked. "What happened then?"

"He left his hand imprint on the rock, thus preventing it from crushing them. It remained where it was for a thousand years, stuck to the cliff face."

I peered over the wall.

"Where is it now, I wonder?" I asked.

"It was stolen by King Amalric of Jerusalem in 1168 when he invaded Upper Egypt to defeat Shirkuh the Kurd,"[110] Mounir replied. "He ordered the section of rock with the imprint of Christ's hand on it to be cut away. Possibly he did so because the imprint possessed healing qualities. It is said a needle could be inserted into fine perforations in the rock, so releasing black collyrium used in treating eye infections."

"Do you actually believe such a story, Mounir?"

"What else can I believe, Mr. James? We know that Amalric passed by here. As the king of Jerusalem, everything in Egypt he would have regarded as his by right. A relic of this nature—one that celebrated the passage of the Holy Family through Egypt—would have been immensely valuable. Just like the foot imprint of Jesus you saw in Sakha. They are the healing stones that the good Lord, in his wisdom, left us as a measure of his love."

My tea was cold, but I did not really care. That Christ's handprint had mysteriously disappeared did not faze me, either. I began to realize that even after two thousand years its mark upon the earth remained as vivid as if it were carved into the rock at my feet. Below, the Nile swept onward to the sea, its earth-laden waters a perennial tonic. It was easy to compare this nutriment with the words of the infant Jesus here at Gebel al-Tair. Each in their own way gave succor to the world.

"I think it is time we pushed on, Mr. James," Mounir advised, getting up from his chair and looking at his watch. Two guards came over to collect our empty glasses. We thanked them, and they dutifully shook our hands as we started toward the car.

"Tomorrow we must pay a visit to Bishop Demetrius in Mallawi," he said. "He is the bishop of Hermopolis Magna and Antineopolis, two ancient cities through which the Holy Family passed. With his permission, we will be able to visit other sites on this side of the river, namely the village of Beni Hassan, where the city of Speos Artemidos once stood. We must first pay our respects to the martyrs of Antineopolis, as well as the Well of the Cloud nearby."

"The Well of the Cloud?"

"Let me tell you about it when we reach the place," Mounir responded, as our driver started the car.

Through the window, as we descended the road from Gebel al-Tair, I caught a glimpse of the Christian graveyard on our right, its tombs and clusters of domes reminding me once more of a miniature city framed against the horizon. Could it be a celestial city, I asked myself? The dead lived a more stately existence here than many of those living in the village above. Pharaonic Egypt is never far away. The tombs in the cliffs along the river still retain memories of the dead—and of those ascetics who died to the world while reciting their poems in stone for the living.

20 One Man's Choice

WE CROSSED BACK OVER TO THE western side of the Nile and made our way south via Al-Minya toward the provincial capital of Mallawi. Mounir made a call on his cell phone as we sped through villages and towns in our taxi, hoping to arrange a meeting with Bishop Demetrius at the diocese headquarters. It was a long shot on his part, as he had no idea as to the bishop's movements. After a period of discussion in Arabic, which seemed to me to be quite animated, he eventually hung up. I looked at him inquiringly.

"Well?" I said.

"It seems that Bishop Demetrius is touring his parish on pastoral duties," replied Mounir, smoothing his moustache.

"Does it mean we have missed him?"

"It depends."

"On what?" The suspense was killing me.

"On whether we are able to meet him in the countryside."

"Is there any way of knowing where he might be?"

"His secretary has advised me that if we make our way to Abu Fana monastery near the village of Qasr Hur, we may be able to catch him. He intends to visit the monks there and perform evening office."

I studied my map to see where Qasr Hur might be. It was very close to Hermopolis Magna, one of the most important cities in ancient Egypt whose tutelary deity had been Thoth, the god of divine speech and of writing. This was a good enough omen for me.

"Shall we head for the monastery, then?" I asked.

"If you wish. We may have to wait some hours, or even a day, however."

For some strange reason, I felt comfortable with the idea that events were outside our control. I was more than happy now to leave it in the hands of fate.

"Abu Fana is a primitive place, Mr. James. It was abandoned for many years, and today only has a few monks."

"We are going there to wait for the bishop. If we wish to gain his blessing for the rest of our journey, then surely we must put ourselves out a little," I said.

When we turned off the main highway near the town of Al-Fiqriya and started along the back roads, it became increasingly evident that the villagers whom we stopped to ask the way were offering us conflicting information. On more than one occasion a chorus of gesticulation greeted Mounir or the driver's inquiry. For a while I began to believe that not only were we lost, but we would never reach the monastery at all. In the end, I sat back in the car and allowed the journey to unfold before my gaze.

Palm groves, well-ordered fields, cattle grazing on levee banks, farmers trudging behind bullocks plowing furrows in the black soil, villages filled with slender minarets, children ambling home from school by the roadside, donkeys all but lost under a load of feed trotting in front of us, these were some of the many images of rural life we witnessed. The driver turned down one road and up another as we slowly made our way to the very fringe of the desert. Then, without warning, we found ourselves on a dirt track leading to a distant monastery surrounded by sand.

"Let's hope the good bishop gets word that we've arrived," I said, half in jest.

"A phone call will alert him, I am sure," Mounir replied. "If he is in the vicinity, then he will surely come."

I climbed out of the car and looked about. There were two monastic complexes associated with Abu Fana, one near where we stood and another perched on a sand hill some hundred yards away. Surrounded by a high wall, the compound on the hill reminded me of a fortress. All I could see was a cupola protruding from the rampart. Not far from the main monastery and to its left was a large Christian burial ground similar to the one I had seen at Gebel al-Tair. Set against the dusty brown sand and the blue of the horizon, its numerous white domes and painted tombs possessed a dreamlike quality, as if this city of the dead were no more than a mirage. I was reluctant to walk toward it for fear it might disappear before my eyes.

The monastery was founded by Abu Fana in the fourth century. According to ancient chronicles, the man was born in the village of Abusir near Hermopolis Magna. At an early age he left home to seek out a cave on the edge of the desert. There he practiced a life of extreme austerity in total darkness for eighteen years. Even while asleep he never lay down on a mat; instead he leaned upright against a wall throughout the night. The result of practicing this kind of asceticism ensured that Abu Fana became disfigured with a humpback, which people compared to a palm tree—a *bane* in the Upper Egyptian dialect. Hence his name, Apa Bane, or Abu Fana. Observers said his feet were like those of an elephant, and tougher than leather. His ability to fast was legendary—up to thirty-seven days, three days less than the legendary fast of Christ. He was a man of deep piety and much loved by the surrounding villagers, who used to entrust their money to him for safekeeping. He was, in a very real way, their spiritual bank.

In 1992 the remains of his body were unearthed from the ruins of the funerary church by a team of Austrian archaeologists. They found his body embalmed and bandaged in linen, resting on a layer of incense in a deep shaft below the floor of the church. Subsequent examination and analysis of the skeletal structure confirmed some of the strange ascetical techniques practiced by this saint. It seems that by the age of twenty-two Abu Fana may have suffered from inflammation and fusing of his vertebrae, making it too painful for him to lie down. This would account for why he slept standing up. Although the calcification of his spine may have had its origin in some childhood disease, Abu Fana believed it to be a trial sent by God to test him. He was to be a date palm and withstand the winds of the desert. He was to be a man whose rigid body was to become a symbol of the strength and conviction of his faith, as well as an inspiration to others.

With the discovery of Abu Fana's remains, the monastery underwent a revival. Already a half dozen or so monks gravitated to the existing structure from elsewhere, and the original compound on top of the dune was soon restored. The sand, which had been slowly encroaching for many years, was dug away from the outer walls of the older building, while these were reinforced from within. I had not yet walked up to visit the monastery on the hill, but already I sensed that it was a haven built to resist time and the elements.

Mounir and I decided to sit on a bench outside the main monastery to wait. It was late in the afternoon, and the light cast a golden glow on all that lay before us. I could hear the sound of livestock drifting toward us from the river land in the distance. But here, in the desert, the atmosphere was altogether different: the world had slipped by like a felucca on the river, leaving us stranded on an island.

A monk appeared through the gateway and walked toward us. We rose from our seats to greet him. I judged him to be around sixty years old, thin, slightly built, with penetrating, limpid eyes. It was hard not to be entranced by his gaze.

"Welcome," he said simply.

Mounir proceeded to explain the reason for our visit—that we were waiting for the bishop to arrive.

"He will be here shortly," the monk, whose name was Father Victor, advised.

"Tell me, Father," I asked. "How long have you been living here?"

"Not long, sir. You see, I am only a novice."

"You have only just decided to become a monk?"

"This is correct, sir. On the death of my mother in Cairo, I decided the time had come for me to dedicate what life is left to me to God. It was not a decision lightly taken, but one that had been with me for many years." Father Victor's voice was respectful yet at the same time filled with humility, as if he had been a monk all his life.

"You never married?"

Father Victor shook his head. "My mother was an invalid. My job at a government ministry as a clerk only made it possible for me to care for her in her last years. With her death, however, I became free of this burden. It was all I could do to deal with the emptiness of my life."

"Is this why you decided to become a monk?" I asked.

Again Father Victor shook his head. "All my life I have wanted to enter a monastery and serve God. There was something about the ascetic life, sir, which drew me to it. Could I indeed practice the austerities demanded of me at such a late stage, I asked myself? Could I subject my aging body to the harshness of the desert? Of course I was afraid, as you can imagine. But now"—he paused to think of what he was about to say next—"now I seem to have renewed strength. The good Lord, in his kindness, has cast his glance upon me. I feel I am being observed."

It was a strange remark to make, and I looked to Mounir in order to gauge his reaction.

"We are all under the gaze of Our Lord," he remarked.

"Sir—eh, Mr. James," Father Victor said, deciding to use my name. "I am a simple man, indeed I think not a very intelligent one at that. I am just thankful that Bishop Demetrius saw fit to allow me to come to Abu Fana to become a monk at my late age. I feel blessed."

"Your good works preceded you, Father Victor," I suggested.

"In the life of the Spirit, sir—eh, Mr. James," Victor again corrected himself. "There is always a voice pressing us toward some heartfelt act. I only know I feel a deep sense of calm now that I am here. Abu Fana, as we know, could not sleep on a mat at night. It was his affliction. The way he dealt with it drew me to his bosom. I feel that he has embraced my faltering soul. I am thankful."

Just then, we noticed a procession of cars driving up the dirt road toward the monastery. Immediately we assumed that Bishop Demetrius was about to arrive, such was the consternation among the monastery servants and monks standing nearby. They ran backward and forward, talking loudly, eager to alert those inside that the bishop was on their doorstep.

Bishop Demetrius climbed from his vehicle dressed in the full regalia of office. He was a man in his early fifties, with gentle eyes that looked out from behind a pair of black-rimmed glasses. His black skullcap was moon-shaped against the evening sky. He possessed a long, rather straggly beard that hung white against his robe. On a gold chain around his neck hung a large plaited leather cross, similar to the one that Pope Shenouda possessed. With a staff of office and brass cross in separate hands, he allowed the monks and servants to come forward in order to kiss his hand. It was an occasion fraught with piety: everyone, including Mr. Bedwani, seemed to be profoundly affected by their encounter with the bishop of Mallawi.

"Ah, Mr. Bedwani and Mr. James," he said, greeting us warmly when Father Victor introduced us. "I was informed by my secretary that you might be here. What is it you wish of me?"

Mounir told the bishop of our desire to visit various monasteries on the eastern side of the Nile associated with the journey of the Holy Family through the region. Out of courtesy, he said to him, we wanted the bishop to know the reason for our visit.

"For my part," I concluded, "I wanted to experience for myself what it must have been like for the Holy Family to travel through a land fraught with memory for most Jews. They knew it as a place of exile only, even in the days of Moses. At the same time, was the journey up the Nile no more than a folktale? I needed to find out for myself."

"The journey of the Holy Family through Mallawi is of course well documented," Bishop Demetrius said. "Only a few years ago, in 1998 I believe, a university in Germany published a report on a fourth-century papyrus which described the visit of the infant Jesus and his family. Dr. Gadwat Gabra, an eminent Coptologist, subsequently confirmed this. It would appear that Patriarch Theophilus, who wrote his story in the fifth century, was not the first to detail the Holy Family's journey into Egypt."[111]

"It would seem that you're right, Your Holiness," I replied. "It would also appear, if you forgive me for saying, that if the infant Jesus was by now nearly five years old, then he would have begun to understood a little about what was happening."

"I believe this to be the case, Mr. James. His mother, Joseph, and Salome would have often talked of their difficulties. Can one not assume that the infant Jesus did not absorb some of their bitterness toward Herod and the Jews? They were exiles, after all. But come," the bishop said, indicating the monastery on the hill. "Since you wish to talk, let us do so while we visit the site of Abu Fana's tomb. It is a beautiful place. There is much atmosphere."

Our group, including Bishop Demetrius, his assistants, several monks, and ourselves, dutifully set off in the direction of the walled monastery among the dunes. The sand slid away underfoot as we walked. On the ground were numerous shards of pottery, which presumably were more than a thousand years old. The sun was beginning to set to our left, and the light over the necropolis was luminous. It was as if we had been thrown back into the fifth or sixth century: everything about our modest caravan bespoke an encounter with antiquity. I tried to picture Abu Fana leaning against a wall, preparing to drop off to sleep at last. Did he ever experience respite from the pain in his back?

"Your Holiness, how do you know the Holy Family stayed in this vicinity for eight weeks?" I asked the bishop as we strode together up the slope.

"There is a report by one of our most eminent martyrs, a man named Wadamon," he replied. "According to him, he came from a town to the south called Armant. It is understood that he met with travelers in his hometown that told him they had recently met a family in Ashmounein accompanied by a child who resembled, they said, a king. Eager to know more about the child, Wadamon journeyed all the way to Ashmounein to see the boy for himself. Such a trip would have taken at least a month to complete on a donkey in those days."

"When you add the return trip of the travelers to that of Wadamon's, then presumably you arrive at a period of approximately eight weeks," I said.

"An extraordinary feat, do you not think?" the bishop said. "While many people might wish to dispute the journey of the Holy Family in Egypt, suggesting that it is little more than a pious folktale concocted by the Coptic people for their own benefit, the truth is that a great deal of careful scholarship has gone into verifying the facts. The church dedicated to the martyr Wadamon at Ashmounein still exists to this day."

"If this man was a contemporary of Jesus, and we know that the persecution of Christians by the Romans occurred more than three centuries later, why then was he martyred?"

"Because Our Lord informed him that he, Wadamon, would be martyred for his belief in him. It was his own people, the pagans of Amant, who killed him for his faith in Christ, not the Romans. They could not accept this new dispensation in their midst. It threatened their gods. Such was the power of the infant Jesus, even in those early days."

"So Wadamon may have been the first Christian martyr," I suggested.

"It is reasonable enough to assume, yes."

Out of breath after our climb, we soon arrived at a narrow gateway through the eastern wall of the monastery. Bishop Demetrius led his entourage along a pathway inside the wall into the courtyard beyond. The place was completely deserted. Inside the courtyard, I suddenly found myself gazing into the partly ruined apse of a church from the sixth century AD open to the sky, containing a fresco of a large cross that appeared to be woven rather than painted on the wall. It reminded me of the braided style of crosses that feature on the ceremonial vestments of priests. Its effect was hypnotic: the background of the painting was made up of what appeared to be blue and red wings, all fluttering in unison, as if the entire fresco was one giant bird. We entered the partly ruined church.

Bishop Demetrius made his obeisance before the iconostasis while the monks gathered to form a choir. Their chanting was spontaneous, and in the evening light, with only a few hastily lit candles to illuminate the scene, the monks proceeded to perform their liturgical office while Mounir and I looked on. We could have been attending a service performed nearly fifteen hundred years ago. Nothing essentially had changed. The braided cross above our heads, its plethora of wings shimmering in the candlelight, only added to the antiquity of the moment.

When the service was over, we walked back through the monastery to the gate. It was almost dark now, so it was necessary to watch our step. But I need not have worried: Father Victor quietly attached himself to me in order to act as my guide. His humility touched me. When we shook hands at the bottom of the hill by the car, he placed the back of one hand to his lips as a gesture of respect.

"Take care, Mr. James." This time he did not stutter my name, but said it firmly, with assurance. "I am sure your journey will bless you with its fruits."

"It has been a privilege to have met you, Father Victor," I said.

"Oh no!" Father Victor became suddenly tongue-tied with embarrassment. "I am a simple man. I do not presume to know anything."

"Perhaps this is the reason why you have come here to Abu Fana," I said, trying to ease his concern.

"I fear I have come too late," the old man responded, conscious of his advanced years.

Father Victor peered at me in the gloom. I could see there were tears in his eyes. Meanwhile, Mounir beckoned me to join him in the taxi. We were on our way to Mallawi to dine with the bishop, it seemed. Yet for all that, I would think of Abu Fana Monastery with fondness. Here I had met a man who had allowed his personal constraints to instill his life with its own simple honesty.

21

Braiding the Iota

I T WAS DARK BY THE TIME WE drove into the city of Mallawi. I was tired after a long day on the road. It was not easy, however, to dismiss my recent memory of having attended evening office in the ruined monastery of Abu Fana with a bishop and his flock, among ancient frescoes and candles, and the sound of psalms echoing against half-ruined walls.

While I lay on my bed in a hostel room overlooking a noisy city street, I began to wonder whether it was all a dream, this constant rubbing shoulders with men who seemed to live not only on the edge of the desert but also on the edge of reality itself. Egypt had begun to dismantle everything I thought to be real. I began to sense that the river and the desert had set up a metaphysical frisson like no other. Men and women were called to worship in this land just as the ancient Egyptians were called to build monuments to the glory of the sun-god Ra.

The darkness outside prompted me to realize how hungry I was. I sat up, rubbed my eyes, and looked out the window. Below, the street was filled with people hurrying home to break their Ramadan fast. Knowing that Mounir would be knocking at my door at any minute, I hastily washed and readied myself for our meeting with Bishop Demetrius at his office.

Mounir and I walked up the street to the bishopric, a large building adjacent to the diocese church. Men were sitting in cafés eating their evening meals, conversing, or smoking hookahs. Some of them politely nodded to us as we passed. Courtesy, it seemed, was innate to the Egyptian's nature: he was ready enough to welcome us.

As soon as we introduced ourselves to the guard at the gate, we were immediately taken across the courtyard to a set of offices. There we were ushered into a room dominated by an ornate gold-leaf desk, a number of chairs on either side of the room, a large marble table in the center, and a line of recently painted icons of saints surrounded by magnificently carved wooden arabesques on the walls. These figures gazed down at us wherever we chose to sit. Looking upward, I noticed a dome dominated by an icon of Our Lord. Presently the door opened and a servant appeared bearing a tray of food. This he placed on the table, then departed.

Mounir and I tucked into the food with relish. Tea was soon brought in at the conclusion of the meal. I decided then to broach the question of where the bishop might be.

"He will arrive soon," Mounir replied. "His job never ends. There will be petitioners outside asking for his help. A marriage contract might need to be discussed, a debt ratified between two parties—in the end, everything is of interest to him. It is all part of Coptic life."

"He sounds more like an old-time Ottoman pasha than a bishop," I said.

"Everything that touches our lives is his business, Mr. James."

Suddenly the glass door at the back of the room opened, and in walked Bishop Demetrius with two assistants. We shook and kissed his hand as we did at Abu Fana, and took our seats once more. Bishop Demetrius, meanwhile, walked around to the other side of his desk and sat down. The audience had commenced.

"You enjoyed your visit to Abu Fana, I trust," he began, nodding politely when a glass of tea was brought to him.

"Very much, Father," I said. "I was particularly touched by the welcome I received from Father Victor."

"He is a man of deep commitment. It is not often that we receive novitiates into monastic life at such a late age. You may be aware that he cared for his mother for many years."

"Could it be that he had taken his vows long ago, but in secret, and was only waiting for the opportunity to enter the monastery?" I said.

Bishop Demetrius nodded, his beard rubbing against his vestment with a certain deliberation.

"It is not important whether one lives in or outside of the monastery," he said. "Some men have a talent for the ascetical life much as if it was theirs at birth. I see it in a child's eyes sometimes. They gaze at you with a look of tranquility. When I see this quality, I always pay attention to the child's development. It may be I am able to direct his final intention with a few well-chosen words. But in Father Victor's case, I suspect his life of solitude helped to forge the tranquility of his nature. He is—though I would never tell him so!—a saint by disposition. We must acknowledge these men's contribution to monastic life. They are, in their own way, *sowah*."

I glanced at Mounir for a translation of his last remark.

"A *saahih*, Mr. James, is a spiritual wanderer, a solitary," he said.

"You have never mentioned these *sowah* to me before," I replied. "Are they monks?"

"You have not heard of the *sowah*?" Bishop Demetrius interposed. "It is because they are men of the inner desert. We do not know them by name, nor do we ever meet them. If we are fortunate enough, we may have intimation of their presence. That is all."

"It is said," Mounir added, "the *sowah* number one thousand, and that when one of them dies, someone from the world steps forward to take his place. Thus the number is always maintained."

"Another hermit?" I asked.

"An anchorite who has reached a sublime level of spiritual understanding, yes. Only he is able to take his place as a member of the one thousand," Bishop Demetrius said. "He becomes a *saahih*, and so disappears forever from the world. He never returns to the monastery, except—and I must emphasize, that he does so not in any formal sense—as someone without visible presence. He appears in his actions, not in any bodily form."

"Does this mean he comes as a spirit only?" I asked.

"He is a man, let me assure you," replied the bishop. "It is just that he does not wish to be seen. Because of his spiritual attainments in the life of Christ, a *saahih* prefers not to engage in normal social intercourse. He no longer speaks our language, either. To put it bluntly: he is not a person as we know it any more."

"Then what *is* he?" I asked.

It seemed inconceivable that there may be men living in the desert who refused all contact with their fellow men, I thought. Nowhere in Coptic literature had I read about their existence. It was as if a fragment of papyrus had suddenly been unearthed on which was written a remark about an obscure desert order altogether removed from the face of the earth. They were shades, ghosts. They were men who had been utterly effaced. Indeed, they no longer possessed names. *Sowah* were the faceless ones. In truth, these men had become fully spiritualized.

"A *saahih*," Bishop Demetrius continued, "is someone who has acquired another sense of how things are. A man in possession of such qualities can no longer bear to be in contact with normal people, not even with another hermit. In order to maintain his state, he must remove himself from all human contact and make the inner desert his home. The *saahih* has developed the faculties to a point where engaging in normal conversation breaks this spell."

"Yet you tell me these people actually exist, Father," I remarked, hoping to draw out more information about the *sowah*.

"Of course, Mr. James," responded the bishop. "We know of them only by accident. Sometimes we might hear chanting in the church late at night and find crumbs of bread on the altar in the morning. Then we know that there has been a gathering of *sowah* to perform holy office in our absence. On another occasion we might find wine stains on the floor of the church, indicating that they have partaken of the blood of Christ in our absence. They enter our lives, alert us to their presence, and then disappear as mysteriously as they have come. It is the way of the *sowah*; they do not have to meet with us because there would be nothing for them, or us, to discuss. What could one say to a man who no longer speaks as we do?"

"I have no idea, Father," I admitted. "The fact is, you are asking me to believe in a group of men who live in the desert, who presumably find food wherever they can, and who wander from one place to another in order to survive. And, moreover, who speak a different language from us. Is all this possible?"

"Certainly," replied Bishop Demetrius. "Only you must accept the existence of different levels of human life removed from that which makes you and I mere flesh and blood. It is we who suffer such limitations, not the *sowah*. They have become—how do you say it in English?—disembodied."

"Even this sounds a little strange, Father. You make these men appear to be 'little people' who live at the bottom of the garden."

Bishop Demetrius flashed a smile; Mounir, though, appeared somewhat strained, almost troubled by my comparison, as he looked at the bishop for further elaboration.

"You must understand, Mr. James, we Copts have been living with their presence for nearly two thousand years. Your difficulties are not ours."

"Their familiarity makes it acceptable?"

"We have many stories, all of them verified by independent witnesses, affirming their existence. We are not talking about garden gnomes, as you infer. These men do exist. Furthermore, they represent the crown of ascetical life, for they have transcended every aspect of the ordinary."

"A state which Father Victor is committed to discovering for himself also," I ventured.

Bishop Demetrius nodded.

"Perhaps he will become a *saahih* one day," he said, then picked up a small book on the table.

"Mr. James," Bishop Demetrius continued. "I had intended to offer you a small gift this evening, one that you might find interesting. It is a book I wrote on the sanctity of letters. One letter in particular is the basis of all that we worship."

"May I ask what this letter might be, Father?"

"The *iota*. You will have seen it in the apse at Abu Fana when we performed holy office this afternoon."

"If I recall, what I saw there was a cross, not the letter *i*."

"That cross was made up of innumerable tiny *iotas* all woven together. The letter, by the way, is the first in the word *Jesus* in Coptic. In our morning praise we ask divine help to direct us to the *iota*, which we see as the name of our salvation, Jesus Christ. It is the basic unit for drawing the braided cross you saw at Abu Fana. Our life is embodied in it. *Iota* represents the essence of our belief, Mr. James."

I picked up the book that Bishop Demetrius kindly passed across his desk. The cover was dominated by an elaborate pattern made up of tiny *iotas* reminiscent of Celtic lettering on medieval Psalters.

"Please take the time to read it when you have a free moment," he said. "It may help you to understand the *sowah*. After all, they communicate in a language that is no longer like ours."

"When I was speaking to Father Victor, I sensed his capacity to talk was becoming more difficult also," I remarked.

"He may be under the influence of the *iota* already," Bishop Demetrius said with a wry smile. "Read the book and then decide."

I suddenly felt very tired. My thoughts were racing. I had not only the Holy Family's journey through Egypt to investigate but also other issues to deal with. Disembodied men and primary letters had become interwoven with a miraculous event. Suddenly I recalled the dream I had experienced in Cairo. Could it be that those strange dancing figures I had witnessed in the hall were my first encounter with the *sowah*? The thought seemed reasonable enough. After all, the figures in my dream were otherworldly, dreamlike.

Meanwhile, Bishop Demetrius stood up and came around the table to offer me his hand to kiss. The audience was now over.

At Ashmounein 22

THE NEXT MORNING MOUNIR AND
I drove out to the ruins of Hermopolis at Ashmounein, a few
kilometers north of Mallawi. In his *Vision*, Theophilus mentions
this place as one where the Holy Family's arrival had a profound
effect on the people living there. Not only did their appearance
cause many of the idols to crash to the ground (as they did at Tel
Basta in the Nile Delta), but their mere presence inspired resent-
ment among the priesthood and civil authorities.

It seems that the priests of Ashmounein felt threatened by the
family's popularity among ordinary folk as a result of the miracles performed by the infant Jesus. A tree at the entrance to the
city had already recognized his divinity and bowed before him.[112]
Theophilus is explicit in the interchange between child and tree:
"Blessed be your coming, O Lord Jesus Christ, the true Son of
God," the tree announced. To which Jesus replied, "Let no worm
be found in you forever." According to the fifth-century historian
Sozomen this tree, known as Persea, possessed prophylactic qualities: its bark could be used to heal the sick.

The Holy Family's visit to Hermopolis became a defining
moment in their journey. When the four horses at the gate were
shattered as they entered the city, even Governor Aphrodosius was
shocked. According to the *Gospel of Pseudo-Matthew* he remarked

to one of his advisors, "If this were the doing of our supreme god, these horses would not have fallen. It is a sign that we must revere this new God, otherwise we will suffer the fate of Pharaoh who was drowned along with his army." It is not surprising that the writer should resort to the book of Exodus for scriptural affirmation; the trouble was that the Egyptian ruler of the time was less reasonable. He overruled his governor, and demanded that the Holy Family be arrested and killed. To achieve his aim he devised an interesting stratagem. Ordering every man, woman, and child from the city, he then asked them to return one by one and be recognized.

At this point the chronicles are confusing. Suddenly a new character appears, that of Lazarus, whom Jesus was later to raise from the dead in Palestine. Lazarus, according to legend, was a court official and much esteemed by the ruler in Hermopolis. How he could be in two places at the same time is not addressed. Nonetheless, when two figures forged in brass overseeing the reentrance of the citizens to the city cried out, "Here is the king!" as the infant Jesus attempted to pass, Lazarus drew Joseph aside and asked him from where they had come. "Palestine," replied Joseph. Lazarus then took pity on the Holy Family and went to the ruler in order to pledge himself on behalf of the child. It is for this reason, so the story goes, that Jesus loved Lazarus and raised him from the dead in Bethany, Mary's hometown. The writer wished to ensure that one of Mary's kinsmen might come to their rescue in far-off Hermopolis. Narrative tidiness is important where hagiography is concerned.

By the time of their visit, the infant Jesus was in full possession of his powers. Not only did he render five camels into stone that had been blocking the road through the market, but he also healed many people of their infirmities. Such actions further angered the temple priests, who saw him as undermining their authority. They sent a contingent to arrest the Holy Family in a house believed to be where they were staying, only to find that someone had alerted them to the danger. According to Theophilus, they hid in an upper room while their host was arrested and taken away to be interrogated. The poor man, whose name was Apelon, so the *Coptic Synaxarium* relates, was later tortured in an attempt to make him confess. "They left my home three days ago," he lied to his captors, "and I do not know where they were going." Bruised and battered, Apelon eventually returned home, and advised Mary and Joseph to quickly make their escape.

In a few short weeks the family had managed to disrupt the entire social fabric of the city. Whereas in most places along the Nile they were warmly received, here in Hermopolis their very existence spelled disaster. Why was there so much resistance to them by the local authorities? Why had they not allowed the infant Jesus to perform his miracles before moving on to another town? After all, he had practiced them with impunity in other places. Why indeed had they wanted to kill him when they were neither associates of nor cared for Herod in faraway Palestine? There must have been other issues going on in the city that the appearance of the Holy Family merely exacerbated. When one considers what the city stood for, and the role of its tutelary deity, it is clear that the infant Jesus might have been perceived as a dangerous iconoclast. His very presence offered a challenge to the old ways by all those who oversaw the Pharaonic cult.

Hermopolis was the home of Thoth, the divine scribe and god of time. Not only was he the inventor of writing, but he was the "weigher of words" (*utcha metet*) as well, and so the god who empowered humanity with the beauty of language. Science was his creation—namely, geometry, astronomy, music, and numbers. In his Greek incarnation as Hermes he was the so-called messenger of the gods, and therefore a popular intercessory figure. He was preeminently the god of the horizon, a symbol of the first glimpse of the divine. Thoth was the consort of Maat, of divine harmony, and so by disposition the god of intellect. It is only natural that the deceased might wish to ask him to intercede on his behalf in the realm of Tuat. "I am the writing palette, O Thoth, and I have brought unto you your ink jar." In other words, make use of my poor body to write on it what you will. As regulator of time and the seasons, and so closely associated with the moon, Thoth was depicted on tomb walls as a mummy standing on *maat*, holding the emblems of life and stability.

Naturally the custodians of the cult of Thoth feared the advent of the infant Jesus arriving in their midst. As the embodiment of the divine Logos, these same attributes of Thoth belonged to Jesus also. The divine child was perhaps, to the Egyptian eye at least, a mirror image of Thoth. Appearing suddenly among them, performing miracles and healing the sick, such actions alone would have placed him in direct conflict with the temple priesthood. It became obvious that there was not enough room in Hermopolis for two such potent deities. A child-god and an ibis-headed god, each responsible for individual transformation, would inevitably clash. It is not surprising that idols crashed to the ground, and government agents were busy trying to discover the Holy Family's whereabouts: a seismic event had shaken the city to its foundations. From here on, nothing would be quite the same.

When Mounir and I walked through the gate into the ruins at Ashmounein that bright morning, all these ideas were on my mind. I tried to picture the sick and the lame clamoring to touch the infant Jesus while the priests of Thoth looked on. Here was the beginning of a popular movement that undermined their authority. By the actions of a child, his mother, and an elderly Joseph, they had been made to look like silly old men. Furthermore, this family was demeaning the deific presence of Thoth, the supreme scribe and weigher of words. Even as we entered the ruins of the temple, built during the reign of Ptolemy III (247–222 BC) in order to look for a Christian basilica constructed within its walls in the fifth century AD, I knew that we were entering a precinct whose demise was founded upon religious confrontation. The old gods were to be no match for the power of the new God in his incarnation as the infant Jesus. The argument between Thoth and Jesus was to end in the destruction of everything that Pharaonic religion stood for.

Walking among the columns of the ruined temple, I tried to locate the foundations of the basilica. Suddenly I recalled an image in Bishop Demetrius's little book that I had read the previous evening in the hostel. One of the figures depicted, the letter *A*, or *alpha* in its original form, was that of a bird. Over the process of time, the head of this bird had slowly metamorphosed into the letter *A*. The bird, possibly the head of the ibis itself, had been transformed into a form capable of bearing the burden of meaning that went beyond its earlier incarnation. The bird had become *A*, none other than the sound "Aaah" one makes when one opens one's lips. This told me something about the way we draw from one world images and ideas that finally express what we want in another.[113]

In the same way, the infant Jesus's appearance in Hermopolis transformed a society from one of allegiance to an ibis-headed god into one recognizing him as a future God-man. It was only natural that the old priesthood sought to rebuff what was transpiring before their eyes. Did not Thoth deserve their loyalty and protection? Equally, Thoth was already in the process of metamorphosis into that of Christ. The writer, the mathematician, the astronomer, and the weigher of words was to become none other than the architect of the world, the lodestone, the Logos. Thoth, it appears, could not be any of these, however, in his present incarnation as an Egyptian avatar. He was too immersed in an older dispensation, which limited his power to "save" humankind.

Mounir called out to me, and I walked over to where he was standing.

"Around here, Mr. James," he said, indicating with a wave of his hand the debris lying about, "you can see the outlines of the Christian basilica inside what was once the temple of Thoth."

"Like a yoke inside an egg," I observed. "In a sense, it reflects the Christian religion emerging from the old Pharaonic belief."

"The old gods have become shadows, Mr. James. The Holy Family's journey through our land has now made us custodians of their reality. We are participants in Christ's infancy and his subsequent realization as the God-man."

"It invites the question, of course: what happens to people like me who find it difficult to suspend our disbelief?"

"Perhaps you need to meet someone who is able to bridge the gap between faith and the physical world," replied Mounir, stepping out of the apse of the church to measure its width.

"I can think of men such as Father Abadir at Saint Bishoy, and Father Victor yesterday," I replied.

"These men possess what the Early Fathers called 'bare intellect' (*nous yimnos*). It is a term derived from the idea of utter simplicity, a state of infinite ignorance," replied Mounir.

"This, surely, is what the *sowah* possess."

"The *sowah* live in a state of ecstatic trance almost all the time," Mounir remarked. They have cast off from the earth like a balloon."

"This doesn't tell me how one reaches a state of 'bare intellect,' however," I said.

"Men join monasteries to learn how to live such a life." Mounir replied, placing his camera to his eye. He pressed the shutter a few times, capturing a line of columns as if they were trees on a country road.

I gazed over the rubble that was Hermopolis. It spread into the distance, brick walls that looked like ant hills, segments of Doric columns on the ground, entablatures half buried among weeds, a broken statue of an eagle and of a baboon, Thoth's sacred beast. Here was a metropolis of rubble, the place where Ra first appeared on earth. Thoth wrote his *Book of Breathing* here too, so that the soul might breathe forever. The eternal wordsmith in his guise as the ibis was thus able to write. It was not hard to sit at the feet of the divine scribe and observe his palette and inkpot.

"Last night," I remarked to Mounir as we made our way back to the vehicle, "I read the bishop's little book on the *iota*. I learned how to make black ink from green thorny gall, myrtle leaves, indigo, and black Arabic gum. This is how ink was made three thousand years ago. I can imagine Thoth preparing his papyrus before committing his words to paper. Hermopolis was a place of words."

"Which is ironic, when you consider that Christ wrote nothing in his lifetime," Mounir added.

"Perhaps the world needs to heed the words of the old gods once in awhile, just so that time might be divested of its impermanence," I added, casting a final glance back at the solitary pillars that were the temple-church of Ashmounein, the home of Thoth, the place of confrontation and miracles.

23

The Well of the Cloud

DURING THE YEAR AD 130 THE
Emperor Hadrian made a voyage up the Nile, ostensibly to
survey his dominion. He was in good spirits, at the height of his
intellectual and political powers, a Hellenist at heart, and in love
with all things Greek. Wishing to emulate his heroes, Hadrian
conceived a passion for a good-looking young man from Bithynia
named Antinius. The boy seemed full of life, and though disliked
by Hadrian's officers, who despised homosexuality as little more
than a "Greek disease," Antinius was always on hand to assuage
his emperor's passion as the entourage made its way south toward
Thebes.

Unfortunately the young man met with an accident, drowning after attempting to row a boat back to shore. The chronicles
suggest that it was no accident; rather, that Antinius wanted to
prove his love for Hadrian in an act of self-sacrifice. Hadrian was
deeply affected by the loss of his friend, and vowed to enshrine
his name by founding a city near the spot where he had died. He
ordered construction to begin on Antineopolis at a nearby necropolis containing the ruins of a temple of Ramses II. According to
the chronicles, Bissa was a permanent settlement for sorcerers who
were later used by Pharaoh to challenge Moses to the legendary
"duel of sticks" as described in the book of Exodus.[114] Built in less

than four years, Antineopolis covered an area of three hundred acres and boasted a population of twenty-five thousand at its peak.

Conceived out of an act of blighted passion, Antineopolis later became one of the four official Greek cities of the kingdom under the Ptolemies.[115] Its inhabitants enjoyed a rare privilege. Hadrian, in a bid to create a new, stronger generation that retained the strength of the Egyptians and the intelligence of the Greeks, granted its Greek citizens the right to marry ethnic Egyptian women. One could argue that Hadrian had been the first to preside over the creation of a superior race by this act of eugenic intervention. Antineopolis was to be a perfect city inhabited by a perfect people. He wanted it to remain a living cenotaph to his lost love— perfect in every way, beautiful, eternal in its grandeur. At its heart lay the tomb of Antinius, his young lover, symbol of his wayward passion for Hellenism. Hadrian had built a monument to his own delusion.

The city was to remain blighted by death in the years that followed the time of the Ptolemies. During the reign of Diocletian, it became a killing field for Christians. It is said that more martyrs died here than in any other part of Egypt. Tens of thousands of men, women, and children were put to death for refusing to confess their allegiance to the emperor as god. Sacred books were burned, churches destroyed, and men removed from office for not making public confession. Even freed slaves were deprived of their civil rights. Antineopolis was turned into a conflagration of bodies in the years following the public edict of AD 303 promulgated by Galerius in the emperor's name.

One of the world's earliest genocidal acts had become a reality. It may be no accident that Diocletian died by his own hand (AD 313), blind and half mad, during the same year that Emperor Constantine issued an act of indulgence toward Christianity. Galerius, Diocletian's henchman, had already passed away in AD 311, his body suppurating with ulcers, worms eating away at his flesh. According to the historian and traveler Ibn Jubayr, Saladin[116] ordered the destruction of Antineopolis in the twelfth century, imposing on all ships sailing north along the Nile the task of carrying one stone to Cairo.[117] Love and death were finally dispersed.

Today, the city is little more than an extended ruin of baked brick walls and abandoned granite columns, many of them recently excavated by Italian archaeologists. In his *Lausiac History* Palladius tells us that he spent four years in the region of Antinoe, residing in numerous monasteries there. "Twelve hundred men are settled around the city," he writes, "who live by their hands and are extremely ascetic."

In spite of its reputation as a death camp, by the fifth and sixth centuries Antineopolis became home to many monasteries for both men and women. This was in part because of the memory of its martyrs, but also because the Holy Family, tradition tells us, stopped by at least two places on their way to Ashmounein. At a place known as Beer el-Sahaba, not far from the ruins of Antineopolis, lies a spring known as the Well of the Cloud. At Kom Mariya, near the village of Dier Abu Hennes, stands a hill upon which the travelers rested. It appears that they were warmly received in the region. In this village, too, Empress Helena three centuries later built a church dedicated to Anba Yehness (Abba Johannis).

The Well of the Cloud is important as the place where a miracle occurred. Apparently a cloud guided the Holy Family to the well (like the Star of Bethlehem?), thus confirming Isaiah's prophecy where it states, "The Lord rides on a swift cloud, and shall come to Egypt."[118] More importantly, Egypt "shall be moved by his presence," and its heart shall "melt in the midst of it." Isaiah uses apocalyptic imagery in his vision of the country's demise, which will occur as judgment for not abandoning the old gods in order to embrace Yahweh. "And the spirit of Egypt shall fail in the midst thereof: . . . and they shall seek to the idols, and to the charmers, and to them that have familiar spirits, and to the wizards."[119] This place of magicians would remain resistant to the coming of Christianity until after the time of Diocletian's persecutions.

Then, suddenly, the magicians were converted, and monasteries blossomed in the wilderness. The burial place of a grief-stricken emperor's lover was transformed forever by the passage of the Holy Family through the region.

Mounir and I boarded a car ferry with our vehicle and crossed the Nile to the village of Deir al-Mulaq. We had left Mallawi early that morning, intent on visiting Hermopolis, Antineopolis, and the Well of the Cloud before returning that evening. According to Mounir, a number of monasteries still survived in various villages scattered below the Ansana Escarpment. Places such as Abu Hennes, Al-Barsha, and Al-Nasara still flourished in this predominantly Islamic community.

Even as we crossed the river on the ferry crowded with farmers, cars, and livestock, I could make out the escarpment extending northward into the distance. It was an arid edifice of stone, once home to Pharaonic catacombs and ascetics' caves. It seemed that the living and the dead cohabited around Antineopolis with little thought of the other. On the riverbank women gathered to wash clothes, and children played in the shallows. Once the ferry had arrived and lowered its ramp, we drove north through palm groves to the monastery of Al-Barsha to pay our respects to Saint Bishoy, its patron saint.

I allowed myself to be jolted along the road from one monastery to another, until we reached the mound known as Kom Mariya outside Deir Abu Hennes. We left the car and, water bottles in hand, clambered up the hill, from which we could see the surrounding river land under cultivation, as well as the ruins of Antineopolis. To the east the Ansana Escarpment was plainly visible, its height reducing the village minarets to ragged needles. Studying the ruins through my binoculars, I could see black-bricked ruins, crumbling monastic cells, sand filled with pieces of pottery and ostraca, arches half buried in sand, Corinthian columns and pediments abandoned in culverts. For six centuries Antineopolis had been a thriving metropolis; now it was all but lost amid sand dunes.

"Imagine building an entire city in memory of a lost lover," I said to Mounir, who was busy excavating what looked like the portion of an ancient amphora with his foot.

"Hadrian was mad, Mr. James."

"He was an old man out of touch with his body and his mind, it seems. Building a new city can be ample excuse for nonreflection, I guess," I replied.

"In contrast, on this mound where we stand, the Holy Family chose to rest one hot afternoon, before making their way into Deir Abu Hennes. Unlike Hadrian, their love for one another was absolute."

"Which passion is more real: that of the Holy Family or Hadrian's, I wonder? They both chose an unlikely place to test their belief in the afterlife. This is an exceedingly barren place, after all," I said.

"A prophecy determined the Holy Family's visit to Beer el-Sahaba, Mr. James. It is why these ruins will eventually turn into dust, whereas the Well of the Cloud down the road will always be here," Mounir observed.

It did not take long to drive the short distance to an outlying Christian necropolis near Beer el-Sahaba where the Well of the Cloud was located. On the way we passed a large hill, which was the burial ground for many of Diocletian's victims. It was hard to imagine that beneath this hard earth lay countless remains of early Christians who gave their lives for their faith, rather than become apostates in the name of Rome.

"I recall visiting the museum in the monastery of the martyrs at Akhmim on my last visit," Mounir remarked as we drove past. "The glass cabinets in one of the rooms contained the mummies of men and women who had been killed during the Diocletian persecutions. On one day alone Arianus, the local governor, ordered over eight thousand executions. It must have been appalling, this savage murder of innocent people. What I saw in these glass cases were the dried-out bodies of people like ourselves. Their hair was still intact, and they were clothed as they had died. Each bore a crack in the skull or a broken neck as testament to the way they had been slaughtered. I wondered then whether I would have shown the courage that they had, should I have been faced with the same choice."

"These poor people, it seems, were incapable of renouncing their faith, not even to save their life," I said.

We drove on a little way to the outskirts of the Christian necropolis, a vast conglomeration of tombs that extended toward a string of ruined monasteries lying on the southern slope of the Ansana Escarpment. Wherever we looked, we found ourselves surrounded by empty tombs. Anchorite caves, Pharaonic tombs, and crumbling monastery walls, they all seemed to blend into one another. That Hadrian had made his small contribution in the form of a city was appropriate. The secular and sacred had merged; the flesh and the spirit had become one beside this great mausoleum of the dead.

Our driver parked the car a few yards from the Well of the Cloud, which turned out to be not much more than a hole in the earth surmounted by a bucket-and-pulley system suspended between cement pillars. We walked over to the structure while the driver proceeded to lower the bucket into the well. He felt that we should at least fill our water bottles with its miraculous fluid.

"The drink alone will be worth the trip," I said.

"Such an insignificant spot, Mr. James. A well in the desert: why should a cloud appear here, I wonder?" Mounir asked.

"Why should a cloud appear at all? And in a country where rain is all but unimaginable," I said.

Meanwhile Mounir filled our water bottles from the bucket our driver had kindly hauled to the surface.

"The cloud stood above this very spot as something unknowable, it seems. The Holy Family quenched their thirst in its shade," he said.

"As we are doing now," I replied, accepting a water bottle. The water tasted cool, and without any hint of salt.

Finally we started walking back toward the car, conscious, I think, that the invisible cloud above us had its own silver lining. We were in the shade of an isolated nimbus in the middle of a desert dedicated to a madman's blighted love and a family forever on the run.

Center of the World 24

IT IS UNLIKELY THAT THE HOLY
family would have stopped at Al-Amarna, the city founded by
Akhenaton, as they passed by its ruins on their way upriver to
Dairut, given that the city had long since been abandoned. After
leaving Hermopolis, their destination, unknowingly, was to be
Mount Qussqam at Al-Muharraq. At this point on their journey, they were under considerable pressure: Herod's soldiers were
rumored to be close by.

Theophilus in his *Vision* maintains that the infant Jesus, now in
full control of his theurgic powers, used them to miraculous effect
among villagers afflicted with disease or mental defects whom they
met along the way. "The inhabitants of this town were very chari-
table," he wrote of a place called Kenis. "And the Holy Family
remained there several days. The infant Jesus wrought many miracles in that place, and all those who had diseases came to Him with
faith, and He healed them in His abundant grace." Indeed, when
a certain carpenter living in Kenis heard of their arrival, he hurried
to meet Joseph, whom he knew as a friend from meeting him in
Jerusalem some years earlier.

According to the *Vision*, this carpenter friend pleaded with
Joseph to intercede with the infant Jesus on behalf of his son, who
had been insane since birth. "In him was a cruel and pitiless demon

that actually provoked the boy to dash himself against the ground in frenzy." So vehement was this demon that it caused the boy to froth at the mouth and utter foul diatribes: "What have I to do with you, O Jesus of Nazareth? Have you come to torment us? We left Jerusalem to you, yet now you come to this town to torment us. Verily you are the Son of God." To which the infant Jesus replied: "Accursed one, leave the boy this instant."

Through Al-Qusia, Sanabu, and Mir the family traveled, stopping for as long as people made them feel welcome. At Al-Qusia the infant Jesus entered a temple and tore down seven veils concealing the statue of a god. Naturally the priests objected to his behavior, fearing that their authority had been undermined. They urged its inhabitants to drive the Holy Family out of town. Accordingly, Jesus placed a curse upon Al-Qusia.

Outside the town of Mir, the family rested for a short while to eat. There, Theophilus relates, the infant Jesus took Joseph's staff of olivewood and planted it in the earth. Immediately the staff sprouted leaves and gave forth olives. The infant blessed the spot, declaring the tree to be a perpetual memorial to his presence there.

Reading the *Vision* closely, one senses that by this time Mary was at her wits' end. The pressure of the past few years of constant traveling had left her in a state of depression. She was no longer the young virgin of Nazareth who had received the archangel Gabriel in a state of perplexity and awe some years before. Any memory she might have had of her conversation with him must have seemed like a distant dream compared to her present predicament. Had she truly found favor with God? Would her son be called the Son of the Most High? Might his kingdom have no end?[120] In her present state, trying to hold the family together against seemingly insurmountable odds, such remarks must have caused her to question her own sanity. Did she recall her days of innocence as a temple virgin in Jerusalem before Joseph had been chosen as her husband, not to mention the birth of her child under difficult circumstances?

One thing was certain: Mary could not forget their hasty departure from Judea under the threat of death. This reality alone surely must have made her realize the precarious nature of their situation. The prospect of preserving a "kingdom not of this world" from desecration because of Herod's desire to kill her child was still very much in her hands.

Mary's despair is vividly described by Theophilus. She feared not only Herod's soldiers but also anyone who might attempt to take Jesus from her. She railed against this foreign land of Egypt, their exile in towns and villages that were not their own, the constant fatigue of travel, and the brigands that accosted them. She still could not forget what had happened at Tel Basta at the onset of their journey, when two men stole her son's sandals. She even despaired of surviving herself. Her constant fear, it seems, was that she might live to see what she called his "great affliction"—namely, the death of her son on the cross. "Would that they might kill me before killing you in order that I may not see your great affliction." This is the talk of a woman stretched to her limit. Nor would this mood change until after her second encounter with the two robbers from Tel Basta, who had continued to follow the Holy Family up the Nile.

One day, they found themselves accosted by these same men as they approached Mount Qussqam. It was a moment of reckoning for Joseph and Mary. The men were armed with daggers, and harangued the family for leading them so far into Egypt, insisting that this time they would not be so lenient. At one point they tore the infant Christ from Mary's arms, stripped him of his clothing, then ripped off her veil for good measure. They reduced Joseph to not much more than an old man standing naked on the road. As for Salome, she quickly summed up what was happening, and threw her clothes on the ground to prevent them touching her.

One can only imagine the utter humiliation of the Holy Family at this moment: they stood on the road wearing little or no clothing, a child no doubt screaming in his mother's arms, under the protection of an old man who was too weak to offer them any real support. How did Joseph feel? An impotent old fool, a doddering idiot? No wonder Mary broke down and implored the angel Gabriel to come to their rescue.

The names of these thieves were Dumachus, an Egyptian by birth, and Titus, a Syrian Jew. Little is known about them except that their destiny, according to tradition, was to be crucified alongside Jesus Christ at Calvary. That their desire was to deprive the Holy Family of their clothing in both Tel Basta and outside Mir suggests a hidden agenda relating to the subsequent scourging of Christ by Pontius Pilate. The future Son of Man must be shown up for what he is—a mountebank, a wizard, no more than a precocious child whose powers are the bane of everyone concerned. If Herod's bravos could not find and eliminate him, then it was up to a couple of thieves to complete the task. While Herod's soldiers represented official disapproval of their existence, these thieves reflected the final approbation of society in general. The Christ child had to be utterly humiliated, even killed, before he was able to inflict upon the world his transcendent view of reality. The world, at least according to the state and its people, could not afford to have a new spiritual dimension imposed *from above*. To overturn the status quo was clearly the first step along the road to destroying the belief systems of Jewish, Roman, and Egyptian society as a whole, not to mention the Roman Empire itself.

Was there any hope left? Only, it seems, if the thieves might argue among themselves. It was the Egyptian villain who first realized the consequence of their actions when he saw Mary in tears. Theophilus relates that he saw "on their faces a light greater than the world. The child resembles a prince, the like of whom I have never seen before." He then suggested to his accomplice that since they would likely rob someone else that night, he, the Syrian, could have his share of the spoils if the Holy Family's clothing might be considered as his share. The Egyptian could then return the clothing to its rightful owners. Was this not a reasonable deal, he asked his friend? Eventually the Syrian agreed, since he probably thought that the night's spoils would be higher in value than these few ragged garments. Thereupon the Egyptian gave the clothes back to Mary and Joseph.

The infant Jesus raised his hand and made a sign of the cross. When the thieves had finally gone their way, he turned to his mother and for the first time prophesied his own death: "O Mary, my holy and virgin mother, one day the Jews will crucify me in Jerusalem, and these two thieves will be crucified along with me. The Egyptian who returned our garments will be on my right hand side. Because he will confess his faith in me and believe in my death on the Cross, he will be the first to enter Paradise, even before Adam and all his other children," the *Vision* relates.

Christ's tragic destiny is thus announced on a dusty back road in Egypt, far from the place where his crucifixion would eventually occur. It was as if the announcement of this momentous event required the anonymity of such an inauspicious spot to authenticate it. Christ was to die for humankind in order that kings, thieves, and men of little faith might realize the error of their ways. Egypt was to become the birthplace of a prophecy that would one day change the world.

The infant Jesus was aware of the implications of his humiliation at the hands of the brigands. "It is on this spot that you have shed sweet tears over my body," he stated. "In future, all who have been stripped of their garments will receive my healing power. They will be made whole." The meaning of his remark is evident: those who find themselves humiliated in Christ's name will receive the "sweet tears" of his being as their only solace. It marks the beginning of Christ's ministry, the embryonic moment of his deific life on earth. The stripping of his body became the leitmotif of his future existence as an avatar, as a teacher, and finally as one crucified. He seems to be telling us that we too must endure such a humiliating disrobing in public if we are to become a witness to our faith. Paradise is for those who are prepared to revoke their former life in pursuit of this final act of apotheosis: being crucified on the cross of this world at the "right hand" of one's own deific nature.

Theophilus tells us also that after the infant Jesus had uttered his prophecy, the "night became slightly darker." Joseph, who by this time was exhausted by recent events, roundly turned on Mary and blamed her for allowing them to be caught out on such a lonely road. "Now that we have reached this desert place, and the night is upon us, I do not know where to go," he said. "If God had not protected us, we would have been killed." The infant Jesus, meanwhile, bestowed upon Joseph his beatific smile. "Father," he said. "Do not speak so harshly to my holy virgin mother. It is the will of my good Father that I should perform these things dealing with humanity. It is not you who direct me, it is I who direct all the world, and conduct you wherever I wish." At last his secret was out.

The entire trip throughout Egypt has been the infant Jesus's doing. He has orchestrated their difficulties for the good of the world. Affliction, pain, and anguish are concomitant with faith, he seems to be saying. The Holy Family itself must stand for and endure what all humankind is called upon to do in the name of spiritual understanding. God wants all people to strip themselves bare of every illusion that makes the journey *seem* worthwhile.

Finally, that night, the Holy Family climbed Mount Qussqam in order to find shelter. Stumbling about in the dark, Salome suddenly discovered a washbasin and a jug near a well outside an abandoned house. When she attempted to raise water from the well in order to bathe the child, she found it to be dry. Informing Mary of their predicament, the Holy Virgin then approached the well with the infant Jesus in her arms. At once the child "stretched forth his finger and blessed it," and the spring once more bubbled forth. They had found a temporary home at last.

In staying here for a period of over six months, the Holy Family would make Al-Muharraq (Arabic: "to burn," alluding to the arid nature of the surrounding countryside, and the local practice of burning the fields to rid them of weeds) into the most sacred place in Egypt, second only to Jerusalem as a place of pilgrimage for Christians. The mountain and the monastery that would later be constructed here, probably in the fourth century, was to become the true *omphalos* of Coptic Christianity. The so-called washbasin residing there to this day, which turned out to be a large slab of marble, would in due time become a part of the altar in the Church of the Holy Virgin inside the monastery.[121] This altar and the church are said to be the first in Egypt, built as they were before that of the church of Saint Mark in Alexandria.

25
On the Holy Mountain

MEANWHILE, IN FARAWAY JERUSALEM, other events were beginning to unfold. Frustrated and angered that his agents had not been able to locate the Holy Family in either Palestine or Egypt, Herod ordered more soldiers to fan out across the country. Through his spy network news reached him of a Jewish family traveling in the Upper Nile region with a son who was able to perform miracles.

Theophilus suggests that it was Satan himself who told Herod of the Holy Family's whereabouts. "Tell the soldiers to proceed as far as Qussqam, and then let them travel to the west side of the mountain. The family is living alone in a house there, since no one will give them permanent shelter in the land of Egypt," the *Vision* tells us. Whereupon Herod directed his soldiers to find the family and bring them back to Jerusalem alive. "I want to kill them with my own hands. Furthermore I will give ten talents of gold to whoever finds them, and you shall be great in my kingdom."

Herod, however, did not take into his calculations the prospect of angelic intervention. According to Theophilus a relative of Joseph who lived in Jerusalem, a man named Moses, heard of Herod's plans and, with "divine help," sped to Mount Qussqam, reaching the house where the Holy Family lived in the space of three days. It was a miraculous journey, enacted mostly at night.

When Joseph saw his friend coming toward him one morning, he was taken aback. Moses and he embraced, before he led his friend into the house, where Salome was bathing the infant Jesus. Exhausted after his journey Moses sat down and told them of the fears he held for their safety, now that Herod's men knew where they lived. He then went on to relate how all the children under a certain age had been killed in Bethlehem, and how Satan had revealed their whereabouts to the king.

"Satan approached me in the desert also," he told them. "'Moses,' he said. 'You have toiled and labored in vain because lo! the soldiers are preceding you and are hastening before you. Do not exhaust yourself in vain.' But I tricked Satan. I told him to let me return home in case Herod's troops killed me also. Satan laughed at me, then disappeared from sight. I think he believed me."

The Holy Family's joy at seeing Moses was thus short-lived. Utterly exhausted, this man who had traveled so far and with such speed to warn them of the threat posed by Herod's soldiers, requested that he might lie down to sleep. Moreover, his news had been received with consternation, particularly by Mary. She broke down and sobbed. But the infant Jesus once more intervened to comfort her, as children often do to their mothers when they feel they are unhappy. He turned to Moses and said, "You have come in order that you might inform us of the danger we face. For that we are thankful. Your labor shall be rewarded. Take hold of the stone on which I am bathed, and put it beneath your head. Sleep and rest awhile."

Thankful, Moses took the stone and placed it beneath his head. Then he turned his face to the east and, according to Theophilus, "gave up the ghost." The poor man had fulfilled his destiny. Instrumental in saving the Holy Family from certain death at the hands of Herod, it seemed that there was no further reason for him to live. "Joseph took his body and buried it in the house under the threshold." To this day, the spirit of Moses watches over the Church of the Holy Virgin at Al-Muharraq. The sacred stone on which the journey of the Holy Family is inscribed in Hebrew also rests within the monastery.

It was to be the lowest point of their journey in Egypt. A friend dead in their arms, the threat of soldiers arriving on their doorstep at any moment, and now a period of relative tranquility all but ended, there was nothing for them to do but leave Mount Qussqam and make their escape. One can imagine the despair of Joseph and Mary. "Woe is me, O light of my eyes!" Mary was heard to say. More than ever she feared for her son's safety. "I have left my country and all other countries to come to this place. Beloved Son, lift up your eyes and look at your lonely and wretched mother. See the anguish in my heart."

The child revealed himself as the world's comforter. He spoke to his mother, saying, "You have wept enough. Your pain has touched me. May the will of my Father be done." On hearing these words, Mary's fears were allayed. She felt renewed strength of purpose. She was the mother not of a child in exile but of the Son of God.

The will of the Father had been uttered. The Christ child was fully conscious of his destiny. His family's burden must be lightened. He, the God-man in waiting, must take charge of his own destiny. It was up to him, through the Father, to bring to a close this painful interlude in their lives. Nearly four years of wandering was enough. No family should have to bear such a difficult period of travail, least of all a divine one. The ever-present threat of death must cease. Now it was time to return to Palestine as its savior, and not as Herod's prisoner. The death of Moses was a sign. He had come to them to impart news, and had died as a result. It was up to him, the Christ child, to begin the journey home.

That morning in Al-Muharraq, Mounir and I were fully aware of the significance our own journey. We too had been in exile—from ordinary life and the responsibilities it entailed. It was hard to define our feelings as we gazed through the window of our taxi while it sped through fields and palm groves toward the western edge of the desert. Weeks on the road, traveling throughout the delta and the Wadi Natrun, from Al-Farma to Alexandria, Sakha to Memphis—indeed, to so many monasteries, churches, and ruins along the Nile, while meeting such a variety of people along the way—had left me bereft of any sense of what it was like to live in the modern world. At this point in my pilgrimage, I could not imagine what life would be like without the reality of the Holy Family's journey tempering my everyday existence. The many worlds that were Egypt had washed away all residue of who I was before.

Although Mounir had made the trip on a number of occasions, and tried to visit Deir al-Muharraq monastery at least once a year to make a retreat, he confessed that he also felt a sense of trepidation. Mount Qussqam was the most holy place in Egypt, and he always approached it in a state of awe. It was not just a monastery in the desert but a state of mind, he told me. After all, Mount Qussqam was the only other place besides Nazareth that the Holy Family had lived for any length of time during the years of Christ's youth.

"It has special significance for us all," he said, as our vehicle approached the monastery.

High walls surrounded Deir al-Muharraq. Palm groves in the area lent a touch of pastel green to the brown, mud-brick tessellations on its ramparts and to the many bell towers breaking up the skyline. The place was like a castle in the sky, a princely haven, a city lost in the desert. Cupolas and crosses protruded above the wall also, as did clumps of palm fronds. Mounir had understated its effect. "Special significance" seemed to me to be the least of its attributes.

The gatekeeper allowed us to pass through into the monastery grounds. Mounir entered an office nearby in search of a friend who he hoped might show us to our rooms. I wandered about the grounds, taking in the buildings and churches. It still felt a little strange to be at Mount Qussqam after so many weeks on the road. The trip seemed like a blur of monastery gates, monks wearing black vestments, and long conversations that went late into the night. I wanted to believe I was here at last, even though my mind was still gazing at Tem's statue among the ruins at Tel Basta, or standing in the church at Gebel al-Tair.

Mounir soon returned, accompanied by a monk named Father Zachariah, a senior lecturer at the Coptic seminary there. He was a younger man, well groomed, and with a pleasant, welcoming demeanor. He spoke perfect English, informing me later how he had attended school at Saint Edward College in Malta. English rather than Arabic was his mother tongue, so I knew that any discussions that we might have together would be of great interest. As soon as Mounir and I had deposited our bags in our rooms, Father Zachariah agreed to show us around the grounds.

"The Church of the Holy Virgin was built during the first century," he told us. "The monastery itself was founded in the fourth century at the time of Abba Pachomius in AD 342. He believed that the site of the Holy Family's house should be incorporated into the structure. That same stone where the Christ child was attended by Holy Mary and Salome is now a part of the altar in the church."[122]

I looked across the courtyard at the old Church of the Holy Virgin, built next to the Church of Saint George, surprised by its size. It hardly looked grand enough to be the home of the most significant relic in Egypt. I remarked on this fact to Father Zachariah.

"We owe its humble appearance to Patriarch Theophilus, the same man who wrote the *Vision* you are carrying," he replied. "On a visit here from Alexandria sometime before he died, he heard a voice in his prayers asking him not to build an imposing edifice. Mary, it seems, appeared on a throne of light to tell him her son did not wish to be remembered in this way, and that he should leave the church as it was, so that subsequent generations would recall her son's humility."

"Theophilus regarded this place as a holy mountain, I presume. He actually compared it to the Mount of Olives," I said.

"It is in this very place, too, that Theophilus was granted his vision of the Holy Family's journey throughout Egypt. He wrote down the *Vision* shortly after his encounter with Mary and the angels Gabriel and Michael. We must accept that Christ did not want the trials of his family to go unremembered. Al-Muharraq, where they had rested for over six months, was to be elevated into that of a second Jerusalem."

"It couldn't be a fabrication, perhaps?" I ventured, determined to test Father Zachariah's credulity now rather than later.

"Patriarch Theophilus was a realist, Mr. James. For him to experience a vision such as the one he relates means that it must surely have happened. Besides, there is enough evidence today to suggest that all he wrote down is correct. The nature of such miracles is not for us to question, however. History and tradition affirm what we have no reason to doubt."

We took off our shoes at the entrance to the Church of the Holy Virgin. It was a strange sensation entering one of the oldest churches in Christendom. It was here, tradition tells us, that the first Eucharist was celebrated after Christ had risen from the dead. In attendance on that day were Christ himself, Mary, Salome, Anna, Mary Magdalene, and the apostles. I tried to picture this remarkable congregation as it arrived on a cloud one evening.[123] Why such a remote place—and in Egypt? But then I decided not to ask any more questions. The ancient iconostasis before the altar was as perfectly made as any I had seen so far on my travels. I thought of Bishop Demetrius and his *iotas*: here they were again, transformed into a dark wooden screen. Hanging at intervals in front of the iconostasis were eight ostrich eggs, symbols of providence.

"The construction of the church fulfilled the prophecy of Isaiah where he said, 'On that day there will be an Altar to the Lord in the center of the Land of Egypt,'"[124] Father Zachariah explained. "For us, it is the most sacred place in Egypt."

Mounir and I paid our respects with a short prayer before the sanctuary. Father Zachariah then led me forward to a square aperture in the iconostasis with a view of the sanctuary beyond. From there one could see the ancient stone altar, covered in velvet cloth, on which the infant Jesus was reputedly washed. This was the center of the world—indeed, the sacred center of Coptic Christianity. I thought of the black stone known as the Kaaba in Mecca, or the Stone of Scone in Scotland, and how certain objects retain a numinosity not imparted to other objects. Of all the significant events in the life of Christ such as his birth, the Last Supper, his baptism, or the crucifixion, this place where the infant Jesus had been bathed and dressed by Mary and Salome was of the utmost importance. It was the outer point on the radius of Christ's life. From here he would return to Palestine to begin his ministry in the years ahead.

Father Zachariah took us inside the adjoining Church of Saint George, built in 1888 by the abbot Qummus Salib. I was immediately taken by the marble iconostasis donated to the church by the Italian government. Several of its icons were of superior artistic merit, relying as they did on a background of gold leaf and a floor effect painted in deep green. Although more elegant than the church next door, incorporating as it did a number of Byzantine features, the sanctuary was no less atmospheric than its older counterpart. Father Zachariah informed me this was in part due to the fact that four monks noted for their sanctity were buried here. It was they who imparted to the Church of Saint George its deep sense of repose.

I asked Father Zachariah whether he might direct me to the monastic library, said to hold some of the oldest codices in Greek, Coptic, Aramaic, and Arabic in Egypt. I wanted to study some of the illuminated manuscripts to see whether Bishop Demetrius's belief was true: that their designs were based upon the principle of the *iota.* Unfortunately, he informed me that the library was not open at this hour. The librarian, Father Angelus, only worked on certain days, and needed to be formally asked to open the room. Was this possible, I asked? Father Zachariah shrugged his shoulder. He then told me that the man normally did not meet with outsiders, particularly foreigners. The omens were not good.

"Does he resent Westerners?" I asked

"Not at all, Mr. James. But he is a man of great piety. Speaking with members of the public disrupts his tranquility. He is happier remaining with his books, with his studies, and with his prayers. There is no man like him in Egypt."

"You seem to have a special affection for him, Father," I said.

"He is my teacher," Father Zachariah confessed. "I will speak to him on your behalf, however. Perhaps he will agree to meet with you this evening, after supper."

"Would it be possible?" I almost pleaded.

"We must leave it in his hands. Father Angelus is a man of deep opinion. Sometimes I think of him as a *saahih*, though he perhaps would not like me saying so."

"I was told that *sowah* do not appear in our world, that they live in the desert."

"It does not prevent me from thinking of Father Angelus as one of them, Mr. James. Perhaps he is a secret *saahih*, who knows! I will inform you after supper whether he will receive you."

I glanced at Mounir. He in turn was looking somewhat quizzically at me. It was clear that between us we were already preparing for an encounter that neither of us really expected might happen. Perhaps Al-Muharraq would indeed turn out to be the center of the world, not just for Egyptians, but for us as well.

26 *Father Angelus Speaks*

AFTER SUPPER THAT EVENING IN
the refectory, I returned to my room to await the call from
Father Angelus, should it come. I had no idea what to expect
from a man whom I had not met, yet whom I already believed
to be someone of considerable insight and experience. The few
words Father Zachariah had said to me about him had aroused
my interest. What sort of man would he be? Would he dismiss
my questions as no more than those of idle curiosity? I thought of
Father Abadir back in Saint Bishoy, his voice a reminder to me of
how delicate and subdued spiritual inquiry can be. Because of the
nature of their quest, men like Abadir and Angelus spend their
lives on a journey that appears to have no end. The Holy Family's
journey throughout Egypt may have been their model, but each
had worked out his own particular route.

Deir al-Muharraq represented the end of my own journey also.
I had traveled so far and for so long in the footsteps of the Holy
Family that all other realities had slipped from my thoughts. I
had become a sojourner along their way. I had steeped myself
in their predicament, and had lost all sense of what it was like
to live a normal life. Was it possible, I asked myself, to attain
to a state of simple intelligence, and admit to no separation or
division in one's capacity to believe?

I kept telling myself that making a demand on the all but impossible is precisely what Father Abadir or Mother Nadeen would do each day, and every hour, of their lives. They were not immune from the same self-questioning that I was prone to. Even Pope Shenouda must have asked the same questions of himself when he was living in his cave. Certainly Dionysius the Areopagite had suffered from this affliction if one goes by what he wrote. He spoke of *agnosia*, of "unknowing," as the basis of his search. It was not that he did not believe; rather, Dionysius knew that only by setting aside all that can be known could the Unknown be realized.

My dilemma was that I understood these things in principle, but lacked the ability to translate them into practice. This is why I had spent so many weeks on the road re-creating the world of the Holy Family in Egypt. Their journey was a prototype for the one I was making in my head. Every crisis along the way was a spiritual crisis for me, as it had been for them. Herod, the robbers, the sick and the afflicted, the temple gods that fell to the ground in their presence, the intervention by angels, and mysterious clouds that appeared above wells, all these things were metaphors for a larger encounter with the idea of divine exile. The Christ child was engaging in an exploration of himself. He was subjecting himself to the "things of this world," to the limitations of created being as he and his family journeyed up the Nile. He had to learn how to deal with what was inherently flawed in its appearance in order to render it in his image as one of perfection. While in Egypt, the Christ child became an acolyte of himself in order that he might transform himself into the master of the world. I understood this now: that the infant Jesus, whom I had probably regarded as a divine yet unruly child, remained in a state of naive innocence throughout the period of his journey.

The years that he spent in Egypt were in every way a preparation for his future life. Even as a near five-year-old he probably spoke a little ancient Egyptian, or Coptic, as well as Aramaic, the language of his parents. It is not unreasonable to believe that he was Egyptian in the cultural sense, since he must have played with children of his own age. By fleeing to Egypt he became a child of the world, not just of Palestine. It brought up a question, of course: was Herod's intention to kill the children of Bethlehem a part of the divine plan, in the same way that Judas's betrayal of Christ was in the Garden of Gethsemane?

These are controversial ideas, of course, but they pressed themselves upon me on more than one occasion during the course of my journey. Egypt had imposed them upon me, whether I liked it or not.

Experience in other parts of the world, on other journeys that I have made over the years, particularly when dealing with indigenous peoples, had already alerted me to the need to "listen to the land." One forgets how important soil and water and weather are in formulating ideas. In Egypt one is always living within the proximity of both the fertile and the arid. There is no escaping the fact that all Egyptian thought, from the predynastic period over five thousand years ago through to its latest transformation under Islam, has been influenced by a river's inundation, clear skies throughout the year, a vast expanse of sand, and rich black earth bursting forth. Such contrasts have made Egypt the land that it is: none other than a place steeped in questions. It is no surprise, then, that the Holy Family *needed* to come here in order to bathe in its waters.

Reaching the monastery of Deir al-Muharraq, I was conscious that the place was extremely important in the history of Christianity, even though few in the West know of this sanctuary. In 4 BC or thereabouts, an old man named Joseph had led a donkey bearing his wife, Mary, and the infant Jesus, along with their servant Salome, to Mount Qussqam in search of a place to rest for the night. They did not know what to find there. They did not even know whether they might discover water. In the glare of history it all seems so precarious; that a simple peasant family from Palestine might hope to find refuge in a harsh but generous land. In the light of this event, was it reasonable for an entire culture to make the flight into Egypt part of its belief in order to fashion a new theology of transcendence? Even now it appears inconceivable that such a lowly condition experienced by four people should have become a premise for living after such a long history of god-kings. It was as if pre-Christianity was reduced to a few basics: a man, a woman and a child, a donkey and a servant, an unmarked track across an alien land, and the prospect of death at the hands of a deranged king in far-off Judaea. What truths, what elements of wisdom could be drawn from these on my part? The question puzzled me. Nor did I know how to answer it, when suddenly I heard a knock at the door of my room.

"Who is it?" I asked.

"Mounir, Mr. James. Father Angelus has agreed to meet us in the library. Father Zachariah has just informed me."

I stood up and went to the door. Mounir was standing in the corridor, smiling.

"This is great news. What made him agree to see us, do you think?" I asked.

"Father Zachariah's powers of persuasion, I am sure of it. He told Father Angelus you were interested in discussing with him certain aspects of the Holy Family's journey to Mount Qussqam."

Together we walked down the empty corridor to a stairwell leading to the courtyard outside. Various people were wandering to and fro in the dark, monks as well as laymen. The monastery would always be busy, given its social and historical importance. Unlike Saint Bishoy or Abu Fana, Al-Muharraq was a cultural institution before it was a place of prayer. My only surprise was that a man like Father Angelus had chosen to make it his home. Perhaps its well-stocked library had lured him there, given that he wrote articles and theological pamphlets for the diocese. Father Zachariah later informed me that Father Angelus had been an engineer, and had lived in various countries in the Middle East during the course of his professional life. Retiring to Al-Muharraq

to study was no more than an extension of his intellectual inter-
ests: now he devoted his hours to the study of the Bible and other
religious texts.

The library was on the second floor in the main building. When
we arrived, we found the door open and the lights on. No one was
there to greet us, so I took the opportunity to wander along the
bookcases and study the codices. In one cabinet there was a display
of illuminated manuscripts, their delicately embroidered designs
glowing in the light. Elaborate mandalas and giant letters rose up
from the text like dragons; intricately designed borders on pages
reminded me of carpets. On one page I noticed a Coptic cross
fashioned from Father Demetrius's beloved *iotas.*

There was a commotion by the doorway. I turned to see Father
Zachariah ushering another man into the room. He was dressed in
black, wearing a monk's bonnet and leather cross against his chest.
His beard was straggly and gray; so too were his eyebrows. The
man's nose was made more prominent by his sunken eyes, which
gazed at us with a piercing stare. I felt uncomfortable in his presence. He seemed to look straight through me, as if I were no more
than a piece of rice paper. Nothing about me was secret anymore.

Father Angelus was in his late fifties perhaps, though it was hard
to be certain. Years of ascetical practice made him appear wizened.
My first impression of him was that of looking at an old icon. His
charisma seemed austere and overpowering.

"This is Father Angelus, Mr. James," Father Zachariah said.

"I am very pleased to make your acquaintance, Father," I said.

"You," he said. "You are Mr. James. Well then, what are you doing
here? Does your wife know where you are? Does she approve?"

I was taken aback by the tone of interrogation in Father Angelus's
voice. He was the first person that I had met in Egypt who had
chosen to question *me*, rather than the other way round.

"Does she approve?" he asked a second time.

"She knows I am here, and accepts my reasons for being here,
Father," I said.

"It is dangerous, what you are doing. Do you realize that?" Again Father Angelus again interrogated me.

"Dangerous?" I inquired.

"Yes, delving into the spiritual life like this: great risks are attached to it. Destruction is ever-present." Father Angelus spoke in a voice like that of an Old Testament prophet.

"People have been most helpful, Father," I said.

"Very good. But you must be careful. The Spirit is not a conversational exercise. It is something you live. With passion, and with heart. To enter monastic life, even as an observer, you must respect what you see and hear. It is a tested procedure, yes. Generations of monks have been working to perfect it. They are not recluses, no. They are men of the Spirit. Pioneers of the Spirit. They travel where few men are capable of going. Faith is an adventure, you see. It demands courage, perseverance, and patience. Patience, above all, yes. One has to wait for the Spirit to enter. It is not some fish or animal easily trapped. Do you understand?"

"I am beginning to, Father," I confessed.

Father Angelus then addressed Zachariah in Arabic. They spoke for half a minute or so, while I tried to come to terms with what the recluse had said. He was talking as one who understood the true nature of asceticism, of inner training. Finally Zachariah turned to me and said: "Father Angelus asks you to forgive him for the abrupt tone of his manner. He wants you to know that his English is not good. He does not wish to sound rude."

"I do understand," I replied, somewhat relieved.

"Yes," Father Angelus said, resuming his tirade. "They are a torrent. My mind is a torrent. You must understand. I live in silence. I hear only the words of God. They batter me like water from a levee that has broken. If I wash you away, cling to what you have. I do not mean to be, how do you say—polite?"

"Rude, I think you mean," Father Zachariah corrected him.

"No, Zachariah. I mean 'polite.' The Word of God is not a cup of tea and a cake. No. Sometimes we should expect the contemptuous nature of words to knock us about. As Saint Anthony once said, fish that tarry on dry land deserve to stink. We need to jump back into the depths. The Spirit is not a shallow place."

Father Angelus sounded like a man speaking in riddles. I began to suspect he wanted me to recognize that the life of a monk was fraught with issues that had nothing to do with asceticism, or indeed the loneliness of the desert. "The Holy Family came to Mount Qussqam because of a prophecy," Father Angelus went on. "God wanted to test his son by placing him in the most arid spot on earth. This was no act of politeness. His son had to be tested, even as a child. We do this with our own children, do we not? The Holy Father is no different: the baby Jesus had to be honed by fire. Otherwise, how could he begin to cut out the evil that was rampant in the world?"

"I have no idea, Father," I admitted.

"Suffering is the only antidote to the poison of the easy life. Mary knew this to be so, as did Joseph. They were like doctors; they administered herbs to their child. He needed to be made resistant to all the slings and arrows of the world. He needed to be made strong in order to prepare himself for the difficulties that lay ahead. The crucifixion was never going to be a—how do you say it? A cake path?"

"A cakewalk, Father," I said.

"Call it what you will, yes. It takes more than a stroll in a garden to find courage enough to be crucified. Egypt made Jesus the man he became, I am certain of that."

"How can you be so sure, Father?" I ventured.

Father Angelus looked at me. I could feel his eyes boring into me.

"Because," he began, "Egypt is the eternal fire of humanity. It is here that every conceivable thought that has ever been has been properly tested. Did not the Greek philosophers come here in their youth to learn? Yes, they did, of course. Did not the Jewish people learn from us before they returned to Israel? Do you not recall the many Christian theologians from the West—men like Rufinus, Johan Cassian, Evagrius, and Hilary of Poitiers—and how they traveled throughout this land in search of knowledge? Egypt is the kingdom of thought, I am certain of it."

"I never quite realized how important the country was in the development of Western thought," I admitted.

"So you understand when I say that religion is dangerous. It is dangerous because it demands much of us. To be fainthearted in the face of the Lord God and his creation is to fail the test of manhood. Of that I am certain. The good Lord wants us to risk everything we have. He wants us to throw down the dice!"

"Gauntlet, I think you mean, Father," Zachariah said.

"No, dice I mean. The spiritual life is a risky game!"

"Of chance?" I asked.

"Chance is another word for 'test,' is it not?"

My head was reeling. Father Angelus was fiery, like a torch. He reminded me of a phoenix in the act of self-immolation.

"I wonder whether I might ask you about the *sowah*," I said at last, hoping to change the subject.

"*Sowah*?" Father Angelus glanced at Father Zachariah, as if to say: who has been talking to this man? What does he know?

"What have you heard about the *sowah*?" he asked.

"Only that they are an anonymous group of men who live in the desert."

"Anonymous? Forgive me. But these men are all known. They all have names. Just because they are not members of a community, this does not mean they are not familiar to us."

"Have you a story or two that might help me to understand them, Father?" I asked.

"I can tell you one or two, yes," replied Father Angelus, warming to the subject. "Years ago, at Saint Macarius Monastery in the Wadi Natrun, there lived a monk called Luca. He was a man of deep learning, a pious man. One day he approached the abbot of the monastery and asked permission to leave. 'Why?' Father Daniel asked. 'Because I feel it is time for me to retire permanently to the desert,' replied Father Luca. 'Are you ready?' asked the abbot. 'I believe so,' replied Luca. And so Father Luca disappeared and was never seen again.

"Recently, Bishop Matthias visited Saint Macarius monastery to ordain a group of new monks. To one of these monks he decided to give the name 'Luca' in memory of the man who had disappeared into the desert long ago. That evening, an elderly monk known as Father Philemon called upon the bishop to inform him that Father Luca was still alive, and therefore it would be inappropriate to bestow his name on another. When Bishop Matthias asked Father Philemon the whereabouts of Father Luca, he was told that the man was a *saahih*."

"Father Philemon remained in contact with Father Luca?" I asked.

Father Angelus shrugged. "Contact? These men speak a divine language. What we say, they are able to hear. I am sure Father Luca conveyed his concerns to Father Philemon about the use of his name in a way we will never understand. Did not your Francis of Assisi speak a bird language?"

I nodded.

"I have another story, if I may," Father Zachariah said.

"Please," Father Angelus said.

"It involves the death of a certain Bishop Demetrius in Cairo in 1996," Father Zachariah continued. "After the funeral service, his body was transported to the White Monastery at Sohag, not far from here, to be buried. The coffin was placed in the church that evening in preparation for a memorial service the next day. That night, men's voices were heard in the church, singing psalms. Not until the next morning did the monks realize that the *sowah* had performed Mass in honor of the bishop. Yet no one ever saw them arrive or depart."

"Sometimes, when you travel in the desert," Father Angelus added, "it is possible to come across a plot of land that has been watered, though there appears to be no water at hand. Obviously this is a small field used by the *sowah* to grow vegetables."

"I have a story about the *sowah* also, if you will permit me," Mounir said.

"Speak, Mr. Bedwani," Father Angelus said.

"I was visiting some friends in a monastery in Al-Fayyum one day," he began. "They asked me whether I might like to accompany them to the cave of Saint Samuel, a sixth-century anchorite revered for his spiritual powers. I was surprised to see that my two friends carried a sack of bread and a few flasks of water on their backs as we walked away from the monastery. On the way to Saint Samuel's cave we stopped by another, where a portion of food and water was duly left inside the entrance. But there was no one there. Later, when we reached Saint Samuel's cave, one of my friends called out, 'Excuse me, Father,' as we approached, but again there was no reply. There, too, the balance of the food and water was deposited inside the entrance. While in the cave, I took the opportunity to look around. All I could see was a very old piece of carpet lying on the floor. Immediately I felt a strange sensation come over me, like pins and needles. Perhaps it was awe, I can't be sure. I felt a presence in that cave, though I was unable to say what had caused it. My friends asked me not to speak of what I had witnessed. To this day I have not."

"These caves belonged to *sowah*, I presume," I said.

Mounir nodded.

"Yet I have never seen one," he admitted.

"Are there any more stories?" I inquired.

"Mother Miriam from the Monastery of the Martyrs at Isna, north of Luxor, told me an interesting tale," Father Zachariah said. "She spoke of how the local bishop paid them a visit at the monastery one day. They decided to hold Mass at midnight in honor of his visit. Mother Miriam instructed one of her nuns to wake her and the bishop before the hour, but unfortunately this did not happen. In the morning, Mother Miriam apologized to the bishop, who agreed that all of them must have been very tired the previous evening. 'But I heard people praying in the church,' she admitted to him. 'Perhaps,' he said, 'they were *sowah* who had come to perform Mass for us, knowing of our fatigue.'

"I recall," Father Zachariah added, "Mother Miriam actually saw a *saahih* once. 'He looked like an eagle with wings extended,' she told me. 'Suddenly he glided down and entered our church at around sunset. There he joined other *sowah*, and together they performed Easter Mass. I saw them through a hole in the roof of the church where I was sitting while enjoying the evening breeze, even though I knew it was forbidden to look at them. Their prayers were all but inaudible.'"

"Is this not enough, Mr. James?" finally Father Angelus asked.

"More than enough, Father," I said. "I hadn't imagined how varied the life of the *sowah* could be."

"They are men of flesh and blood, of course. But they have attained to a state bordering upon the nonphysical. It is for this reason that they perform such extraordinary feats," Father Angelus said.

"We have no way of explaining their behavior," Mounir said.

"You are beholden to them, I suspect, for granting you at least a glimpse into their remarkable world," I said.

"The *sowah*," continued Father Angelus, "are men who submerged themselves in the true darkness of mystical ignorance. They are able to close their eyes to all that they see. In doing so, the *sowah* are able to reach out to what is entirely untouchable and unseen, belonging not to themselves or another, but to the good Lord, who is above all. Their very unknowing helps them to know what surpasses understanding. Such men continue to live among us, even though we do not see them."

"Now I think I understand what 'simple intelligence' really means," I said. "I have been wrestling with its meaning for some time."

"The *sowah* are masters of the mystical life," Father Angelus added. "These men do not know the difference between what they see and what they feel. All realities have merged for them. The good Lord no longer presents himself to them as an object. They do not require more knowledge of him, but union."

"They are urging us to seek after the good, and go back to the beginning within ourselves," I suggested.

"Very good, very good. I like that. You, sir, have presented your case very well. I like that also."

Father Angelus spoke rapidly to Father Zachariah in Arabic, to which the latter interpreted for me: "Father Angelus is conscious of the time. He feels that you may wish to rest after your journey today. Our discussion has been vigorous. He does ask, however, whether you might be interested in continuing our talk at the conclusion of a short break."

"At nine o'clock, or thereabouts?" I proposed, aware that Father Angelus may want to resume our dialogue as much for his own benefit as mine.

"He is of the opinion that we have not yet exhausted the subject of the *sowah*, or of certain issues which have been raised during the course of our discussion."

"May I ask what sort of issues?" I asked.

"Father Angelus feels you may have a question you might like to put to him. A question relating to your own life perhaps."

I glanced at Father Angelus, who sat in his chair, composed but silent. The fire in him had momentarily gone out. His gaze struck me, however: he seemed to be looking not into space so much as toward some distant light. Nothing about him indicated the type of man he was. Father Angelus had become someone whose inner being had resumed a secret life of its own. Could he have been, secretly, a *saahih*, as Father Zachariah believed?

"I could talk all night with Father Angelus," I said. "That is, if he has enough time and energy left to listen to me."

"Your wish is his command, Mr. James. Father Angelus admits himself that he draws pleasure from his conversation with you. I, unfortunately, do not offer him such a challenge."

"You are being too modest, Father Zachariah. I am sure you are equal to the task."

"He wants to talk about *you*. By coming all the way to Deir al-Muharraq, you have presented yourself as someone willing to seek out more than most. This has impressed him."

"Father Angelus challenges me beyond what I believe I am capable of understanding," I said.

"It is not a question of what you think you are capable of, Mr. James. But what the good Lord believes you are ready *for*," Father Zachariah said.

"Father Angelus can help me in this respect?"

"Of course. After all, he continues to help me. He is my teacher."

Father Angelus stood up then, and made his way toward the door to the library. He hardly glanced at me in passing. For him I had become a ghost. I looked at Father Zachariah and Mounir for confirmation of what might happen next.

"He will return at nine o'clock this evening," Zachariah said. "I will leave the door open for you to come back here at your leisure."

The light in the room shone on the illuminated manuscripts in the cabinet, as if they were on fire. Then I realized that the light was coming from the hallway beyond. Father Angelus, it seems, had left a glow in his wake.

A Dream Interpreted

MY HEAD WAS POUNDING. IT WAS difficult to contain all the ideas that tumbled about in my mind. I returned to my room to rest for an hour or so.

The intensity of Father Angelus's personality was like nothing I had experienced before. His verbal agitation seemed to have been a sign of his overwhelming belief in the mystery and ineffability of God. There was nothing else that could account for it. The man was not mad, but everything about his behavior resembled a kind of mental derangement. All his thoughts were engaged in a battle with divisiveness. He wanted to bring his entire being into a state of union—with what? Only he knew. His charisma was infectious, however. The man was incandescent. He made the spiritual life seem like a cauldron of fire into which we must plunge.

I pulled out my bottle of whisky from my bag. Pouring a stiff nip, I went out onto the balcony and sat down with my feet on the railing. I needed to calm down. Going back over our conversation that evening, I tried to find a common thread. What did Father Angelus mean by the spiritual life being dangerous? What did he mean when he said that suffering was an antidote to the poison of the easy life? And that one needed to have courage to endure crucifixion? Danger, suffering, courage, crucifixion: all these images struck a chord. He was trying to tell me something—that we must always put ourselves in a position where defeat stares us in the face. Even in the spiritual life, he seemed to be saying, the chances of success are infinitesimal. We are like frogs' eggs on a pond: there might be a lot of them, but few will reach maturity in order to become tadpoles.

Taking another sip of whisky, I recalled that I had journeyed halfway up the Nile in pursuit of what now appeared to be an illusion. I was looking for something that did not exist—or, if it did, I had failed to discover what it might be. I began to realize that there might be a separate reality out there waiting to be encountered. One needed certain attributes, however—attributes cultivated at the fringe of everyday reality—in order to make such an encounter possible. Did I possess them? Did I know what belief meant, what faith represented, what grace actually signified? These were qualities that both baffled and fascinated me. They were lying there like stones on the path: they simply would not go away.

The conversation with Father Angelus made me feel as if a bomb were going off in my head. Everything that was ordered and cataloged, every piece of information I possessed about the spiritual life was now like so much confetti thrown in the air. Philosophy, history, theology, aesthetics, and logic, even science—none of them meant anything to me any longer. It seemed that a conversation with one man, an eccentric monk fueled by a passion for the Absolute no less, had left me feeling less than honest with myself. He had shown me up for what I was: a spiritual itinerant, one who wandered from one experience to another like a vagrant searching for a place to sleep.

Resisting another glass, I sat there as calmly as I could. The night sky was filled with stars. The Bear, the Dipper, and Orion, even the Pleiades above me, they all drifted past my gaze. I all but counted each star in a bid to slow down my breathing. You have seen too much on this journey, I told myself. You have heard too many strange things. Egypt is not a place but a dialogue with the infinite. Its desert is a palimpsest of words. As soon as one layer is put down on the land, it becomes erased by another. How can one ever begin to comprehend so many eons of thought? No one, not Zoser, Ramses, Akhenaton, Moses, Plotinus, Clement, Origen, Philo, Athanasius, or Anthony—none of these men have ever been able to comprehend Egypt. So why should I even try?

Slowly I could feel myself coming down to earth. The sensation was pleasant. It was almost as if Father Abadir had stepped into my room. His tranquil presence was close by. Had he appeared invisibly like a *saahih*, ready to utter a silent prayer on my behalf? I began to feel fortunate, even privileged, as if I had been chosen to carry a torch in a relay. I had been asked to carry the fire forward to the next runner—and so on until the cauldron was lit. We are all merely runners in a relay across time, I told myself.

When Mounir knocked on my door a few minutes before nine o'clock that evening, I was more than ready. My head was clear again, though I felt I had been on a long journey through space. Walking with him down the corridor to the stairwell was to experience both the loneliness and the exhilaration of space travel. Father Angelus, I realized, had been into orbit before, and knew well what to expect.

"How do you feel, Mr. James?" Mounir inquired as we crossed the deserted courtyard on our way to the library building.

"Tonight I feel different, very different," I replied.

"Talking to Father Angelus has had this effect on you?"

"As well as everything else that has happened to me these past months."

Mounir shook his head in disbelief. "It is not something I have experienced myself. Father Angelus is a remarkable man."

"You have lived with it all your life, Mounir. It is second nature to you to encounter what Father Angelus stands for. He is not a man so much as an energy. Don't you feel his heat when he speaks?"

"This is natural in a man who has dedicated his life to God, Mr. James. Father Angelus has become a part of the good Lord's grace. There is no power on earth that can match it."

"It takes some getting used to, I agree," I said.

"Try to relax. I am sure Father Angelus understands."

We climbed to the second floor and made our way to the library. When we entered, Father Angelus and Father Zachariah were already seated. This time I could only see these two men, as well as the glass cabinet full of illuminated manuscripts behind them. It was as if the library of books had disappeared.

"Welcome," Father Zachariah said. Father Angelus nodded, but did not speak. "I trust you have been able to rest, Mr. James."

"I confess, Father, I took the time to study the night sky. It is very clear tonight. Sirius, King Zoser's favorite star, was quite bright."

"Like the star over Bethlehem," Father Angelus commented.

"I had never thought of it like that, Father."

"It was, as we already know, a conjunction of Saturn and Jupiter. A miracle in its own way."

"Obviously," I said.

"Let us begin," Father Angelus then remarked, as if we were about to start a meeting.

"I don't quite know how to," I confessed, conscious that more was expected of me this time.

"You have been traveling throughout Egypt, Mr. James. Surely there are questions that remain unanswered. The *sowah* must have left you wondering what limit there might be to the question of spiritual commitment."

"Some weeks ago, Father, I had a dream," I said, realizing that expressing something personal might help. "It was a mysterious dream, one that left me feeling elated, I don't know why. The dream revealed nothing to me, however."

"Tell me, then, what you dreamed, Mr. James," Father Angelus responded.

Taking a deep breath, I recalled what I could of my dream in Cairo. I spoke about the strange hall, the mysterious players dressed in black and gold sitting in orderly rows on the floor, the strange apparition of a number of pairs of creatures, themselves dressed in black and looking like gazelles in flight, and my reaction to them while in the company of Father Abadir. I also told Father Angelus of Abadir's concluding remarks as we watched the performance: "Let them continue the dance. My appearance, and our lecture, is not important at this stage. These creatures are giving us a taste."

No one spoke for quite some time after I concluded my story. It was as if I had presented them with a riddle.

"And you felt a deep sense of well-being?" Father Angelus eventually inquired.

"As if all was right with the world, Father," I replied.

Father Angelus got up from his seat and began pacing the room. He did not seem agitated in his gestures but, rather, unusually alive. Evidently he was examining what I had told him. At last he returned to where we were sitting and settled in his chair.

"This is an important dream, Mr. James," he began. "Yes, very important. You realize, of course, that you have been visited."

"Visited: by what, Father?"

"Why, the good Lord, of course. In your dream he has come to rest in your life."

I made no response.

"Think about what you have dreamed, Mr. James. You are in a hall that you recognize but at the same time do not, and all this in the one instant. The hall is familiar to you even as you believe it may be somewhere else. This is your life. The hall, when it is empty, is how you are. When it is so, it is no longer a familiar place. You long to see it filled. In your dream it becomes crowded, but by men dressed in strange garb, playing music you do not recognize, sitting in a way that implies order and certainty. The blackness of their clothing suggests rigor, austerity, a timeless sense of truth."

"And the gold of their clothing?" I asked.

"It is the glow of truth that breaks forth from the darkness which the performers represent," Father Angelus explained. "It reveals itself only as an instantaneous and illuminating brightness. You see it, but you also see the darkness, and your mind cannot determine which it prefers—the solidity of truth or how it reveals itself. Such is its—how do you say it in English?" Father Angelus spoke quickly in Arabic to Zachariah, asking him his advice.

"Ambivalence, Father," Father Zachariah said.

"Yes, that's it! Ambivalence," responded Father Angelus, his voice rising with excitement. It was as if he had caught something beautiful in a net, a rare butterfly perhaps.

"Am-biv-alence." Again he pronounced the word slowly to assure himself of its worth. "You are ambivalent about the nature of truth. One side of you accepts is as a reality, something intrinsic; the other part of you expects it to glow like gold simply because it exists. This tells me you want to be titillated. For you, truth must be seen as something that is not only beautiful, but is seen to be beautiful."

"Perhaps I am too much enamored of how things appear in the world, Father," I said.

"Clearly it is a superficial encounter with the world that you are having," Father Angelus replied. "Nevertheless, its deeper aspect is there to charge your heart with the energy that governs all forms. At present, however, you are immune to it. The things of this world are the nature of being; they exist to prop up a visible intention. What lies behind this intention is the essence of things, not what we see. In your dream you were still struggling with this problem. The men on the floor, playing an otherworldly music while at the same time remaining conscribed by the strict orderliness of their posture, reveal to you the nature of being. Between them they acknowledge both the purity and fragility of visible things. In a very real sense, they are what you are only when your own intention is pure."

"And the gold on their clothing?" I said, returning to the same question.

"It is your vision of paradise, Mr. James, of which you are far too much enamored. In a sense, you are putting the load before the donkey."

"I think you mean "cart before the horse," Father," Father Zachariah quietly interposed.

"Yes, yes! Carts, donkeys, loads: you know what I mean."

"Of course, Father," Zachariah half apologized.

"We are plunging deeper now, Zachariah, remember that. We must not let words waylay us!"

"I know, Father. I am sorry."

"No matter. This is where we stand. We look for paradise more than we do *at* the process of understanding. We want to taste the ripened date without cultivating the ground nearby. The sweet taste of a date, as you well know, is the product of careful husbandry. Farmers teach us everything, even if we do not learn from them. But to return." Father Angelus clasped his hands with evident intensity. "Now we know what the performers were there to do: to alert you to a false way of thinking. They were there to conceal and to reveal truth, provided that you did not concentrate too much on only one aspect of it."

"What about those strange creatures that flitted about the room in pairs, and in perfect unison?" I asked. "Were they linked to the performers below?"

"Of course." Father Angelus stood up again, this time walking over to the cabinet behind us. I turned to observe him. He stood in front of one of the illuminations—the mandala, I think—his hands clasped behind his back. His fingers twitched. Then he slowly turned about to gaze at me.

"These creatures, Mr. James, I believe are the full and unbridled intimation of the Spirit," he said. "They exist as its affirmation. Each pair of dancing creatures represents the perfect union of our dual nature, the physical with the spiritual. Traveling in pairs, so utterly unified in their every movement, they are the way the Spirit expresses itself in the world. There is always unity in diversity, as you are aware. Until it is achieved in each one of us, then we will never realize the resolved movement of all aspects of our nature. These gazelle-like creatures are the summation of existence—your existence—not only in this world but also in the world beyond, the realm inhabited by angels."

"Are they angels, perhaps?" I ventured.

"In a way, they are," replied Father Angelus. "But you must be careful not to believe that the form in which they appear in your dream is their only form. Angels are beyond appearance. They delight in presenting themselves to us in a multitude of guises. What Mary encountered when the archangel Gabriel appeared is not the same angel that appears in your dream. Your angels are masked, as you mentioned. The one that appeared to Mary was open-faced. So you see, angels only appear in the garb we are capable of seeing. Their spiritual dimension is entirely determined by our understanding of their essence."

"I have never heard it explained to me this way before, Father. Thank you," I said.

"The truth is that you have never dreamed of them before. It is the beginning of your spiritual journey, Mr. James."

"And my appeal to Father Abadir to help me: what does this mean, exactly?" I asked.

"He is alerting you to the most important issue that you face, Mr. James."

"What association could I possibly have, then, with Father Abadir's remark: 'These creatures are giving us a taste'?"

"He is telling you not to try to intervene in the great dance of the Spirit," Father Angelus continued. "It is beyond you; it goes on around you; it is the supreme act of joyous expression by the good Lord himself. What you see is but a taste. You must be patient because you have not yet acquired the skill to enter into a full relationship with him. Father Abadir is telling you to hold back on your questioning, on your interrogation of the Spirit. This is the first step into the abyss, I am afraid."

"Maintaining my allegiance to critical thought, you mean?" At this point my head was reeling under the pressure of Father Angelus's argument.

"Patience, Mr. James, is derived only by recognizing the limits of such thinking. He is not telling you to abandon critical thought, no, but to accept that logic must be used only when the right circumstances exist. It is clearly not the most apt tool for trying to understand the workings of the Spirit."

"Then what is, Father?" I asked, feeling now that I must know.

For the first time Father Angelus looked at me as if I were there in his presence as a friend. I felt that he wanted to embrace me—not with his arms, but with his mind.

"Grace is," he said. "It is a quality that can only approach you when you are prepared and ready. It does not approach those who are still obligated to a certain way of thinking, a logical way of thinking. The great ascetics of the desert, men like Anthony, Paul, and Evagrius, these men spent their whole lives breaking down such constructs in their minds. The caves they inhabited were none other than the deep solitude of the Spirit. They began to understand that these constructs were a high wall barring them from entering into the domain of the Spirit. All Anthony's temptations, all Evagrius's attempts at building a rational theology for others, everything of this nature prevented them from reaching out to what they believed was theirs to experience. Uniquely so, of course. It was only when both these men returned to the simplicity of being that any real advance in the spiritual life could be achieved by them personally."

"In other words, when they finally attained to a simple intelligence," I said, recalling our earlier conversation.

"The world is maintained by a simple intelligence, not one like we humans use. In fact, I should say we have lost this gift. 'Be as little children,' the good Lord said. What he was really trying to tell us was to return to a state of simplicity. Is this not so, Father Zachariah?"

"It is, Father."

"Good. My English is improving! I have entered into your language at last, Mr. James. It has begun to fit me, like an old coat."

"You wear it well, Father," I replied.

"So now you begin to understand the hidden nature of your dream," Father Angelus said. "It is telling you that, until this moment in time at least, you are merely an observer of the spiritual life. It is as if you are looking at a play. You have not learned how to participate in it. You are not one of the actors. The flitting creatures in the hall are but a taste of what is in store for you only if you choose to become a member of the company. Yes, the good Lord has granted such a gift to you! For that you must be thankful. At least you have been offered a vision of another world. Many people would give their life to have such a vision. Tonight you mentioned to me that you counted stars while sitting on your balcony. Do you not have an expression for that also?"

"We do, Father. We say to count your lucky stars."

"Then do so. Your dream is a fortunate star. It is the star that guided the Magi to Bethlehem. The manger, after all, is but a glimpse of paradise, is it not?"

I turned to look at Mounir. He sat there, utterly still. Clearly he was also moved by Father Angelus's explanation. He had no words either to explain what was happening. How could a man peel away the surface of reality with such consummate ease?

"Your dream is now your guide, Mr. James. You must follow its intent."

"But I cannot join you here in Al-Muharraq. That would be impossible," I said.

Father Angelus shook his head.

"Your dream does not demand this of you," he said.

"Then what does it ask of me, Father?"

"To become an actor in the great drama of the spiritual life. Not just to observe. It asks you to regard such a life as the only life, to give up the phantom of modern existence. This is no more than an empty hall, as you now know. From here on, you must listen to the voice inside that demands from you an act of courage. As I said before: the spiritual life is no cakewalk. You must be prepared to suffer. You must be prepared to doubt. You must be prepared to experience failure too. These form the primary pillars of the temple you must build anew. If you rest in its peristyle, and choose not to leave, then you will be safe. Remember, such a temple was built a long time ago, and has endured many earthquakes and storms."

"I will, Father," I replied.

"Now rest, Mr. James; it is time. We have traveled far together this evening. Your visit to us here at Al-Muharraq has been one we have all enjoyed. Is this not so, Zachariah?" Father Angelus inquired.

"It is, Father. Mr. James has provoked you to engage in certain—how shall I call it, volcanic activity?"

"An eruption! Yes, I like that," Father Angelus said with a warm smile. It was the first time he had done so. "On certain occasions we monks need to quit our cave. I perceive in you a man on the brink of great things, Mr. James. The choice is yours. Now that you have a taste for the spiritual life at its most basic level, traveling as you have in the footsteps of the Holy Family, it is up to you whether you wish to go further. I cannot advise you on your limit; only you in converse with the good Lord will be able to work that out for yourself."

"What should my first steps be then, Father?" I asked.

"Read and consider. Inquire, and then meditate. And finally, pray. I mean the prayer of stillness, the one that is not of words. Finally the *iota* must be put aside. Articulation is the furniture of the mind only. Of course we enjoy moving it around, but it does not say what cannot be said. Your task is to find a way to embrace every subtle movement of the heart and of the soul. This is the essence of simple intelligence, assuredly. Physical beauty, in its true sense, is the plow: it digs deep into the subsoil of our being. No, into the ground that is the good Lord himself. I want you to feel his presence as a seed in the earth that is you. Egypt teaches us to understand the workings of growth. Let him grow in you. Let him inundate you with his ineffable waters. Let him flood what is the parched earth of your being. Such is the lesson of Egypt. As you are aware, in ages past, the Nile was our god. Today the river is still a metaphor for he who made us."

"I will try to put your advice into practice, Father," I said. "I just hope I have what it takes."

"Enjoy your stay here. It is unlikely we will meet again. I must return to my cave," Father Angelus said.

I gazed into his deep-set eyes. Father Angelus may not yet be a *saahih*, but the moment of his disappearance into the desert must be near at hand. He had shown me the way; for that I was thankful. He had taken me on a journey more eventful than that of the journey of the Holy Family itself.

The Last Supper

28

JOSEPH, WITH HIS OWN PROCLIVITY for dreaming dreams, was instrumental in the change of fortune for the Holy Family. One night at Al-Muharraq, while Mary and the infant Jesus were asleep, he awoke to an apparition and a voice telling him that Herod was dead. It must have come as a shock to him: the cause of their suffering was finally no more. The long years of wandering in Egypt were now over; they could return to Israel and begin normal life at last.

As old as he was, Joseph must have understood the significance of this event. His task as protector of the divine child in an alien land was nearing its end. Recalling how his staff had blossomed in the temple in Jerusalem over six years ago, an event that had changed his life forever, his jubilation at the news from that city nonetheless must have been tempered by sadness. Old men have a way of looking back at the past as an object of nostalgia, one never to be repeated. They cannot go back; their life is over. What they are left with are their responsibilities and their memories. His in particular would have been colored by the knowledge that he had been chosen above all other men to care for a future God-man in the years when it most counted.

After hearing Joseph recount his dream, the news must have proved to be overwhelming for Mary also. They were free at last!

The day-to-day anxiety of caring for a child that was to change the world had finally entered a new phase. From now on, perhaps, she could simply be a mother rather than a woman imbued with the conviction that as the Holy Virgin she occupied a pivotal place in history. Her gift of inexpressible grace and love had achieved its objective. The infant Jesus, already fluently engaged with the world, was now of a certain age. He could think, reason, and speak in a way that the world understood. His powers had been refined. Under her guidance he was now able to affect the lives of all whom he met, and to alert them to their destiny. Human existence was no longer going to be a disjointed and largely meaningless journey from birth to death, but a real, existential encounter with divinity. One could *be* deified through him. One could experience the unsurpassable moment of beauty that was God in his name. Her role in this drama had been important. No one—not man, woman, or child; not ruler, priest, or sage—could take her place in the realization of the divine nature of the Christ child. She was, and always would be, the chosen vessel.

In their house on Mount Qussqam, the Holy Family had lingered in a state of fear and expectation for over six months. They had prayed that Herod's soldiers would not find them. Equally, they had pondered the future. One day they had hoped to return to Palestine not necessarily in triumph, but at least as a humble family destined to impose their presence on history. This was to be the enduring tabernacle in which they lived. Mount Qussqam was to be the place of gestation, a holy mountain where a God-child realized the uniqueness of his nature. Call it what you will, this remote place in Egypt, far from the centers of power, was to become the object of affection and awe for generations of Coptic Christians. It was to be the first home of Jesus Christ, the place where the first Mass was performed, and the location of the first church in Christendom. Nowhere, not even the cities of Jerusalem or Rome, could lay claim to any such distinction.

The Gospel of Matthew alludes to the return of the Holy Family to Palestine in almost dismissive tones. "And he arose, and took the young child and his mother, and came into the land of Israel."[125] What this remark does not allude to is the pain and suffering that the family endured whilst in exile. Only Coptic Christians understand what Joseph, Mary, Salome, and Jesus went through. They have made the journey real by identifying where the family lived during their time in Egypt. For that we must be thankful. The churches and monasteries that have sprung up in their wake are part of the myth-line of the journey itself. Equally, Patriarch Theophilus, through his *Vision*, has given us insight into the childish workings of divinity. We now learn that the God-man, even as a child, is not averse to travel. Moreover, he is prepared to encounter alien places and endure unpalatable experiences for the sake of alerting us to the redemptive effects of displacement. We are all exiles in this world. The journey of the Holy Family teaches us to endure such exile as a transition to another plane altogether.

Bidding goodbye to the few friends that they had made at Mount Qussqam, the Holy Family set sail down the Nile toward Babylon (Old Cairo). The *Coptic Synaxarium* maintains that the route they followed was similar to the one they had used on their journey south. If this is so, then we must assume they passed by Hermopolis and were greeted by a more accommodating citizenry. Even Theophilus, who was no great lover of Hermopolitans, said that they welcomed them there with "great joy and jubilation." The consensus is that they revisited many of the places of their earlier visit, presumably to thank those who had helped and succored them along the way. We hear from Antoninus Martyr (AD 560–570) that he personally saw a piece of linen in a church in Memphis upon which was a portrait of the boy Jesus.

"As the people said," he wrote, "He wiped His face upon it, and His image remained there. This image is adored at certain times, and we adore it, but because of its brightness we were not able to look fixedly upon it, because the more earnestly you fixed your gaze upon it, the more it changed before you eyes." The God-child's trace was everywhere, it seems: on stones, imprinted on mountain-sides, at rest in pieces of cloth.

From Al-Maadi the Holy Family passed through Matariyah, Musturud, Al-Mahammah, and on to Leontopolis. From there they began their journey westward through Vicus Judaeorum to Onias, where they stayed with old friends. Onward they continued through Bilbeis, the Wadi Tumilat, and across the isthmus at Al-Qantara, before traveling the caravan route from Egypt to Palestine along the Mediterranean coast. According to tradition, the Holy Family rested a few days near Gaza, in a garden by Gebel Muntar.

When they finally entered Israel, news reached Joseph that Herod's son Archaelus now reigned in Judea, which forced the old man to reconsider going to Jerusalem to live. He decided it might be safer for the Holy Family to turn "aside into the parts of Galilee," as Matthew relates, in order to dwell "in a city called Nazareth," thus fulfilling the prophecy that "He shall be called a Nazarene."[126] The family was home at last.

Jesus was now nearly six years old, and we do not hear any more of his early life in the Bible until he was twelve, when he conversed with priests in Jerusalem. There are numerous apocryphal stories relating to this period, however, most of them dealing with his supernatural powers. We hear, for example, of how the boy Jesus was swimming with friends in a stream, which he soon transformed into a series of fishponds.[127] At the same time he fashioned twelve clay sparrows, which he arranged around one of the ponds. When a pious Jew came along and reprimanded the boys for working on the Sabbath, Jesus dutifully began destroying the ponds. The sparrows, however, he gave life with a clap of his hand. They immediately flew away, presumably to be transformed into the apostles at a later date. A son of the Jew, a boy called Hanan, then attempted to kick down the levee around one of the fishponds in a gesture of contempt. Immediately the water disappeared. Jesus said to the boy, "As this water has vanished, so will your life disappear." The boy dried up like the water.

We are never allowed to distance ourselves from Jesus as a young boy of miraculous abilities. Naturally this is in keeping with his avataric nature. We do know from less reputable sources that he was present at the death of Joseph, his adopted father, when the latter had reached the ripe old age of 111! Jesus was then sixteen years of age. It is said that he took up a position standing by Joseph's head during the vigil, with his mother positioned at the foot of her husband. It is an image we see in Egyptian tomb painting showing the death of Osiris, with his son Horus and wife Isis occupying similar positions by his deathbed. One is never far from the primordial images central to Egyptian religion. Joseph, that grave old man whom we have learned to love and respect, finds himself transformed into one of the most fascinating figures in the Egyptian pantheon.

I was aware that I had made a journey of significance in their footsteps. It is one thing to travel through a country, enjoying its people and its culture; it is quite another to feel that you have participated in a journey with consequences for the future of humankind. Without the generous embrace of Egypt, where would Christians of the world be today? Egypt is like a scroll containing an ageless and continuing story. It tells us more about ourselves, and our need to find fulfillment in the mysterious actions of deity, even if they are not immediately apparent, than any other place on earth. I had walked the pathways that the Christ child had likely walked; I had sat in the cell where Saint Bishoy slept standing up, supported by his hair. These were more than experiences; they form the very bedrock of this ancient land. The Nile might sustain it, but ultimately the country is grounded in another order of reality derived from the constant interplay between human minds and these enduring images of the spirit.

I had grown to respect and love the Nile. It is a slow-moving river that yearns for the sea. On the banks and in the fields date palms and papyrus offer their green stubble to Ra, the sun's incarnation. Cattle and other livestock graze on its banks. Mud villages blend into its luxuriant growth. River craft drift by, offering up their vast triangle of sail to the chrism of the breeze. In the distance, along ridge and mountain, lie Pharaohs' tombs, savoring of death and the hieroglyphs of eternal life. Canopic vases lie buried in the soil, each one filled with ibis or cats' mummies. Because of this river, gods, humans, and animals, thoughts, visions, and miracles, all are refracted through its prism. Its apotheosis is to rise and fall in season. A donkey brays. The cries of crows transcend antiquity as they greet the morning sun. Can one not marvel at this river, which has given us so much? It is one of the world's miracles, its civilizing spirit, Hapi, always there to emerge from the black earth in order to renew each day. The river celebrates death, adores death, and surrenders to its embrace. Finally, it is a river of repose.

Toward the end of my stay in Egypt, Mounir and I spent some days in and around Al-Muharraq, visiting various places linked to the return journey of the Holy Family. One of these was the convent of the Virgin Mary built into the cliff face of Western Mountain, a few kilometers south of Assyut, where the philosopher Plotinus was born. The family stayed in a large cave there, which has now been turned into a church. Uniquely so, the iconostasis stands in the center of this cave as a four-walled wooden structure housing the altar. From its terraces one can see the river threading its way north.

On the morning of our departure for Luxor and the monasteries of Upper Egypt that Mounir promised to show me before we headed back to Cairo, I paid a visit to Father Zachariah in his office. Though I had no expectation of seeing Father Angelus again, my head was nonetheless filled with impressions of our recent conversations in the library. The days of sightseeing since then had not obliterated anything of his vivacity, or of what he had said that evening. It was hard to believe it had really happened. I kept thinking that I had met a *saahih*, not a monk. Father Zachariah asked for tea to be brought in when I sat down.

"Father Angelus is a man of unusual insight," Zachariah began.

"It is almost as if he is a visitor from another realm. Where does his knowledge come from, I wonder?" I asked.

"Who knows? He has not experienced any evident suffering in his previous life, before becoming a monk."

"His inner life may well have been one of deep conflict—of a battle, perhaps, between discordant spirits," I ventured.

"It is the way of the ascetic, Mr. James. Unlike the rest of us, these men live close to the abyss. They are constantly looking into it. What they see is a glimpse of final things, each according to his capacity. I suspect Father Angelus has seen more deeply than most. I know from my discussions with him over the years that he is often unable to express what he feels. Nor is language a constraint for him, as you may have noticed."

"His English attained heights that few of us who are familiar with it ever reach," I remarked with a smile, recalling how Father Angelus had manipulated it to suit his thoughts.

Then I said: "Was it not Dionysius the Areopagite, that legendary recluse from Syria, who acknowledged what he called the 'invisible and incomprehensible' as being the only reality?"

"And also the 'unsearchable and past finding out'!" replied Zachariah. "Using such words makes us realize how inadequate our tools of expression really are."

"One thing Father Angelus has taught me is to be more patient with myself. I probably thought that the spiritual life could only be attained simply by applying oneself to its tenets. He suggests otherwise—that we need to allow things to evolve in their own time, and not in the time we would like."

"It is the time of souls Father Angelus puts his faith in most. Our time means nothing to him. Often, when I see him looking tired or wan in the face, I ask him what might be wrong. 'Are you feeling ill?' I ask. He tells me, 'No, but I have been in long disputation with certain friends.' These friends, I might add, are no longer with us. He is talking about Saint Anthony or Pachomius, even John

Climacus, the monk from Raithu Monastery on the Red Sea who died in the seventh century! These men come to his cell at night to converse."

"Like the *sowah*," I said.

Father Zachariah laughed.

"One could argue he is in communication with invisible *sowah*."

"Especially if time has been overcome in his eyes, as you rightfully suggest," I said.

"Father Angelus would argue that a man's life is not determined by bodily function, but by the emanation of his thoughts and his actions. For him, these early ascetics continue to live on in his memory. They are alive. Their every gesture is for him an affirmation of their ongoing existence."

"And for yourself as well, I gather, Father," I suggested.

Father Zachariah sipped his tea pensively.

"Mr. James, I am like you, no more than a wayfarer. I deal in ideas and concepts. This is my way. I am born to be a teacher, not an ascetic. We each have our vocation. For me, men like Father Angelus are my fountain. I go to them to be refreshed. For others, however, I am their fountain. I teach them the ways of the Spirit."

"Do you think that our actions as thinkers or teachers exclude us from making the final ascent?" I asked.

"It is not for us to decide. Remember what Father Angelus told us—we must prepare ourselves for the advent of grace. We are masters of our destiny only to the extent that we ready ourselves for a helping hand should it come. This is the great gift. Until then, we simply attend," replied Zacharias.

"As good farmers, we keep cultivating the fields," I suggested.

"How the Nile, in the end, ensures that our feet remain firmly planted on the ground!" responded Father Zacharias with a smile. "In the meantime, I wish you a safe journey, Mr. James. I understand you are heading north as far as Aswan."

"To the ruins of Saint Simeon, yes. Mounir feels that this is an appropriate place for us to end our trip."

"By the time you get there, the Holy Family will almost be back in Israel," Zachariah laughed.

"Ready to embark on the next stage of their lives, perhaps," I replied.

"As Father Angelus told us: the spiritual life is a dangerous game. It requires courage, faith, and endurance. It is not a tea party, Mr. James."

"It seems that the earth, as perfect as it may seem to be, is made up of volcanoes, tidal waves, and destructive storms. Why should not the spiritual life be the same, Father?"

"Just so long as we understand the risks entailed. This is what Father Angelus is advising us to do, I am sure."

Father Zachariah and I shook hands as we bid one another good-bye. We both confessed that it was rare indeed for men to become such good friends in so short a time. Probably it was the effect that Father Angelus continued to have on us both.

Before stepping out to meet our taxi, I took the opportunity to spend a few additional minutes in the Church of the Holy Virgin. I wanted to gaze one more time at the altar where the infant Jesus was bathed, and to imagine his presence. I peered through the aperture in the iconostasis into the smoke-stained sanctuary. This time I noticed an icon of Christ enthroned hanging in the niche beyond. He was gazing down upon an altar covering of white cloth surmounted by a painted box containing the host. On the side of the box was an icon depicting the Last Supper. Christ was portrayed dispensing his flesh and blood as bread and wine to his disciples. Two brass candlesticks stood on either side of the altar stone.

Here was the Altar of the World, I said to myself. Here a child was groomed to become a man. But he was to become no ordinary man. He was to become someone destined to change the world. Not as Alexandria the Great or Julius Caesar or Genghis Khan might have done, but as the son of a carpenter who had traveled extensively in his youth, learning all that he could from a people wedded to a river and their history. His story was always going to be miraculous in that it celebrated vicissitude. In the long history of religion and of belief, no man has voluntarily given up his life to affirm the reality of a life beyond death. The man believed in something. He believed in what the Father stood for as an invisible agent of transformation. For him *kenosis*, the self-emptying and abasement of himself before the proconsul of empire, was to be his supreme act of renunciation. His will needed to be hammered into a state of will-lessness, so that the will of the Father might be accomplished.

My journey had ended. To gaze upon this altar and know that at some time around 4 BC Mary had gathered up her child in her arms in this very place and said a prayer for his well-being was enough for me to realize the significance of what I had accomplished. I might leave Egypt and return home in the next few weeks, but the country would not leave me, I knew that. Such is the nature of *kenosis*, I told myself. In *kenosis* I empty out all my preconceptions of what might constitute the early life of Jesus Christ. I could venture forth into a new world now where the physical and the spiritual commingled, just as the Nile waters commingle timelessly with the earth.

At the same time, I had come to understand what it is like to suffer in the pursuit of sacred knowledge. Men and women throughout present-day Egypt, most of them Copts, had alerted me to the eternal nature of restraint, and of ascesis, that together make up the discipline of self-emptying, which in turn forms the true bedrock of all human understanding. The Holy Family, as wayfarers and exiles, embodied virtues that only now was I able to acknowledge and accept: humility in the face of adversity, and patience as the aftermath of those who choose to revile truth when it appears in their presence. Living in a faraway land, the Holy Family, along with loyal Salome, stood for the principle of flight as a bulwark against the forces of evil masquerading as titular power, in this case in the hands of a tetrarch without scruple or courage.

There were deep metaphors at work here—metaphors that could equally be applied to a modern life such as mine. We are all on a journey to an unknown place, all subject to forces and opinions that threaten to destroy us. At the same time, we are surrounded by miracles that protect us whenever we feel ourselves to be most vulnerable. A footprint in stone here, a golden sandal there, a solitary cloud somewhere else. Are we not looking for such signs that tell us that we are protected by an invisible hand? Certainly I was beginning to believe this to be so.

No amount of any occasional incredulity that I displayed throughout the trip could erase the fact that the Holy Family's journey across the ancient land of Egypt and up the Nile was, by its very nature, a sacred event. It has no linearity, no timeliness, and no reality other than as the fulfillment of prophecy. But this is enough, surely. More than history, more than hagiography, the Holy Family's travails are the stuff of humankind's need for certainty in the face of those ever-shifting values that plague our daily lives. Fear of soldiers, fear of robbers, fear of a mad king bent upon massacre, these are but symbols of the abyss that we, too, find ourselves in and long to escape. I for one knew that on this journey at least, I had been forced to face up to my own level of incertitude, and my willingness to *dis*believe in the wake of hard evidence to the contrary. In the end, I had to find a way to accept the power of sacred events as a vehicle for transformation and change on a very personal level if I were ever going to see myself as part of an enduring mystical tradition. Belief is a many-faceted gemstone, I told myself, cut to reveal an inordinate beauty that has always been there to view, if ever a person so desires. I needed to acknowledge the gemstone that is belief.

My journey, too, had been somewhat unworldly. I had experienced an Egypt that did not conform to a land that we normally associate with mummified kings and pyramids. The Egypt that I traveled through was one wedded to the idea of sanctity ever on the move, ever fleeing the concept of its own aridity, as well as a family that knitted together various levels of its unique historical reality. This had come as a revelation to me. In turn, I had found a way to enter into the importance of the sacred journey as a way of deepening my own commitment to understanding how an infant God-child was fashioned into a future savior for the benefit of humankind in this ancient land. Simple, really. The great River Nile, long honored for its contribution to religious thought and practice, had entered into Christian history before Europe and the West had partaken of Christ's message—indeed, had even heard of his existence. This struck me as important: the river, too, was a part of Christ's education and growth.

Finally, recognizing that my journey was now over, I stepped away from the dark wooded iconostasis before which I stood, and started back toward the entrance to the church. Beyond the wooden iconostasis I knew, standing alone in the apse, was a rough-hewn stone upon which the original *saahih* had performed the first Mass in his bid to heal the world. He, the vagabond child Jesus from Judea, the wanderer and miracle-worker, had found in Egypt the perfect altar for the expression of his divinity. On it he would sacrifice himself one day, so that all people might become whole in his name.

Postscript

DURING THE NEXT WEEK, MOUNIR and I traveled along the Nile toward Luxor and Aswan to the south. We stopped at the White Monastery at Sohag to visit the great basilica inside its high walls, and to study the fine fresco of Christ Enthroned in its apse. The image reminded me that the seated figure of Ramses as Pharaoh was never far from the thoughts of those early Christian painters. Here the two cultures collided. We passed through Nag Hammadi, where the Gnostic Gospels were discovered in 1945, and stopped at numerous smaller monasteries such as Deir al-Salib, Saint Abadif, Saint Bestantaos, Saint Boktar, and Saint Michael.

Everywhere we went we were greeted by monks and nuns living in small congregations, and in places that had been in continuous occupation since the sixth and seventh century. The Thebaid, named after the ancient capital of Thebes, is home to simple mud-brick compounds boasting a humble church with only a few domes, and a battered iconostasis with a number of poorly executed icons. In them were men and women with no thought of the world other than to welcome us.

In the Monastery of the Martyrs (Deir al-Shuhada) near Isna, we were served lunch by Mother Miriam, a woman of calm demeanor whose gaze was always welcoming. She informed us of how 160,000 martyrs in the region were killed on the orders of Arianus, the governor of Antinoe, during the Roman occupation of Egypt. It was impossible to grow mango trees in the area, she informed us, as the land around the monastery had become the graveyard for these martyrs. Mother Miriam showed us a room where many bones still lay, a reminder perhaps of the legacy that the monastery felt bound to preserve. It was she who had told Father Zachariah her stories of the *sowah* that he had earlier related to me.

By the time we reached Aswan, a popular tourist city and gateway to distant Abu Simbel on the shores of Lake Nasser, we were both ready to return to Cairo. There is a point on every journey when the idea of home becomes more attractive than the prospect of discovering some new place of interest. Mounir confessed to me that his wife was missing him, as his daily telephone conversations with her were peppered with pleas to return. I understood his predicament. Still, he insisted that I should visit the ruins of Saint Simeon outside Aswan before we caught the train back to Cairo. For some reason the monastery had captured his imagination on an earlier visit. We booked a small hotel in downtown Aswan, within walking distance of the corniche overlooking the river.

After dinner we decided to stroll along the corniche, taking in the sight of holiday riverboats moored along the riverbank. Eventually we found a park bench where we decided to rest. Not far away I could see the lights of the Old Cataract Hotel, a landmark of the city going back to the days when European travelers sailed up the Nile as part of the grand tour. Now it is a five-star hotel with guards on its gates, and ordinary people are not encouraged to enter. A number of feluccas drifted past us on the river with their cargo of tourists. Reflected street lights rippled in the water below us.

"Agatha Christie wrote some of her books while staying in the Old Cataract, I believe," Mounir observed, gazing at the hotel compound on our left.

"*Murder on the Nile*, I suppose. It sounds quaintly British, doesn't it?"

"Such people came here to see only one aspect of Egypt. It was largely a projection of their own expectations."

"A country filled with exotic splendor—sphinxes, tombs, pyramids," I remarked.

"All you needed in those days was to wear a linen suit, drink gin, and lie about on riverboats," Mounir added with a rueful smile.

Below, a felucca berthed, and its captain began to tie down the sail. We watched him methodically wrap up his boat for the night. Then he stepped ashore and climbed some steps, to be greeted by a cup of tea that a man brought to him from across the road. It all looked so mysteriously ordered, timeless.

"What they came to see is nothing like the Egypt we have encountered, Mounir," I said at last.

Mounir pursed his lips. "Mr. James," he said. "I must thank you for what has happened to me on this trip. The Egypt you have revealed through your curiosity and inquiry is vastly different from the one I thought I knew."

I thanked him, knowing that he meant what he had said.

"Tomorrow, we will visit the ruins of Saint Simeon Monastery. I wanted you to see the place for a very particular reason."

"What might that be?" I asked.

"You will find that the monastery has its own voice," Mounir replied. "I need not say anything."

We sat there by the river for quite some time, taking in the evening. It was very restful. In part, I suppose, because our thoughts were still firmly centered on the events of recent days. Eventually Mounir ceased his reverie and spoke. "I will miss your company, Mr. James."

"We have traveled a long way together. Sometimes I was never quite sure what world we were involved in most."

"In the monasteries, you mean?"

"As well as following in the footsteps of the Holy Family. It became a thread that seemed to join everything together."

"Like a string of pearls," Mounir added, as he made a move to go back to our hotel.

The next morning we hired a taxi to take us to the ruins of Saint Simeon Monastery, located on a hill in the desert about a kilometer from the western bank of the Nile, and opposite the island of Elephantine. The road passed through the desert, and we were soon engulfed in sand dunes. We drove down a bumpy road until at last what looked like a ruined castle greeted our gaze. The khaki-colored mud-brick walls were largely intact; so too were various defensive towers on distant corners. The entire structure reminded me of a Crusader fortress in Turkey. Near the gate a number of cameleers stood about resting on their beasts, hoping we might take a ride through the sand dunes.

Mounir purchased our tickets at the gate, and we entered the monastery along with a few other tourists. We soon found ourselves walking among foundations, broken blocks of stone, through archways and along narrow passages. It was a large complex that had probably housed several hundred monks in its heyday. The monastery was originally dedicated to Anba Hadra, an anchorite of the fourth century who later became bishop of Aswan. The oldest vestiges went back to the seventh century, even though the present structure was part of a period of reconstruction completed in the tenth and eleventh centuries. This may have occurred, also, after a particularly violent attack by Saladin's troops on their expedition south into Nubia in 1173. The severe architecture of the complex was almost majestic in character: one sensed that throughout the centuries the monks had been prepared to defend their way of life with their lives. Since then, not even the desert has been able to claim the place as its own.

For some hours we wandered through the living quarters, peering into ill-lit cells where the monks' rough, earth beds were still extant. Even the toilet block was still visible, bathed in sunlight. I had the sense that the monks were working in the fields somewhere, if that were at all possible in this arid place. The table in the refectory was bare of eating utensils or mugs; but still I thought of the monks as perhaps attending holy office in the church nearby.

However, when we entered the ruined basilica, and gazed down the aisle toward the apse, I knew that they had gone. The peeling fresco in the half dome of the apse, all but destroyed by vandals over the centuries, was the last remnant of what was once an entire coenobitic culture. The spirit, it seemed, had finally departed.

I climbed up on to one of the walls and gazed out over the desert as the sun slipped low in the sky. Beyond, I could see the fields beside the Nile; whereas in the other direction all that was visible were sand dunes. The monastery straddled two worlds, each one imposing its own limit. I felt myself being drawn by one world, then by the other. I had been involved in this tug-of-war for the duration of my journey, it seemed. One moment I was leaning toward what the desert represented, its dalliance with asceticism and the enormity of otherworldly visions; the next, I found myself drifting back in my mind toward the fertile fields of the Nile.

That night, I would climb aboard the train to Cairo with Mounir and travel back to the world of modernity. Yet right now I was standing on a battlement in the desert, gazing into the distance, my thoughts filled with my recent experiences. Even to juxtapose Father Angelus with an airport lounge made it difficult to integrate the world he reflected with my own. It was a question that returned repeatedly as I gazed across the desert.

"Ah, there you are, Mr. James," I heard Mounir say. He had climbed up onto the wall to join me. In his hands he clasped some dates, which he generously offered to me, knowing my liking for dates.

"Has the answer revealed itself to you, perhaps?" he asked.

I looked at the man, confused.

"Saint Simeon: has he not delivered his message?" Mounir said.

This time I looked behind me into the ruins of the great basilica below bathed in afternoon light. Its broken pavement looked like a half-finished jigsaw puzzle. The apse, partly in shadow now, reminded me of a frozen tear.

"I think he is trying to tell me that in life we straddle two worlds," I remarked at last.

"He is also saying not to pressure yourself into believing that you should remain in one world or the other, Mr. James," Mounir replied. "The world of Father Angelus is not ours, we must remember that. Equally, living in a world devoid of spirit would destroy us; we know that also. It is our task to bring them together, somehow. Father Angelus is the needle. With him to help us, we are able to sew the different pieces of this fabric into one piece. As a needle, he is there to serve us."

"Is it the reason why he left the seclusion of his cell to talk to us, do you think?"

Mounir nodded.

"I believe he knew how important he was to both of us; indeed, to everyone who calls upon him to receive his advice," he said. "The monastic life is a partnership between the sacred and the secular. Without us, how could the monastery possibly survive? It is we who provide the funds, the resources, and the opportunity for it to sell its wares. Every monk knows he must pay for the privilege of leading a solitary life by giving back to the community the benefit of his experience and knowledge. This is the compact between us, Mr. James. And it is why Saint Simeon Monastery survived for so long. A complex such as this one was a marketplace for ideas. Every man who lived here understood his role in society. He was to knead the bread of the Spirit into a loaf fit for our consumption."

"So what you are saying, Mounir, is for me to cast my eyes over both worlds—to see for myself how each can live in harmony with the other," I reasoned.

"Yes. Egypt may seem to many like a locked vault. Yet it is necessary for us to find the key to its treasure."

"Father Angelus is it, then; he is the key," I added.

"Let's face it, Mr. James. He is a *saahih* in his own way, masquerading as a door to be opened," replied Mounir.

"Probably you are right," I agreed.

Which meant that the desert would one day lay claim to him, I thought, and he would join the mysterious one thousand. And us, too, if we but allow ourselves to be drawn into the solitude of our individual deserts.

Meanwhile, our taxi driver beckoned to us with a wave of his hand from below the outer wall, where he stood conversing with the camel drivers. It seemed that he wanted to get back to Aswan before dusk enveloped us.

Acknowledgments

MANY PEOPLE HAVE HELPED MAKE this book possible, and I wish to acknowledge at least some of them for their valuable contribution to the project. Chief among these is His Holiness Pope Shenouda of the Coptic Patriarchate in Cairo. His courtesy and unfailing interest in ensuring that I was able to visit the numerous places associated with the journey of the Holy Family in Egypt were a blessing. Those who attended to the practical details on his behalf included Bishop Yohanna at the Patriarchate; Miss Gehan Ameen, who accompanied me throughout my stay and was unfailingly responsive to my every wish; and Mr. Mounir Bedwani, my guide, whose knowledge of Coptic archaeology was unparalleled. Both he and Miss Ameen were perfect traveling companions, their good humor a balm when incidents occasionally tested us.

My thanks also are extended to the Australian Ambassador to Egypt, Mr. Robert Newton, and to his personal assistant Ms. Dagmar Emmery. It was through Mr. Newton's approach to His Holiness that I was able to obtain an audience with this most esteemed cleric. Bishop Biemen of the Diocese of Nakada and Bishop Demetrius at Mallawi gave generously of their time and knowledge during my travels up the Nile. Mr. Samir Gayed, the President of Electro Mitry, and Mr. Mounir Ghabbour, CEO of

Mirage Hotels in Egypt, were most supportive of my endeavors. In this respect, I should not forget Miss Ireny Eid, who opened doors that might normally have remained closed to me while in Cairo. Mr. Wasfi Doss, owner of the Windsor Hotel in Cairo, together with his wife, Yohanna, director of the Ramses Wissa Wassef Arts Center, were stalwart friends and generous hosts. I thank them for their interest. Their son, Wanil, provided encouragement.

In the provinces there were many people whose help I valued. Mother Nadeen at Saint Damiana Monastery, Dr. Zachariah Fakhoury and Father Angelus at Al-Muharraq Monastery in Upper Egypt, Father Abadir and Father Luca at Saint Bishoy and Deir es-Suriani Monasteries in the Wadi Natrun, Gerges Sobhi, my guide at Aswan, as well as the many monks and nuns in every part of the land who so generously gave of their time. Some of their names appear in this book, and I wish to extend my thanks to them for sharing a little of their knowledge with me. The author Jill Kamil patiently answered my questions, and gave me the benefit of her vast knowledge of Coptic spirituality and culture. I would like to thank the guest masters at the various monasteries where we stayed. Their unfailing courtesy, hospitality, and all-round welcome on arrival were always deeply appreciated.

I would further like to thank all those who carefully went through the manuscript to correct points of style and to alert me to any inconsistencies in the text. In such a large manuscript these inevitably occur. Their attention to detail is deeply appreciated. Mr. Mounir Ghabbour was extremely helpful in this area too. To the people of Egypt I must extend my heartfelt thanks. They are a generous people, full of friendship, and always willing to open their hearts to the visitor. In this respect, it is perhaps worthwhile to remind oneself of how important all those Egyptians of the past are who made it possible to journey through their land and their thought. A country, after all, is made up of more than the sum of its landscape or its inhabitants. It is built from the miracle of individual aspirations, and how these have been translated into the creation of culture itself.

The journey of the Holy Family in Egypt is a remarkable tale of endurance. Looking at it from a modern perspective, it is hard to imagine how three people and a child managed to survive what must have been extremely trying conditions even in those days—and, moreover, with little or no money in their possession. Though Mary and Salome were young women, and so more than able to deal with the physical difficulties of such a journey, one must remember that Joseph was a relatively older man who on occasions would have struggled to keep up. Though the Gospels are circumspect about the nature of their journey or its duration, or indeed how they managed to survive in Egypt, we must assume that they received help from many caring people as they made their way up the Nile. The Egyptian people offered them sanctuary, as they have done to innumerable visitors throughout the ages. I would like to think that the hospitality they extended to a family fleeing persecution is the same hospitality that they continue to extend to the traveler today.

James Cowan
Saint Simeon Monastery, Upper Egypt

Bibliography

Aldred, Cyril. *Akhenaten, King of Egypt*. London: Thames and Hudson, 1996.

Ashe, Geoffrey. *The Virgin*. London: Arkana, 1988.

Athanasius. *The Life of Antony and the Letter to Marcellinus*. The Classics of Western Spirituality. New York: Paulist Press, 1980.

Bachelard, Gaston. *On Poetic Imagination and Reverie*. Dallas: Spring Publications, 1971.

Barns, Jonathan. *Early Greek Philosophy*. London: Penguin, 1987.

Bettenson, Henry, ed. *The Later Christian Fathers*. London: Oxford University Press, 1970.

Bevan, Edwyn. *Hellenism and Christianity*. London: George Allan & Unwin, 1921.

Borges, Jorge Luis. *The Aleph and Other Stories*. New York: Dutton, 1978.

Brock, Sebastian, ed. *The Syriac Fathers on Prayer and the Spiritual Life*. Collegeville, MN: Cistercian Publications, 1986.

Brown, Peter. *The Body and Society: Men, Women, and Sexual Renunciation in Early Christian Society*. London: Faber and Faber, 1991.

Budge, E. A. Wallis. *The Gods of the Egyptians*. New York: Dover, 1969.

———, ed. *Coptic Biblical Texts in the Dialect of Upper Egypt*. Vols. 1–4. AMS edition published in 1977 from an original in the collections of the University of Michigan Library, 1912.

Cavafy, C. P. *Collected Poems*. London: Hogarth, 1984.

Chitty, Derwas J. *The Desert a City*. Crestwood, NY: St. Vladimir's Seminary Press, 1995.

Cioran, E. M. *Tears and Saints*. Chicago: University of Chicago Press, 1995.

Climacus, St. John. *Ladder of Divine Ascent*. Willits, CA: Eastern Orthodox Books, 1959.

Cooke, Harold P. *Osiris, a Study in Myths, Mysteries and Religion*. Chicago: Ares, 1979.

Coptic Orthodox Diocese of Malawai. *The Visitation of the Holy Family to Mallawi*. Unpublished pamphlet.

Corbin, Henry. *Spiritual Body and Celestial Earth*. Bollingen Series. Princeton: Princeton University Press, 1977.

Cumont, Franz. *Astrology and Religion among the Greeks and the Romans*. New York: Dover, 1960.

———. *Oriental Religions in Roman Paganism*. New York: Dover, 1956.

Curzon, Robert. *Visits to Monasteries in the Levant*. London: Century, 1983.

Daniélou, Jean. *The Infancy Narratives*. London: Compass Books, 1968.

Demetrius, Bishop H. G. *Write and Pray Little by Little*. Mallawi, Egypt: Coptic Orthodox Diocese of Hermopolis and Antenoepolis, 1991.

Desroches-Noblecourt, Christiane. *Tutankhamen: Life and Death of a Pharaoh*. New York: Penguin, 1978.

Diogenes Laertius. *Lives of Eminent Philosophers*. Vols. 1 and 2. Loeb Classical Library. Cambridge, MA: Harvard University Press, 1972.

Dionysius the Areopagite. *The Celestial Hierarchies*. London: The Shrine of Wisdom, 1935.

———. *The Divine Names*. Translated by C. E. Rolt. London: SPCK, 1940.

Doresse, Jean, *The Secret Book of the Egyptian Gnostics*. Rochester, VT: Inner Traditions, 1986.

Eliade, Mircea. *The Two and the One*. London: Harvill, 1965.

Evagrius Ponticus. *The Praktikos and Chapters on Prayer.* Translated by John Eudes Bamberger, OSCO. Cistercian Studies 4. Kalamazoo, MI: Cistercian Publications, 1981.

Feiler, Bruce. *Walking the Bible.* New York: HarperCollins, 2001.

Fideler, David. *Jesus Christ, Sun of God.* Wheaton, IL: Quest Books, 1993.

Flaubert, Gustave. *Flaubert in Egypt.* London: Penguin, 1996.

Gardiner, Sir Alan. *Egypt of the Pharaohs.* Oxford: Oxford University Press, 1966.

Gibbon, Edward. *The Decline and Fall of the Roman Empire.* Oxford: Oxford University Press, 1907.

Hadot, Pierre. *Plotinus or the Simplicity of Vision.* Chicago: University of Chicago Press, 1998.

Herodotus. *The Histories.* Loeb Classical Library. London, 1926.

Hultgren, Arland J., and Steven A. Haggmark, eds. *The Earliest Christian Heretics: Readings from Their Opponents.* Minneapolis: Fortress, 1996.

Ibn Jubayr. *The Travels of Ibn Jubayr.* London: Darf, 2003.

Jabes, Edmond. *The Book of Questions.* Middletown, CT: Wesleyan University Press, 1991.

Kamil, Jill. *Christianity in the Land of the Pharaohs.* Cairo: American University in Cairo Press, 2002.

Lacarriere, Jacques. *The Gnostics.* London: Peter Owen, 1977.

Leroy, Jules. *Monks and Monasteries of the Near East.* London: Harrap, 1963.

Levi, Peter. *The Frontiers of Paradise.* London: Collins Harvill, 1988.

Lewis, Naphtali. *Life in Egypt under Roman Rule.* Oxford: Clarendon Press, 1985.

Lossky, Vladimir. *The Mystical Theology of the Eastern Church.* Cambridge: James Clarke, 1968.

———. *The Vision of God.* Bedfordshire, UK: Faith Press, 1963.

Makar, Adeeb Bassili. *The Visit of the Holy Family to Mallawi.* Coptic Diocese of Mallawi, Egypt, 1999.

Marlowe, John. *The Golden Age of Alexandria*. London: Victor Gollancz, 1971.

Mattaos, Father. *Saint Samaan, the Shoemaker*. Cairo: The Church of St. Samaan, 1994.

Meinardus, Otto. *Coptic Saints and Pilgrimages*. Cairo: American University in Cairo Press, 2003.

———. *The Historic Coptic Churches of Cairo*. Cairo: Philopatron, 1994.

———. *The Holy Family in Egypt*. Cairo: American University in Cairo Press, 1986.

Moschos, John. *The Spiritual Meadow*. Translated by John Wortley. Kalamazoo, MI: Cistercian Publications, 1992.

Moussa, Bishop. *An Introduction to the New Testament*. Egypt: Dar el Geel Press, 1996.

Nerval, Gerard de. *Journey to the East*. London: Peter Owen, 1972.

Otto, Walter. *The Homeric Gods*. London: Thames & Hudson, 1979.

Pagels, Elaine. *Beyond Belief*. New York: Vintage, 2004.

———. *The Gnostic Gospels*. London: Penguin, 1979.

Palladius. *The Lausiac History*. Translated by W. K. L. Clarke. New York: Macmillan, 1918.

Plotinus, *The Enneads*. London: Faber & Faber, 1969.

Plutarch. *Isis and Osiris*. Loeb Classical Library. London, 1936.

Regnaut, Lucien. *The Day-to-Day Life of the Desert Fathers in Fourth-Century Egypt*. Petersham, MA: St. Bede's Press, 1999.

Rist, J. M. *Stoic Philosophy*. Cambridge: Cambridge University Press, 1990.

Robinson, James M., ed. *The Nag Hammadi Library in English*. Rev. ed. Leiden: Brill, 1996.

Schwaller de Lubicz, R.A. *Sacred Science*. New York: Inner Traditions, 1982.

Souriani, Fr. Yehnnes. *The Visit of the Holy Family in Egypt*. Private monastic publication of the Monastery of the Syrians. Wadi Natrun, 1999.

Symonds, J. A. *A Problem in Greek Ethics*. New York: Haskell House, 1971.

Tarn, Sir William, and G. T. Griffith. *Hellenistic Civilization*. London: Edward Arnold, 1966.

Tony, Girgus Kamal. *Antenoepolis*. Mallawi, Egypt: Saint Mina Monastery Press, 1999.

University of Geneva. *Le Site Monastique des Kellia (Basse-Egypte)*. Recherche des annees 1981–1983. Louvain, Peeters, 1984.

Vasiliev, A. A. *History of the Byzantine Empire*. 2 vols. Madison: University of Wisconsin Press, 1984.

Ward, Benedicta, trans. *The Sayings of the Desert Fathers*. Cistercian Studies 59. Kalamzoo, MI: Cistercian Publications, 1984.

Watterson, Barbara. *Coptic Egypt*. Edinburgh: Scottish Academic Press, 1988.

Yourcenar, Marguerite. *Memoirs of Hadrian*. London: Penguin, 1986.

Notes

Prologue

1   Exodus 4:19 (NRSV): "Go back to Egypt, for all those who were seeking your life are dead."

1 The Audience

2   Pope Shenouda III was born Nazir Gayed Rufail in 1923. He attended the American school in Banha. In 1943, Nazir matriculated at the University of Cairo, and four years later received his BA in English and history. He was a reserve officer in the army during the Arab-Israeli war of 1948. He became a monk at the Monastery of the Syrians in 1954, where he was placed in charge of the library. In 1959, he was appointed by the previous pope, Cyril VI, as his personal secretary. Later, he returned to the monastery and selected a cave ten kilometers away, on the edge of Wadi al-Faregh. His time in the desert prepared Nazir for his ascension to the papacy in 1971. It was in 1981 that President Sadat ordered him into exile in the Monastery of Saint Bishoy. He was released only after President Mubarrhaq came to power.

2 A Vision

3   In the Old Testament, Pelusium was known as Sin, which, like Pelusium, means "clay" or "mud" in Chaldaic and Greek.

4   *Itinerarium Bernardi Monarchi.*

5   Judges 14:20.

6   Numbers 13:22.

7   *Armenian Infancy Gospel.*

8   Genesis 10:19.

9   Zechariah 9:9.

10   The clothes the Holy Family wore ultimately became the model for the ecclesiastical vestments known as the alb, tunicle, and chasuble.

11   See Luke 2:1–5, which refers to the census. In AD 526, Dionysius Exiguus, who is responsible for the change from the *Anno Urbis Conditae* (AUC: Roman era) to *Anno Domini* (AD: Christian era), made an error of four years in his calculations. He placed the birth of Christ in the year 754 AUC, yet we know that Herod died in April of 750 AUC. The true date should be 747 AUC, or thereabouts.

12   The so-called wise men from the East were likely priest-sages, attached to the Zoroastrian religion of Iran, which was related in some obscure way to Judaism and borrowed several of its doctrines. It is not clear why the Magi might have been interested in seeking out a "king of the Jews," apart from the suggestion that the lost tribes of Israel may have lived beyond the Euphrates, and in hearing of the birth of a Messiah were drawn to Israel to offer their allegiance. By the time that Matthew wrote his Gospel, this tradition would have lost all meaning since Israel was no longer interested in a reunion with the lost tribes of the East.

13   The Serapeum treasure was reputedly that of Alexander the Great, so that in removing it Theophilus was removing all trace of Alexander's heroic past.

14   Aside from his attempts to destroy paganism in Egypt, Theophilus was active in church politics in Byzantium. We know, for example, that he attempted to stop John Chrysostom from being consecrated bishop in AD 398 because of his passionate dislike of the man. In AD 401, he also attacked the monks living in the Desert of Nitria because of their support for Origen and his symbolic view of the Gospels. He was a man of strong intellectual gifts marred by a somewhat violent disposition.

15   *Vision of Theophilus*, trans. A. Mingana, Woodbrooke Studies, vol. 3, Fasciculus 5 (Cambridge: Heffer, 1931).

16   See Luke 2:49 (KJV): "And he said unto them, How is it that ye sought me? Wist ye not that I must be about my Father's business?"

17   Papyrus of Nu, British Museum, No.10477, Sheet 6, trans. E. A. Wallis Budge.

18   Ibid., Prisse Papyrus.

3 *Journey into Exile*

19   Matthew 2:13 (KJV).

20   See Hosea 2:1: "Out of Egypt I called my son." Isaiah 19:1: "Behold, the LORD rides on a swift cloud, and will come into Egypt; the idols of Egypt will totter at His presence, and the heart of Egypt will melt in its midst." Isaiah 19:19–21: "In that day there will be an altar to the LORD in the midst of the land of Egypt, and a pillar to the LORD at its border. And it will be for a sign and for a witness to the LORD of hosts in the land of

Egypt. Then the LORD will be known to Egypt, and the Egyptians will know the LORD in that day, and will make sacrifice and offering" (All quotations NKJV).

21   Among these children was the infant John the Baptist, whose father, Zechariah, was killed for not revealing his whereabouts. *The Book of James—Protevangelium* 23.2–3 relates: "And Herod said unto Zachariah: 'Say the truth, where is thy son? For thou knowest that thy blood is under my hand.' And Zachariah said: 'I am a martyr of God if though sheddest my blood. I am innocent.' After his death, his blood turned to stone by the altar in the forecourt of the temple. The truth was that Elizabeth, John's mother, had taken the boy into the wilderness until the crisis was over." According to the *Encomium of St. John the Baptist*, an ancient Coptic text purportedly written by John Chrysostom, they lived in a cave that was idyllic and all-beneficent, where they suffered from neither heat nor cold, living on locusts and wild honey (See E. A. Wallis Budge, ed. and trans., *Coptic Apocrypha in the Dialect of Upper Egypt* [London, 1913]).

22   See Matthew 2:4–5 (NKJV): "And when he had gathered all the chief priests and scribes of the people together, he demanded of them where Christ should be born. And they said unto him, In Bethlehem of Judaea: for thus is written by the prophet."

23   Matthew 2:13.

24   *The Book of James—Protevangelium.*

25   *Gospel of Thomas* 42 ("The Gospel of Thomas (II,*2*)," trans. Thomas O. Lambdin, in *The Nag Hammadi Library in English*, ed. James M. Robinson, rev. ed. [Leiden: Brill, 1996], 131): "Jesus said, 'become passers-by.'"

26   Tacitus, *The Histories*: "Yet [it] is divided and unsettled by strange cults and irresponsible excesses, indifferent to law and ignorant of civil government."

27   Philo wrote that the population of Alexandria was in the vicinity of one million.

28   *Arabic Gospel of the Infancy of the Savior* 38.

29   It was Archaelus who instigated the death of John the Baptist, perhaps at the urging of Salome. Pontius Pilate attempted to shift to him the responsibility for trying Jesus, but failed.

30   Ibid., 39. It is suggested in the text, however, that two spans of the throne are found to be of unequal length, which forces Joseph to call upon his son for help. Jesus says to him: "Fear not, and do not lose heart. Take hold of one side of the throne, while I take the other." Between them, they are able to fix the throne. The story is probably there to emphasize Jesus's theurgic powers, even as a child, at the expense of Joseph's carpentry skills.

31 Hosea 11:1 (NKJV).

32 See Luke 3:46–47 (KJV): "They found him in the temple, sitting in the midst of the doctors, both hearing them, and asking them questions. And all that heard him were astonished at his understanding and answers."

4 Confronting the Old Gods

33 Genesis 45:10.

34 Genesis 12.

35 Herodotus, *The Histories* 2.107.

36 Ibid., 2.30.

37 Ibid., 2.111.

38 Exodus 1:11.

39 There is some evidence that the so-called oppression Pharaoh may have been Ramses II's son Merenptah.

40 At another, deeper level he was also "self-created." This may have occurred as a later development of Egyptian theology. Pharaonic religion went through a slow process of evolution over many thousands of years. It stands to reason that all the gods have a primitive prototype that in time gave way to a more sophisticated concept of deity.

41 There is a certain inconsistency in the character of Tem, for he is also known as the god of the setting sun, and therefore of the refreshing breeze of evening. As the oldest of the gods, and therefore the ancestor of the sun-god Ra, one senses that his contrasting nature is essential to understanding the complexity of any god. In a papyrus hymn, we hear this merging of opposites: "O Ra-Tem, in your splendid progress you rise, and you set as a living being in the glories of the western horizon."

42 E. A. Wallis Budge, ed. and trans., *Coptic Apocrypha in the Dialect of Upper Egypt* (London, 1913), 521.

43 "He is the Sun of the sun, the intelligible object behind the object comprehensible by sense, and from invisible fountains he supplies the visible beams which our eyes behold." Philo, *The Special Laws.*

44 Isaiah 11:6 (NKJV).

5 City of Women

45 See John 1:1–5 (NEB): "When all things began, the Word already was. . . . The Word then was with God at the beginning, and through him all things came to be."

46 In some accounts a dove emerges from his staff. The symbolism remains the same, however.

47 Herodotus, *The Histories* 2.59.

48 E. A. Wallis Budge, trans., *Legends of Our Lady Mary the Perpetual Virgin and her Mother Hanna* (London, 1922).

6 The Tree That Cried

49 Anthony (ca. AD 252–256) is the founder and father of Christian monasticism. A disciple of Paul of Thebes, he lived much of his life as a hermit at Mount Colzim, in the eastern desert. He was the first spiritual to embark upon a program of interior cleansing in a bid to attain to a state of stillness and calm. His so-called temptations in religious art have become a part of the European canon, denoting the battle against the sins of externality and physical excess. His influence on Western monasticism and religious thought was profound (see James Cowan, *Desert Father: A Journey in the Wilderness with Saint Anthony* [Boston: Shambhala, 2004]).

50 Evagrius Ponticus, *Praktikos* 67 (Evagrius Ponticus, *The Praktikos and Chapters on Prayer*, trans. John Eudes Bamberger, OSCO, Cistercian Studies 4 [Kalamazoo, MI: Cistercian Publications, 1981]).

51 See Evagrius, *Praktikos* 64: "The proof of *apatheia* is had when the spirit begins to see its own light, when it remains in a state of tranquility in the presence of the images it has during sleep and when it maintains its calm as it beholds the affairs of this life" (ibid., 33–34). Mircea Eliade explores the same idea in Hindu spirituality when he speaks of concentrating on the "lotus of the heart."

7 On the Road

52 Theodoret of Cyrrhus, *Historia Religiosa*, Patrologica Graeca 1364 D.

53 See Peter Brown, "The Rise and Function of the Holy Man in Late Antiquity," in *Society and the Holy in Late Antiquity* (Berkeley and Los Angeles: University of California Press, 1982).

8 Wastelands

54 Herodotus, *The Histories* 2.28.

9 *The Heel of a Prince*

55 Known as the Lady of the West, Neith is one of the oldest gods in Egyptian cosmology, and often took the form of a sacred cow with stars on her back. She may well have been Nut, the goddess of the sky. Her name is derived from the root "to weave or knit," and her symbol was the shuttle.

10 *Into the Desert*

56 Rufinus (AD 345–411) was a Roman priest, writer, theologian, and translator of Greek theological works into Latin at a time when knowledge of Greek was declining in the West. After study at Rome, where he met Jerome (later a saint and one of the doctors of the Western church), Rufinus entered a monastery at Aquileia.

57 Saint Cyprian (AD 200–258) was an early Christian theologian and bishop of Carthage who led the Christians of North Africa during a period of persecution from Rome. Upon his execution he became the first bishop-martyr of Africa.

58 Also known as Macarius the Great (AD 300–390), he was a monk and ascetic who, as one of the Desert Fathers, advanced the ideal of monasticism in Egypt and influenced its development throughout Christendom. A written tradition of mystical theology under his name is considered a classic of its kind.

59 See my *Desert Father: A Journey in the Wilderness with Saint Anthony* (Boston: Shambhala, 2004) for more details about Saint Anthony's life.

60 Julian, an Ionian, had gone to Egypt to spread the message that human beings are incorruptible by nature, and that their corruptibility is the result of original sin. Christ was considered to be the new Adam, and therefore his incorruptibility was regarded as being anterior to the birth of sin. Such a concept led to the reduction of Christ's humanity in the eyes of orthodox theologians since it implied Christ's sinlessness was derived from an earlier, paradisiacal condition. The monks who believed in this heresy were forced to quit nearby Saint Bishoy and found a monastery of their own. Deir es Suriani became a splinter expelled from the body of orthodoxy.

61 Daniel 2:34 (NKJV; see also Daniel 2:45).

62 Ezekiel 44:2 (NKJV).

63 Luke 1:28 (NKJV).

64 Isaiah 7:14 (NKJV).

65 Exodus 3:2 (NKJV).

66 Isaac of Nineveh, *Discourse* 63.

67 See Exodus 24:10 (KJV): "And they saw the God of Israel: and there was under his feet as it were a paved work of sapphire stone, and as it were the body of heaven in his clearness."

68 Isaac of Nineveh, *Discourses* I/23 (116–17).

11 *A Chance Conversation*

69 Palladius, *The Lausiac History* 10. This is the same Melania who advised Evagrius Ponticus to quit Jerusalem for Egypt.

70 Saint Bishoy Monastery is where Pope Shenouda served his monastic apprenticeship, and also where he was interned by President Sadat for five years.

71 This cell happens to be downstairs in the Church of the Holy Virgin in Deir es Suriani. It is still possible to clamber below and see a portion of rope hanging from a metal spike in the ceiling.

12 *Under the Tree*

72 Jeremiah 43:10–13 (KJV): "I will send and take my servant Nebuchadnezzar, the king of Babylon, and I will set his throne upon those stones I have hidden; and he shall set his royal pavilion over them. . . . He shall break also the images of On, that is the land of Israel; and the houses of the gods of the Egyptians shall be burnt with fire."

73 These two men met in August 1217 in Damietta, where Sultan al-Malik was under siege by a crusading army, where they spent some days conversing on themes pertaining to their respective religions. It has been contended that Saint Francis learned certain spiritual techniques from the Sufis at the sultan's court, which profoundly affected his conduct after his return to Italy (see my *Francis: A Saint's Way* [Liguori, MO: Liguori Publications, 2001]).

74 According to Diogenes Laertius, Pythagoras actually spoke Egyptian, which suggests that his relationship with his hosts was quite close.

75 Plato, *Laws* 2.657b.

76 Plato, *Timaeus* 49a.

77 Laertius tells us that Thales learned geometry from the priests in Heliopolis, and that he was the first man to inscribe a right-angled triangle in a circle.

78   Herodotus, *The Histories* 2.73.

79   In an ancient Egyptian text we read an invocation that could have easily described the risen Christ: "As truly as Osiris lives, he also shall live; as truly as Osiris is not dead, shall he not die; as truly as Osiris is annihilated, shall he not be annihilated."

80   Qur'an 14:25–30.

13   *The Dream*

81   In Arabic, *mokattam* means "cut up."

82   The skeleton of Saint Simeon was discovered during restorations of the ancient Church of the Holy Virgin in Babylon al-Durag in Old Cairo, in 1991. He is described as "short in stature, small in size, of brilliant and beautiful features." Though bald, his hair was still intact on each side of his head. This concurred with an early icon of the saint, which depicts him as baldheaded and carrying two jars of water. His relics are now shared between three churches, among which is that of Mokattam.

14   *Heart of a City*

83   The quarter's name, *Bab il-On*, may also be derived from the "Gate of On" or "Gate of Heliopolis." Most likely the Nilometer gauge measuring the height of the Nile floodwaters was located at this spot. It became the Christian quarter after Roman persecution of Greeks in Alexandria. The fortress itself was built by Emperor Diocletian.

15   *Voyage on the Nile*

84   The Bible was a Smith–Van Dyck version published in 1865.

85   Isaiah 19:19–20, 25 (NRSV): "On that day there will be an altar to the LORD in the center of the land of Egypt, and a pillar to the LORD at its border. It will be a sign and a witness to the Lord of Hosts in the land of Egypt. . . . The LORD will make himself known to the Egyptians; and the Egyptians will know the LORD on that day. . . . 'Blessed be Egypt my people.'"

86   See the *Arabic Infancy Gospel* 48, and the *Gospel of Saint Thomas* 7, Greek text A and B (Oxford: Clarendon, 1924).

87   *Gospel of Saint Thomas* 7.

88   Ibid., 8.

89   Dionysius the Areopagite, *The Divine Names* 1.1.

90   *The Mystic Cross* 101. In *The Hymn of Jesus*, sections 96–102, http://gnosis.org/library/hymnjesu.html.

91   Dionysius the Areopagite, *The Divine Names* 3.1

16 Toward Memphis

92   See Pyramid text 1635–36: "Isis comes to Osiris joyous in his love; your seed rises in her, penetrating like [that of] Sirius. The penetrating Horus comes forth from you in his name of Horus-who-is-in-Sirius."

17 Sailing South

93   "The Oxyrhynchus Papyri are a group of manuscripts discovered by archaeologists including Bernard Pyne Grenfell and Arthur Surridge Hunt at an ancient rubbish dump near Oxyrhynchus," near modern el-Bahnasa. "They include thousands of Greek and Latin documents, letters and literary works. They also include a few vellum manuscripts, and more recent Arabic manuscripts on paper. . . . Among the Christian texts found at Oxyrhynchus, were fragments of early non-canonical Gospels," as well as "*The Shepherd of Hermas* (3rd or 4th century . . .), and a work of Irenaeus (3rd century . . .). There are many parts of other canonical books as well as many early Christian hymns, prayers, and letters also found among them" ("Oxyrhynchus Papyri," Wikipedia, last modified August 16, 2012, http://en.wikipedia.org/wiki/Oxyrhynchus_Papyri).

18 A Heavenly City

94   *Historia Monachorum in Aegypto* 5.1-4.

95   More recently, in 1947, another major discovery of Gnostic papyri occurred at Nag Hammedi in Upper Egypt by a local farmer. These consisted of some sixty gospels of Gnostic origin, known today as the Nag Hammedi library. The full text of the *Gospel of Thomas* was also found here in Coptic, so that a comparison could be made with the Oxyrhynchus version in Greek.

96   Epiphanius, *Panarion* 24.5.4. See Arland J. Hultgren and Steven A. Haggmark, eds., *The Earliest Christian Heretics: Readings from Their Opponents* (Minneapolis: Fortress, 1996), 72.

97   *Gospel of Thomas* 1 ("The Gospel of Thomas (II,2)," trans. Thomas O. Lambdin, in *The Nag Hammadi Library in English*, ed. James M. Robinson, rev. ed. [Leiden: Brill, 1996], 126).

98   *Gospel of Thomas* 3 (ibid.).

99   *Gospel of Thomas* 5 (ibid.).

100 *Gospel of Thomas* 11 (ibid., 127).

101 *Gospel of Thomas* 8 (ibid., 127).

102 *Gospel of Thomas* 19: "If you become my disciples and listen to my words, these stones will minister to you" (ibid., 128).

103 *Gospel of Thomas* 16 (ibid.).

104 Otto Meinardus, *The Holy Family in Egypt* (Cairo: American University in Cairo Press, 1987), 45.

105 One should recall Simon Magus, the Samaritan, who saw himself as a holy man similar to Christ. It is noteworthy that Simon Magus learned his skill in magic in Egypt, and was active during the time of Emperor Claudius (AD 41–54), which therefore makes him a contemporary of Christ. Clement of Rome also accuses him of rejecting Jerusalem as the home of Christianity in favor of Mount Gerezim (Mount Qussqam, near al-Muharraq, the home of the Altar of the Lord?). See *Clementine Homilies* 2.22–25.

106 *Gospel of Thomas* 22 (Lambdin, trans., "Gospel of Thomas," 129).

107 *The Apocryphon of James* 23–30 (Francis E. Williams, trans., "The Apocryphon of James (I,2)," in Robinson, ed., *Nag Hammadi Library in English*, 34.

108 *The Tripartite Tractate* 4 (Harold W. Attridge and Dieter Mueller, trans., "The Tripartite Tractate (I,5)," in Robinson, ed., *Nag Hammadi Library in English*, 65.

109 *Gospel of Thomas* (Lambdin, trans., "Gospel of Thomas," 126).

19 *Language of Stones*

110 Amalric, the son of King Fulk of Jerusalem, had been count of Jaffa and Ascalon before succeeding his elder brother Baldwin III to the throne in 1163.

20 *One Man's Choice*

111 The German university the bishop spoke of is the University of Cologne. An Al-Ahram newspaper report on June 6, 1998, in Cairo recounted that the papyrus gave an estimate of the Holy Family's stay in Egypt as three years eleven months. Modern computation has suggested that they spent

six months in Deir al-Muharraq, at least eight weeks at Ashmounein, and a period of three months completing the homeward journey to Palestine. If Christ was about one year old when he entered Egypt, he was probably at least five by the time he arrived home in Nazareth.

22 *At Ashmounein*

112 According to the historian Abu 'l-Makarim, the governor of the city attempted to cut down the tree in the seventh century, but was prevented from doing so by the patriarch of Alexandria Agathus (AD 568–677), who stood under the tree. When the woodcutter attempted to strike the tree with his ax, the tool flew back in his face. The governor abandoned any further attempt to have the tree cut down.

113 See Plotinus's remarks on the hieroglyph: "The wise men of Egypt—whether in precise knowledge or by native intuition—indicated the truth where, in their effort towards philosophical statement, they left aside the writing-forms that take in the detail of words and sentences—those characters that represent sounds and convey the propositions of reasoning—and drew pictures instead, engraving the temple-inscriptions a separate image for every separate item: thus they exhibited the absence of discursiveness in the Intellectual Realm" (*Enneads* 5.8.6).

23 *The Well of the Cloud*

114 Exodus 7:9–12 (KJV): "When Pharaoh shall speak unto you, saying, Shew a miracle for you: then shalt thou say unto Aaron, Take thy rod, and cast it before Pharaoh, and before his servants, and it shall become a serpent. And Moses and Aaron went in unto Pharaoh, and they did so as the LORD had commanded: and Aaron cast down his rod before Pharaoh, and before his servants, and it became a serpent. Then Pharaoh also called the wise men and the sorcerers: now the magicians of Egypt, they also did in like manner with their enchantments. For they cast down every man his rod, and they became serpents: but Aaron's rod swallowed up their rods."

115 The others were Alexandria, Ptolomeas, and Nokratis near Aten in the delta.

116 Saladin (1137–1193) was the sultan of Egypt, Syria, Yemen, and Palestine, founder of the Ayyubid dynasty, and the most famous of Muslim heroes. In wars against the Christian crusaders, he achieved final success with the disciplined capture of Jerusalem (Oct. 2, 1187), ending its eighty-eight-year occupation by the Franks. The great Christian counterattack of the Third Crusade was then stalemated by his military genius.

117 *The Travels of Ibn Jubayr*, p. 51.
118 Isaiah 19:1 (NKJV).
119 Isaiah 19:3 (KJV).

24 Center of the World

120 Luke 1:30–33.
121 This stone has an alternative history. According to tradition, the sanctuary in the monastery is located on the exact spot where the Holy Family's house once stood. The present stone on top of the altar dates from AD 747, when its use was changed from an altar to a funerary stele, before reverting to its original function when the church was rebuilt in the twelfth or thirteenth century. (Massimo Capuani, *Christian Egypt: Coptic Art and Monuments Through Two Millennia* [Kalamazoo, MI: Liturgical Press, 2002], 197). The actual "washbasin" stone, however, features in another part of the story that is related later in this chapter.

25 On the Holy Mountain

122 According to the historian Abu Salih, the church itself was built around AD 60. Pachomius was the founder of coenobitic monasticism in Egypt, the model later used by monasteries throughout Europe.
123 It is said that they gathered at Mount Qussqam in order that Christ might divide the nations up among the apostles. According to tradition also, Christ asked Peter to celebrate the Divine Liturgy in order to bring the Holy Spirit down upon the congregation. At that moment a large bird flew down from above, carrying wines and delicacies to earth. It alighted in the center of the church, thus inaugurating the "first church in the world" (Otto Meinardus, *Monks and Monasteries of the Egyptian Deserts* [Cairo: American University at Cairo Press, 1961]).
124 Isaiah 19:19.

28 The Last Supper

125 Matthew 2:21 (KJV).
126 Matthew 2:22–23 (KJV).
127 *The Arabic Infancy Gospel* 46.

Glossary of Terms

Abba: an older monk, or spiritual advisor.

Agape: "to love" in Greek; a meeting of men or women wishing to celebrate the Christian mysteries in a state of fraternity and love.

Agnosia: A state of unknowing whereby one may know him who is above all possible knowledge. The rational faculties have, in consequence, been stilled.

Anchoresis: Literally, to "withdraw" in Greek. A condition of social and spiritual disengagement. An "anchorite" is thus one who withdraws from society to practice an eremitical life in the desert.

Apatheia: A state of serenity, when all passions are stilled. For the early Christians in the East such a state represents the beginning of deification. For Evagrius Ponticus, it reflects a state of impassability.

Apophaticism: The isolation of the qualities of God by pointing out who or "what" he is not. The practice of negative theology, as it is called, was popular among mystics, especially Dionysius the Areopagite.

Apostasis: A complete and resolved state of ascetic renunciation.

Ascesis: Literally "to exercise" or "train" in Greek. It is a condition of voluntary restraint in all actions pertaining to bodily comfort and pleasure. The practice of spiritual self-discipline.

Autarkism: To live in a state of absolute self-sufficiency, beyond all social structures. It is the condition of the hermit.

Copts: Indigenous Egyptian Christians, as distinct from Greek or Latin Christians living in the East.

Desert Fathers: A name given to the early fathers of the Egyptian church who lived in the Nitria Desert north of modern-day Cairo, and in certain regions along the Nile. These men, by their example, formulated the early statutes for eremitical and monastic living.

Diakrisis: The gift of discernment, detachment, and discrimination. Also known as discretion.

Eschaton: The condition of Last Things, or the ideal (heavenly) time after death.

Eudaemonia: A state of bliss, being in the proximity and presence of God.

Gnosis: Spiritual knowledge. The term "Gnostic" was also applied to a dualist heresy in the early Christian church.

Hesychasm: A meditative practice designed to invoke a condition of "holy quiet" (apatheia), and the suspension of all appetitive qualities. Literally, it means a "turning inward." In Greek Orthodoxy and beyond, it involves the repetition of the Jesus Prayer: "Jesus Christ, Son of God, have mercy upon me." The monks on Mount Athos in Greece perfected this discipline.

Isochristoi: A state of oneness and equality with Christ in Eastern Orthodoxy. Another way of saying "Theosanir," the perfect man.

Katastasis: Implies a state of stillness in the soul, tranquillity, or peace.

Kosmikos: A man of the world who understands and accepts the spirit in this life.

Parresia: A state of intimacy with God.

Theophany: The visible manifestation of God to humankind.

Xeniteia: The process of social disengagement toward "living as a stranger" (autarchy) in a voluntary state of exile.

Note: Some of the terms and definitions listed here also appear in my previous work, *Desert Father: A Journey in the Wilderness with Saint Anthony*.

ABOUT PARACLETE PRESS

WHO WE ARE

Paraclete Press is a publisher of books, recordings, and DVDs on Christian spirituality. Our publishing represents a full expression of Christian belief and practice—from Catholic to Evangelical, from Protestant to Orthodox.

We are the publishing arm of the Community of Jesus, an ecumenical monastic community in the Benedictine tradition. As such, we are uniquely positioned in the marketplace without connection to a large corporation and with informal relationships to many branches and denominations of faith.

WHAT WE ARE DOING

Books Paraclete publishes books that show the richness and depth of what it means to be Christian. Although Benedictine spirituality is at the heart of all that we do, we publish books that reflect the Christian experience across many cultures, time periods, and houses of worship. We publish books that nourish the vibrant life of the church and its people—books about spiritual practice, formation, history, ideas, and customs.

We have several different series, including the best-selling Paraclete Essentials and Paraclete Giants series of classic texts in contemporary English; A Voice from the Monastery—men and women monastics writing about living a spiritual life today; award-winning poetry; best-selling gift books for children on the occasions of baptism and first communion; and the Active Prayer Series that brings creativity and liveliness to any life of prayer.

Recordings From Gregorian chant to contemporary American choral works, our music recordings celebrate sacred choral music through the centuries. Paraclete distributes the recordings of the internationally acclaimed choir Gloriæ Dei Cantores, praised for their "rapt and fathomless spiritual intensity" by *American Record Guide*, and the Gloriæ Dei Cantores Schola, which specializes in the study and performance of Gregorian chant. Paraclete is also the exclusive North American distributor of the recordings of the Monastic Choir of St. Peter's Abbey in Solesmes, France, long considered to be a leading authority on Gregorian chant.

Videos Our videos offer spiritual help, healing, and biblical guidance for life issues: grief and loss, marriage, forgiveness, anger management, facing death, and spiritual formation.

Learn more about us at our website:
www.paracletepress.com,
or call us toll-free at 1-800-451-5006.

SCAN
TO
READ
MORE

You may also be interested in . . .

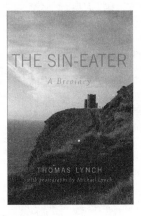

The Sin-eater: A Breviary
Thomas Lynch

The *Sin-Eater* is a collection of two dozen twenty-four-line poems—a book of hours in the odd life and times of Argyle, the sin-eater. Celtic and druidic, scapegoat and outlier, a fixture in the funerary landscape of former centuries, Argyle's doubt-ridden witness seems entirely relevant to our difficult times. His "loaf and bowl," consumed over corpses, become the elements of sacrament and sacrilege. By turns worshipful and irreverent, good-humored and grim, these poems examine the deeper meanings of Eucharist and grace, forgiveness and faith, atonement and reconciliation. With photographs by Michael Lynch, the author's son.

80 pages | ISBN: 978-1-55725-872-4
$22.99, Hardcover

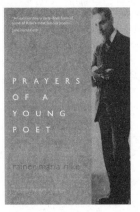

Prayers of a Young Poet
Rainer Maria Rilke
Translated by Mark S. Burrows

This volume marks the first translation of these prayer-poems into English. Originally written in 1899, Rilke wrote them upon returning to Germany from his first trip to Russia. His experience of the East shaped him profoundly. He found himself entranced by Orthodox churches and monasteries, above all by the icons that seemed to him like flames glowing in dark spaces. He intended these poems as icons of sorts, gestures that could illumine a way for seekers in the darkness. As Rilke here writes, "I love the dark hours of my being, / for they deepen my senses."

112 pages | ISBN: 978-1-61261-076-4
$21.99, Hardcover

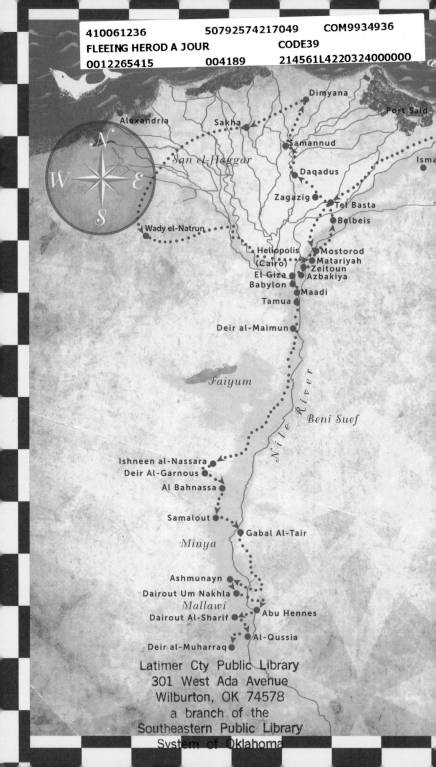

Dimyana

Port Said

Alexandria

Sakha

Samannud

San el-Haggar

Daqadus

Isma

Zagazig

Tel Basta

Belbeis

Wady el-Natrun

Heliopolis
(Cairo)

Mostorod

Matariyah

Zeitoun

El Giza

Azbakiya

Babylon

Maadi

Tamua

Deir al-Maimun

Faiyum

Nile River

Beni Suef

Ishneen al-Nassara

Deir Al-Garnous

Al Bahnassa

Samalout

Gabal Al-Tair

Minya

Ashmunayn

Dairout Um Nakhla

Mallawi

Dairout Al-Sharif

Abu Hennes

Al-Qussia

Deir al-Muharraq